C-SPAN
America's
A Town Hall

By Brian Lamb and the staff of C-SPAN

ACROPOLIS BOOKS LTD.
WASHINGTON, D.C.

You have created in C-SPAN *America's Town Hall*. I don't know if all of you fully appreciate the greatness and the strength of what you've done. Not since men would come together on the street corners in Athens and in the forum in the marketplace and debate together the policies of how that city-state would be governed has any nation had quite what you developed in C-SPAN. It is the town hall for the nation . . . . I appreciate it. America ought to appreciate it. You have satisfied many Americans with the creative and wonderful gift that you have given us, the privilege of viewing our government, our Congress, as it is—unvarnished and whole. I want to thank you for that as a member of Congress and as a citizen of the United States. Not only have you provided an opportunity for people to see that which they own and which is theirs, but, indeed, you have given them the privilege of being better citizens in so doing.

Speaker James C. Wright (D-Texas)
U.S. House of Representatives
in a March 1986 speech to
The National Cable Television Association

To the Chairmen:
Bob Rosencrans
John Saeman
Ed Allen
Jack Frazee
Jim Whitson
Gene Schneider

Authorization to photocopy items for internal or personal use, or the internal or personal use of specific clients, is granted by Acropolis Books Ltd., provided that the base fee of $1.00 per copy, plus $.10 per page is paid directly to Copyright Clearance Center, 27 Congress Street, Salem, MA 01970. For those organizations that have been granted a photocopy license by CCC, a separate system of payment has been arranged. The fee code for users 'of the Transactional Reporting Service is: "ISBN 0-87491-889-8/88 $1.00 + .10"

© Copyright 1988, Acropolis Books, Ltd. All rights reserved. Except for the inclusion of brief quotations in a review, no part of this book may be reproduced or utilized in any form or by any means, electronic or mechanical, including photocopying, recording, or by any information storage and retrieval system, without permission in writing from the publisher.

ACROPOLIS BOOKS, LTD.
Alphons J. Hackl, Publisher
Colortone Building, 2400 17th St., N.W.
Washington, D.C. 20009

Printed in the United States of America by COLORTONE PRESS
Creative Graphics, Inc.
Washington, D.C. 20009

Attention: Schools and Corporations
ACROPOLIS books are available at quantity discounts with bulk purchase for educational, business, or sales promotional use. For information, please write to: SPECIAL SALES DEPARTMENT, ACROPOLIS BOOKS, LTD., 2400 17th St., N.W., WASHINGTON, D.C. 20009.

Are there Acropolis books you want but cannot find in your local stores?
You can get any Acropolis book title in print. Simply send title and retail price. Be sure to add postage and handling: $2.25 for orders up to $15.00; $3.00 for orders from $15.01 to $30.00; $3.75 for orders from $30.01 to $100.00; $4.50 for orders over $100.00. District of Columbia residents add applicable sales tax. Enclose check or money order only, no cash please, to:
ACROPOLIS BOOKS LTD.
2400 17th St., N.W.
WASHINGTON, D.C. 20009

Library of Congress Cataloging-in-Publication Data
America's town hall.
    1. United States. Congress—Television broadcasting of proceedings.   2. Television audiences—United States.   3. Political participation—United States.   I. Lamb, Brian, 1941–
JK1129.A44 1988   328.73   88-14384
ISBN 0-87491-889-8

Cover design, book design and Art Direction by Kathleen K. Cunningham

Acknowledgments

"America's Town Hall," like C-SPAN itself, has been a collaborative effort. A sizable portion of the network's 150-person staff has contributed to this production. A core group—pictured in the photo pages—devoted late nights and long weekends to this project; friends outside the company lent their research, writing, and editing talents. Susan Swain, C-SPAN's vice president of corporate communications, guided and directed the entire effort from start to finish. Carrie "Scoop" Lamson, our managing editor and writer, made all the pieces come together.

So, to Susan and Scoop and *writers* Pat Watson, Caroline Ely, Sheila Quinlin, Penny Pagano, Mark West, Susan Lamontagne, Rosemary Harold; *researchers* Peter Kiley, Suzanne Stahl, Nan Gibson, Kathy Murphy, Rosemarie Colao, Mary Holley, Eileen Quinn, Greg Barker, Bruce Collins, Terri Sorensen, Rob Lee, Mike Michaelson, Jana Dabrowski, Paul Sinclair, Kathleen Brown, Chris Maloney, Martha Gallahue, Michelle Lynch, Connie Doebele, Susan Bundock; *administrative support staff* Lea Anne Long, Jenna Eudaley, Molly Breeden, Joanne Wheeler; *graphics assistants* Clint Smith and Robin Garber; and *research coordinator and photo editor* Maura Clancey, our sincerest thanks for this exhaustive undertaking. But, thanks, also, to our viewers for making it possible in the first place.

Table of Contents

Introduction: Brian Lamb

Foreword: Jeff Greenfield, ABC News

Roy Allen
Savannah, Georgia — The Typical Viewer   1

Richard Armey
Denton, Texas — The Challenger   5

Tuckerman Babcock
Wasilla, Alaska — The Legislative Aide   8

Howard Baker, Robert Byrd, Robert Dole
The Leaders
Huntsville, Tennessee; Sophia, West Virginia; Russell, Kansas   11

Philomena Benevides-Rogers
Washington, D.C. — The Interpreter   17

Bruce Berman
Boston, Massachusetts — The Channel Zapper   20

Margaret Blair
Fayetteville, Arkansas — The Ozark Caller   23

Walter Blevins
Morehead, Kentucky — The Legislating Dentist   27

Sandra Bradford
Standish, Maine — The High School Teacher   31

Barbara Brian
Plaistow, New Hampshire — The Sample Voter   35

Lewis Brierley
Columbia, South Carolina — The News Designer　　　38

Howard Bronson
San Antonio, Texas — The Colonel　　　41

Lillian Brown
Omaha, Nebraska — The Golden Ear　　　44

Robert Browning
West Lafayette, Indiana — The Archivist　　　47

Lee Carle
St. Thomas, The Virgin Islands — The Island Newscaster　　　51

Elaine Carlyle
Pittsburg, Kansas — The Special Viewer　　　54

Pete Carril
West Windsor, New Jersey — The Coach　　　57

Syd Cassyd
Los Angeles, California — The Television Pioneer　　　60

Dick Cheney Sr.
Casper, Wyoming — The Congressional Dad　　　63

Richard Cohen
McLean, Virginia — The Congressional Correspondent　　　66

Jack Cole
West Palm Beach, Florida — The Talkmaster　　　69

Baltasar Corrada del Rio
San Juan, Puerto Rico — The Fifty-first Stater　　　73

Gene S. Crockett
Irving, Texas — The Flag Waver　　　76

James Crosswhite
San Diego, California — The Wordsmith　　　79

Kay Cutcher
Sioux City, Iowa — The Watchdog　　　82

Robert Desramaux
Ottawa, Ontario, Canada — The Canadian　　　86

Phil Donahue
New York, New York — The Moderator　　　90

John Duncan
Phoenix, Arizona — The Ex-Trucker　　　93

Russell Epperson
Moberly, Missouri – The Prisoner 96

Harry Fletcher
Montgomery, Alabama – The Historian 99

Robert Fox
St. Paul, Minnesota – The Recovering Lawyer 102

Helen Frank
Somers, New York – The Poetic Psychologist 105

Stephen Frantzich
Annapolis, Maryland – The Naval Professor 108

Ann Funck
Denver, Colorado – The Volunteer 112

Winnie Gill
Baton Rouge, Louisiana – The Retired Housewife 114

Newt Gingrich
Jonesboro, Georgia – The Conservative Opportunist 117

Gladys Glickman
Wichita, Kansas – The Congressional Mom 121

Albert Gore Jr.
Carthage, Tennessee – The Techno-politician 124

Joe Grandmaison
Rye, New Hampshire – The Party Chair 128

Ellen Greenberg
Dobbs Ferry, New York – The Writer 131

Gary Greene
Holland, Michigan – The C-SPAN Junkie 135

Brian Greenspun
Las Vegas, Nevada – The Desert Editor 138

Paul Griffith
Black Mountain, North Carolina – The Good Neighbor 141

Brian Gruber
Albuquerque, New Mexico – The Cable Marketer 144

William "Bud" Harris
Cherry Hill, New Jersey – The First Friend 147

Larry Hart
Inglewood, California – The Collector 151

Dan Henninger
Ridgewood, New Jersey — The Wall Street Editorialist   154

James Hood
Madison, Wisconsin — The Civil Rights Pioneer   205

Ruth Janger
Oklahoma City, Oklahoma — The Close Up Matriarch   208

Nicholas Johnson
Iowa City, Iowa — The Commissioner   212

Michael Kelley
Fairfax, Virginia — The Capitol Connector   215

Edward Kienholz, Nancy Reddin Kienholz
Hope, Idaho — The Artists   219

Keith Knautz
Glendale Heights, Illinois — The Page   222

Suzanne Lauer
Decatur, Georgia — The Feminist   225

Stephen J. Liesen
Wyandotte, Michigan — The Letter Writer   228

Nackey Loeb
Manchester, New Hampshire — The Union Leader   232

Katherine Loew
Honolulu, Hawaii — The Leaguer   235

Manny Lucoff
Tampa, Florida — The Communications Professor   238

Patrick Lynn
Bismarck, North Dakota — The Anchorman   241

Tony Maidenberg
Marion, Indiana — The Small-Town Mayor   244

Aimee Maxfield
Marietta, Georgia — The Teen-age Politico   248

Bob McBarton
Redondo Beach, California — The Guest Columnist   251

Michaël McGough
Pittsburgh, Pennsylvania — The Area Man   254

Bob Michel
Peoria, Illinois — The Minority Leader   257

Jack Nelson
Bethesda, Maryland – The Bureau Chief   261

Marian Norby
Arlington, Virginia – The Monitor   265

Robert O'Brien
Dover, Delaware – The County Administrator   268

Raymond O'Dette
Foster, Rhode Island – The Caregiver   271

Thomas P. "Tip" O'Neill
Harwichport, Massachusetts – The Speaker   274

Mike Peters
Beavercreek, Ohio – The Cartoonist   278

William Proxmire
Madison, Wisconsin – The Golden Fleecer   282

John Putka
Cincinnati, Ohio – The Priest   285

Ronald Reagan
Washington, D.C. – The President   289

T. R. Reid
Denver, Colorado – The Camscammer   293

Barbara Reynolds
Washington, D.C. – The Role Model   296

Brent Riley
Logan, Utah – The Crusader   299

Joyce Robinson
Great Falls, Montana – The Rancher   302

Tom Rose
Stillwater, Minnesota – The Doctor   305

Bob Rosencrans, Ken Gunter
The Risk-Takers
Greenwich, Connecticut; San Angelo, Texas   308

Shirley Rossi
Pueblo, Colorado – The Mountain Belle   313

Sally Salmon
Jackson, Mississippi – The Presidential Questioner   317

Ray Schwartz
Dover, New Jersey — The Conference Caller   320

Stan Singer
Harrisburg, Pennsylvania — The Legislative Addict   324

John Stolarek
McAllen, Texas — The Lone Star Reporter   327

John Sununu
Salem, New Hampshire — The Governor   330

Shani Taha
Seattle, Washington — The Independent Thinker   334

Nelda Thompson
Applegate, Oregon — The Runner Up   338

Unknown Viewer
Yankton, South Dakota — The First Caller   343

Ken Uston
San Francisco, California — The Gambler   347

Jane White
Scottsdale, Arizona — The Neighborhood Organizer   350

Lawrence White
Culver, Indiana — The Eternal Optimist   353

Kendall Wild
Rutland, Vermont — The Localizer   357

Lee Wing
Durham, North Carolina — The Stateside Producer   360

Tom Winslow
Philadelphia, Pennsylvania — The Park Ranger   363

David Yepsen
Des Moines, Iowa — The Caucus Pundit   366

Joe Yerkes
Jacksonville, Florida — The Special Educator   369

Andrew Young
Atlanta, Georgia — The Big-City Mayor   372

Frank Zappa
Los Angeles, California — The Political Rocker   375

Appendix One   378
— *The C-SPAN audience*

Appendix Two   384
— *Growth in C-SPAN households*
— *Growth in affiliated cable systems*
— *C-SPAN penetration in U.S. households*
— *Call-in program participation*
— *C-SPAN programming "first run" hours*
— *Senate hours in session*
— *House hours in session*
— *Public affairs television audiences*
— *C-SPAN Board of Directors*
— *Book research staff*
— *C-SPAN Press: Then and Now*

Introduction

C-SPAN, the Cable-Satellite Public Affairs Network, has now been in operation for almost a decade. We program two 24-hour channels, C-SPAN and C-SPAN II. Nearly 40 million U.S. homes are able to receive our programming; another 300,000 new C-SPAN homes are added each month. Yet whenever the network comes up in conversation, people still invariably ask, "Who watches C-SPAN?" *America's Town Hall* is our attempt to answer that question.

During the course of C-SPAN's history, we've answered this inquiry through more conventional means. Four extensive national surveys of cable television audiences have determined what kind of people watch C-SPAN and why. (The results of the latest such survey can be found in Appendix One of this book.) For C-SPAN, which is a cable industry public service, these audience numbers are fascinating; for all other television programmers they are a business necessity. But statistics never provide the whole story; understanding the people behind those numbers helps supply a context.

Inside *America's Town Hall,* you'll meet 104 people who bring C-SPAN's demographic profiles to life. They are individuals who have had an impact on C-SPAN's growth or who have found interesting ways to put C-SPAN programming to use in their daily lives. Their stories are sometimes inspirational, sometimes entertaining, and occasionally quite ordinary—just like C-SPAN programming itself.

Like C-SPAN, *America's Town Hall* was a collaborative effort. It took over eight months and more than 30 C-SPAN staff members to produce this work. At the outset, we knew we wanted to profile viewers from each of the 50 states, Canada, Puerto Rico, the District of Columbia, and the Virgin Islands— all places where people tune in to C-SPAN each day. We also wanted the people we selected to be representative of larger groups of viewers, a mix of politicians, press, celebrities, and everyday citizens. C-SPAN viewers are everywhere and come from all walks of life. The effort to find our subjects was extensive and the process undeniably imperfect.

The interviewing process yielded some interesting personal experiences for our staff. Greg Barker, our call-in guest coordinator, had to accompany Georgia Congressman Newt Gingrich on one of his 6:00 A.M. walks around the Capitol in order to get his interview. Staff editor Mary Holley had to work through the intricacies of the Missouri state correctional system to talk with Russell Epperson, an inmate in the Moberly prison. Twenty-four-year-old Peter Kiley, our program listings coordinator, heard a dramatic, first-person account of President Kennedy's effort to desegregate southern colleges from civil rights pioneer James Hood.

And, like any big project, this one has its tales of the ones that got away. There was the Hawaiian fisherman, who repeatedly caused the alarm clocks of two of our colleagues to ring at shockingly early hours as they unsuccessfully attempted to "net" his story. There were celebrity C-SPAN viewers like tennis star Ivan Lendl (whose "television is always on C-SPAN," according to the *Atlanta Constitution*) and actor Harry Hamlin (who confessed to *People* magazine that C-SPAN is his favorite television program because "it's real and reality gets to me"). Unfortunately, even our dogged interviewers couldn't get to them.

We talked to a wide variety of people about their C-SPAN viewing, even though some stories simply didn't develop into full profiles. Former President Richard Nixon wrote to say that for him "C-SPAN is an indispensable tool. . . . C-SPAN offers what neither [network news or newspapers] can or is willing to offer: complete, unedited, uninterrupted, immediate accounts of what is actually happening and what is actually being said without the . . . editor's hatchet." And of course there were technical problems like inaudible audio tapes that left actor Peter Falk's completed interview on the cutting room floor. (We did salvage his observation that "anyone wanting to make a film about politics or the political world, a film that has any truth to it, would have to sit down and watch C-SPAN.")

In retrospect, we really should have included our story about Guam. Lee Holmes, who manages the cable system in that U.S. territory's capital city, has found a way to bring C-SPAN to the 125,000 U.S. citizens who live there. Technically unable to pick C-SPAN programming off the satellite, he has it taped in Pasadena, California, each week and flown 4,500 miles to his system in Agana. We are sure there are other significant tales we missed. We hope that the publication of *America's Town Hall* will lead us to other such stories.

We also hope this book will interest readers who are unfamiliar with C-SPAN programming to seek out our network. Last year, TV watchers in 10.9 million households—potentially 27.3 million Americans—watched C-SPAN. Viewers in 1.3 million of those homes—potentially 3.25 million people— spent 20 hours or more each month watching C-SPAN telecasts. What C-SPAN has done for them is to take public affairs programming out of the Sunday morning ghetto of broadcast television and make it accessible 24 hours a day. Those who watch our channel regularly see moments of high drama and controversy and stretches of undeniable tedium. For, unlike conventional television, C-SPAN does not edit events to make them more interesting or entertaining. Our network covers public events simply by turning on its cameras and letting people watch. Events unfold in their entirety, without analysis or commentary.

At every turn, C-SPAN programming defies conventional television wisdom. A decade ago, those who helped create C-SPAN were taking a big risk with their dollars and personal support. Politicans and journalists were skeptical of public acceptance of the C-SPAN concept. In truth, acceptance of C-SPAN was not instantaneous and will probably never be universal. Ten years later, however, C-SPAN is on the road to becoming something of an institution for politicians, reporters, and segments of the public alike.

Nonetheless, it is unlikely that C-SPAN programming

will ever appeal to mass audiences (this is a country, after all, where only 54 percent of those who were eligible voted in the last presidential election). What has made C-SPAN significant, however, is *who* watches. Our viewers are public officials, the press, educators, and voters. C-SPAN attracts those people already involved in public-policy making and inspires others to become involved. C-SPAN viewers are the kind of individuals who affect our nation's political process.

One of the most surprising things readers of this book will learn about our network is that, despite its mission of televising the government process, C-SPAN is a product of private business. Without being required to do so by government regulators, the cable television industry created and continues to fund C-SPAN as a public service for the nation.

In the pages of this book you will meet two of the network's earliest cable supporters, Bob Rosencrans and Ken Gunter. Many others, in cable and on Capitol Hill, such as Gary Hymel, Bob Schmidt, Tom Wheeler, John Evans, Steve Effros, Henry Goldberg, Rep. Charlie Rose, and the late Bill Hartnett, also deserve mention. This book, however, is not an attempt to tell C-SPAN's history; rather, it is the story of C-SPAN today. Nonetheless, the stories of *America's Town Hall* stand as one small testament to those in the cable television industry, on Capitol Hill, and in grassroots America who were willing to take the chance to support truly different television in the interest of a more open political process.

Brian Lamb
June 1988
Washington, D.C.

Foreword

The revelation came for me in the spring of 1979, as I sped my way through the channels on our newly cabled television set. As newly dubbed media critic for CBS News, I was re-affirming my conviction that, during the daylight hours, at least, television was still best described by the immortal words of one-time Federal Communications Chairman Newton Minow: "a vast wasteland."

And there, wedged somewhere in between a rerun of "The Brady Bunch," three game shows featuring blow-dried Ken and Barbie dolls smirking at the bug-eyed wheel-spinners, and a roomful of leotard-clad exercise freaks, was the U.S. House of Representatives, live and in color, in my bedroom.

Now, I realize that for most of my fellow citizens, even those with a strong sense of public responsibility, the discovery that the lower branch of Congress was now available to cable television households would not be the sort of revelation that ranks with a life-changing experience on the road to Damascus. In my case, however, it was as if I had been a professional butterfly collector and discovered the "Lepidoptera Channel" on my TV set.

I have been hopelessly obsessed with the spectacle of American politics ever since, as a nine-year-old, I was seduced by the drama of the 1952 national nominating conventions as broadcast through a static-filled radio. The idea of tuning in to the work of the United States Congress was, for me, one of those utopian notions long-ago promised by men in beards, pince-nez spectacles, and stiff-necked collars gathered around a giant-sized prototype of what would become the radio or TV set. ("Someday men will be able to observe their leaders assembling the laws of governance; then there will be no war.") It was a promise long-ago betrayed by the perfectly understandable idea of squeezing every last dollar from the broadcast media.

That day, however, the fantasy was being played out. Arizona Rep. Morris Udall (D) and Louisiana's John Breaux (D) were battling each other over an Alaskan lands bill that would set aside millions of acres of wilderness for our national parks system. Udall argued for the protection of our priceless national heritage; Breaux cited the urgent need for energy exploration on the other. It was better television than anything else on the tube. And from that moment on, I was hooked on C-SPAN.

There is no magic to the C-SPAN formula, and certainly no massive infusion of cash to account for its performance. Its $12-million-a-year budget wouldn't last three weeks at a commercial network news division.

Instead, C-SPAN relies on a blend of modern technology and a Jeffersonian faith in the people. Using lightweight video equipment and reasonably priced satellite time, C-SPAN simply shows up at a political event, turns on the cameras, and lets the viewer see what is happening.

Ironically, although the cable channel began as the electronic outlet of record for the House of Representatives, I now regard the floor coverage as the least valuable of C-SPAN's work. For me, the real pearls of great price come when C-SPAN picks up its cameras and winds up at a coffee klatsch in Iowa, or a lobster dinner in New Hampshire, where a presidential hopeful is speaking. Or when it covers a conversation between a political strategist and a group of reporters and editors over coffee and doughnuts. Or when it shows up at one of the hundreds of seminars in Washington on "Media Coverage of Politics."

In this sense, I treasure C-SPAN for the most selfish of reasons. Oh, sure, I pay lip service to its capacity to bring detailed, utterly unbiased information to citizens from Bangor to Maui. While I publicly salute its contribution to an informed, involved citizenry, my real affection for the network is firmly rooted in self-interest. C-SPAN lets me keep up with the presidential campaign while wrapped in a bathrobe drinking coffee in my living room. It lets me follow Sen. Bob Dole (R-Kansas) through a luncheon reception in Des Moines as if I were perched on his left shoulder. It permits me to hear the speeches of Jesse Jackson and Pat Robertson in full, the better to evaluate the rhetorical skills of both. For a writer whose two professional interests are politics and the media, C-SPAN is like having a $12-million research operation at my beck and call.

For those in the arena of public policy making, C-SPAN may be having an equally significant, though much more ambiguous, impact. It has long been said that, in an age of mass media, public figures must assume that every word they say will be heard from one end of the country to the other. And it has certainly been true for two decades or more that, with the advent of network television, a candidate could no longer be the champion of civil rights in Boston and the friend of segregation in the South.

With C-SPAN, however, the presence of the greater public has become a reality for every candidate in most every living room and church basement in America. Ask former presidential hopeful Joseph Biden. As he painfully learned, a few careless words late at night, captured by C-SPAN cameras, can fatally undermine a presidential candidacy. What C-SPAN has done, then, is to bring a potential national audience into the most intimate of political events.

Is this change dangerous? Only if you assume that public figures seeking high public office need not care about the consequences of the words they speak and the ideas they proffer. If the men and women seeking to lead us actually come to discover that the country is listening to what they say, it just may result in a more serious level of public discourse. And Lord knows, that is long overdue.

Jeff Greenfield
ABC News

"The Typical Viewer"

Roy Allen

Savannah, Georgia

Roy L. Allen II, 38, has represented the 40,000 citizens of District 127 in the Georgia State Assembly for the past eight years. Mr. Allen is also an attorney who represents clients in Savannah and Atlanta. He received a bachelor's degree from Howard University in Washington, D.C., in 1971, and a law degree from the University of Connecticut in 1975.

Many regular C-SPAN viewers will recognize themselves in Mr. Allen's words. For this reason we have chosen simply to print his transcribed interview. For those who are new to C-SPAN, he helps set the stage for many of the people you will read about in the following pages.

"I can't recall how I first learned about C-SPAN. Savannah was slow in getting cable service, and four or five years ago the system expanded and added C-SPAN. It caught my interest on the day I first heard about it. I'd gone to school in Washington, I'd been around politics for a while up there, and I had a feeling that this would be right up my alley. . . .

"I watch C-SPAN about 10 to 12 hours a week. I'd watch even more, but I have to make a living. . . .

"I read a lot, but C-SPAN is not the kind of channel you watch while doing other things. It's the kind of channel you watch because you want to watch it and nothing else, unlike a football game or a Western, where you can do other things. I always watch alone. My two-year-old daughter is obviously not interested; my 17-year-old is into music videos; and my wife is into other kinds of television. We have six TVs in the house. I watch C-SPAN either in the game room or in the private library—rarely are we in the bedroom watching C-SPAN.

"I read about a magazine a day—*U.S. News & World Report, Newsweek, Jet*—but I don't have time to read everything in depth. I try to read three national publications minimum per week. . . .

"The C-SPAN viewer is the true politico, the activist, the person who has in his or her blood a penchant for being on top of all key issues, national issues. Probably the one thing I've learned about America is that most people aren't into politics. A tiny few are heavily into it, but the average man would probably not know the names of his two U.S. senators. C-SPAN fills the appetite for that real zealot with political yearnings. . . .

"Politically I guess I'd call myself a moderate. In some issues I find myself in bed with the Falwells and the Robertsons of the world, and on others I'm with the Jesse Jacksons. For example, I'm against aid to the contras. On the other hand, I'm Catholic and anti-abortion. So it depends, I guess, on the issue. It would be hard to take a brush and paint me as a liberal or a conservative. Family issues—conservative. Social issues—more liberal.

"I met with Daniel Ortega twice in Nicaragua. I'm interested in Nicaragua because it's going to loom as a very important issue in this decade and the next. . . .

"Those who watch C-SPAN have probably broadened their perspective on the national political debate. I think now, because I'm on the speaking circuit quite often, it has allowed me a wealth of inside or back room information that I would never have gotten watching Dan Rather or Tom Brokaw. It has also kept me abreast of some of the inner workings of politics, so when I go around with politicos—true politicos—I can honestly discuss things in more depth now. . . .

"I watch network news by accident. If, when I come home, the time is right I'll flip it on. If I don't make it home at the right time I know CNN is there, so I don't worry about missing the conventional news. . . . Conventional news says, 'John

Doe spoke today and sponsored a bill on trade legislation.' OK, well and good. You've got 30 seconds to put it all together. C-SPAN goes quite a bit more deeply into the history, and you get a chance to watch the full flavor of legislation. . . .

"When I supplement C-SPAN with the *New York Times,* which I read at least two or three times a week, I'm really ahead of the ball game. And I'm around politicos all the time, be it Jesse or [Georgia State Sen.] Julian Bond [D], or people who make a living speaking about politics, and it's good when you can get together and hold your own with folks who do it 24 hours a day. . . .

"I have a buddy who is a banker, and we talk about forming a book club and a political discussion club. He's one of the few folks who can name the senator from Nebraska from 20 years ago. He's become my alter ego. But there's no one else here in Savannah, for all practical purposes, who I can sit down with and ask, 'What do you think about Jesse's arguments about [Louis] Farrakhan when he debated Bill Buckley?' This is football territory.

"Even among the members of the state legislature, it's hard to tell who does watch because 90 percent of them— with the legislature only in session three months out of the year—stay in hotels, and I haven't stayed in a hotel room yet that had C-SPAN. . . .

"But if I see an issue being discussed on C-SPAN, I might be inclined to write to the clerk of the House for a copy of the bill so that I can use it as a model for a bill I might want to introduce in Georgia. For example, I caught a glimpse of [Rep.] John Conyers [D-Michigan] speaking about his fair elections bill, which basically allows a wider input or broader list of persons who wish to run for national office. It removes some of the barriers to running for president. That piqued my interest in trying to broaden the opportunities for those wishing to run for offices here in the state. By sending for the bill and reading it, which I have, I have some fuel for matters here at the state level. And, believe me, it has an impact when you get to the well of the House to argue for the passage of a bill and you can say, '. . . because at the national level they have H.R. whatever.'

"Another federal bill I used as a model in the legislature concerned divestiture from corporations that do business with

South Africa. [Gov.] Mario Cuomo has a similar bill in New York, which I learned about from C-SPAN and the *New York Times*. I sent for that one, too. I would have never gotten the information from the conventional media.

"I write to my representatives in Washington. For example, I wrote to [Sen.] Sam Nunn [D-Georgia] about the nomination of [Alabama Judge Jefferson] Sessions to a federal judgeship. I used my political stationery—it has more weight. . . .

"C-SPAN hasn't changed my life, but I do make some use of it." —*M.C.*

Roy Allen watches C-SPAN by way of Savannah TV Cable Co.

"The Challenger"

Richard Armey_____
Denton, Texas

In 1983, Richard Armey, then an economics professor at North Texas State University in Denton, decided to run against incumbent Congressman Tom Vandergriff, a conservative Democrat. Before running, Dick Armey had never served in public office. He had never written to his congressman. In fact, until he was elected, the only member of Congress Prof. Armey had ever met was his opponent.

"C-SPAN changed my life," says Rep. Richard Armey (R) of the 26th District of Texas. As a result of a few years of intense C-SPAN viewing, "I gave up the most secure position in the world, that of a tenured college professor, to enter the first political race of my life."

As a professor and a self-described conservative economist, Mr. Armey's interest in politics had been purely academic: "I was always asking what those darn fools in Washington were doing when I saw the policies that were made. I had no idea how they did what they did, but I knew I wasn't happy with what I was getting."

But watching Congress on television—something Rep. Armey was able to do after subscribing to cable—helped to demystify the workings of Washington, which had always seemed a remote and inaccessible place to him. His C-SPAN viewing became an everyday affair. "I watched everything I could," he says. "My wife used to think I had Saturday night wrestling on, because I would talk back to the television." Rep. Armey became so involved that he cut out most other television viewing. He even cut back on football, except, of course, Dallas Cowboy games.

"And I began to feel a more intimate relationship to the process. I began to understand that these folks weren't bigger than life, and that, in fact, most of them weren't bigger than me."

But one thing bothered Dick Armey. After seeing hours of debate, he was convinced that he could make the arguments better than anyone else he had seen on the House floor. "I finally just said, the job's not being done right. I need to go do it myself. I wouldn't have known that if I hadn't been watching day in and day out as I did." In 1983, after a year of observing Congress from the sidelines, he decided to take the plunge, waging an energetic campaign against Rep. Vandergriff. From the start, reported the *Almanac of American Politics,* he had been perceived as the underdog in a race that even seasoned and prominent Texas politicians tended to shy away from. Dick Armey won by a narrow margin.

Congress-watching did not stop when Rep. Armey joined the club. The floor proceedings are on constantly in the office, and Rep. Armey, 48, says he always watches late in the evening, when he's alone there. Observing his colleagues on television has helped the Texas Republican gain a new respect for some members—Rep. Bill Gray (D-Pennsylvania), for example. "I had the impression that he was a cliché-spouting ideologue until I watched him and saw his skill. I've never swung to the point where I agree with him, but I am convinced that he is a skillful, articulate, thoughtful member and that he would be a more than adequate opponent on any issue."

And, now that the Senate is also being televised, Rep. Armey says he finds himself watching the "other body" of Congress on TV (although he readily proclaims the Senate to be "a much duller show" than the House). "It's helped me to understand the way they work over there, their rules, or what seems to be their lack of rules," Rep. Armey says. "Because I do have to work with the Senate, just learning about the personalities has been helpful."

One particularly helpful Senate debate that Rep. Armey

watched on TV concerned the Gramm-Rudman-Hollings balanced budget legislation, especially the speech by Sen. Phil Gramm (R-Texas). For Rep. Armey, it was the most memorable congressional event he's seen on TV. "I saw a master presentation on the merit of the bill by a man who is a master at speaking as well."

Of course, being on the other side of the camera has left Rep. Armey as open to scrutiny as anyone else. Take, for example, the time he did a Special Order—a speech members can make at the end of the day on any topic—about the labor agenda. He received a point-by-point rebuttal of the speech from a viewer who was obviously a staunch liberal. "I didn't know who the letter was from until I got to the bottom line," Rep. Armey says. The letter was signed, "Love, Uncle Joe." —M.C.

Congressman Armey watches C-SPAN in his Capitol Hill office through the Congress' internal cable system.

"The Legislative Aide"

Tuckerman Babcock
Wasilla, Alaska

Each January, Alaska's state legislature begins its 120-day session in the capital city of Juneau. Tuckerman Babcock, 27, primary legislative assistant to State Representative Curt Menard (R), travels by boat or plane through two time zones to get there. "There are no roads to Juneau," he explains.

They do have C-SPAN in Juneau, however, which is more than Mr. Babcock can say for his hometown of Wasilla. Long interested in politics, he used to be a regular C-SPAN viewer, especially when he was in graduate school in Virginia. Now his watching is limited to his time in Juneau, or when he's visiting his parents in Anchorage.

Tuckerman Babcock has been watching the network since he was a senior in high school. "Our representative from Alaska, Don Young [R], was on a call-in program about gun control and I called in." While a call to Washington, D.C., might sound like a major investment for a high school student, Mr. Babcock says that it's cheaper for Alaskans to call the nation's capital than to phone their own state capital.

Tuckerman Babcock's parents moved to Anchorage in 1966 because they wanted to be near the tallest mountains in North America. By the age of five their son Tuckerman was an old hand at mountain climbing. "I climbed my first mountain when I was four weeks old—on my daddy's back," he says. Each of his three sisters have climbed Mt. McKinley. So compelling were those 20,320 feet of Mt. McKinley that his father traded in his career as a sociology professor to become an instructor in mountaineering and wilderness survival.

Today, Mr. Babcock lives part of the time in Wasilla, a small town some 50 miles north of Anchorage, with his wife and daughter. As much as he enjoys mountain climbing, he was drawn to a less dangerous career. "I was already smitten with politics by the time I was a freshman in high school," he recalls. He attended an alternative high school that was "very public policy-oriented at the time." And since "candidates for governor and for different legislative offices debated at our school," he got a good deal of exposure to politics.

That was enough to convince Tuckerman Babcock to chart a course through college that would lead to a career in state government. He selected one college in the East and another in the West, and attended both of them. "I wanted to see attitudes about politics and government in different parts of the country. There really is a tremendous difference in attitudes."

After managing several campaigns for Alaskan politicians, Tuckerman Babcock accepted a job in state government. His boss, Rep. Menard, is a freshman and a member of the Republican minority. When the 40-member Alaska legislature is in session, Mr. Babcock manages office activities for his boss. He prepares research on the bills Rep. Menard sponsors and lays groundwork for their passage. Mr. Babcock says that Alaska's size, location, population, wealth of natural resources, and relationship with the federal government make state government there unlike that of most other states.

Alaska, with more than half a million square miles of vast, untamed wilderness and almost 34,000 miles of rugged coastline, is more like a country than a state. It stretches across three time zones and makes up one-fifth of the continental United States, yet its population is the smallest of all the states. One U.S. congressman represents the state's entire citizenry. Most of the state is virtually uninhabited: The majority of Alaska's 534,000 citizens live in Anchorage or Fairbanks.

Alaskans are constantly assessing the pros and cons of resource development. Future oil exploration in the Artic National Wildlife Reserve is one such issue. "This will be decided completely at the federal level, yet it affects Alaska tremendously," says Mr. Babcock. "It could mean billions of dollars to us."

Alaska abolished its state income tax and sales tax in the late '70s when, thanks to the new pipeline, the income from the oil fields started gushing in at several billion dollars a year. "As it is now, our oil fields produce about 85 percent of our state budget. But that is going to decline steadily from now on," Mr. Babcock says. "The price of oil has gone down enough that we're really aching to get a chance to explore in other areas." But the area they hope to start exploring is home to 180,000 caribou. Not surprisingly, environmentalists are at odds with those who'd like to drill.

"That's the big battle up here," he says, "balancing resource development, which is vital to our economic survival, with protecting enough of our environment to let us enjoy the kind of frontier recreation that motivated many of us to be here in the first place."

Since the federal government owns and has jurisdiction over 59 percent of the land, many Alaskan issues are resolved in the U.S. Congress rather than in Alaska's statehouse. So Mr. Babcock keeps up on what's happening in Congress—for his own knowledge and because his constituents want to know. "With C-SPAN, you actually get to hear members of a committee say what they are leaning toward or what concerns they have on these issues that are so critical to us."   —C.M.

Mr. Babcock tunes in C-SPAN on Cooke Cablevision when he's in Juneau.

Howard Baker
Robert Byrd
Robert Dole

Huntsville, Tennessee
Sophia, West Virginia
Russell, Kansas

Bringing television to the U.S. Senate in 1986 was a matter of much debate, vote-counting, and several changes of heart. The story of Senate television is a long one and many actors played a role in the deliberation. Three leaders in the Senate approached the issue of Senate TV in three different ways, each of which varied with their perspectives, positions, and experience.

Sen. Howard Baker (R-Tennessee), Senate majority leader from 1981 to 1985, had long dreamed of making the Senate's proceedings available for viewing on TV. He retired from the legislative body to begin a tentative campaign for president before his efforts to lead the Senate into the TV age could become a reality. Sen. Robert Byrd (D-West Virginia), who was the minority leader when the bill to televise the Senate finally passed, had originally opposed Senate TV but modified his stance over the years. Once he'd changed his mind, he took the lead on Senate TV. He worked hard behind the scenes and on the floor to get the Senate to accept cameras in its chambers. The 1986 majority leader, Sen. Robert Dole (R-Kansas), another presidential hopeful, approached Senate television with a position best described as benign neglect. He thought the Senate had more pressing issues to deal with, but said, "At least, let's experiment," as the proposal moved along.

Politicians had debated the proposal to televise the Senate

and the House of Representatives since the 1940s, but Sen. Baker was the idea's first real champion in the postwar era. Opening up the government for citizens' scrutiny on television had always appealed to him. In a 1986 interview, he said that he "wanted [televised Senate debate] to be one of the major achievements in my career in Congress, especially in my career as leader."

Howard Baker came from a longtime political family. His mother and father had both served in the House of Representatives, and he had married the daughter of Senate minority leader Everett Dirksen. His arrival in the Senate in 1966 marked Tennessee's first election of a Republican in generations. During his congressional career he earned a reputation as a master of negotiation and compromise.

As the ranking member of the Senate Communications Subcommittee in the 1970s, Sen. Baker had become aware early of cable television's potential to carry public affairs programming. He put forward the idea of Senate TV as early as 1976. "Television has an extraordinary effect on the public's awareness of the legislative and government process," he said at the time. "And, based on that, I think there ought to be total free access to live coverage for anybody who wants to take proceedings of the House and Senate. . . . It's certainly ready-made for the multiple-channel capacity that cable systems have."

As the new majority leader, Sen. Baker offered the first resolution for Senate TV coverage in 1981. It was soundly rebuffed. In 1986, the senator recalled his experience with Senate TV as "running into a political buzz saw. There were people in the Senate who were violently opposed to it, and that's what surprised me—the depth and emotion of the opposition to television. . . . It started out as a mistrust in the Senate of an unknown element."

During his term as majority leader, the senator tried several times to get the Senate to consider a motion on Senate TV. Each time, the measure went through committee, but met with no success on the floor. "I was very careful—maybe more careful than I should have been—about putting the issue up in its final form and losing it. . . . So I held back and I counted carefully, and I negotiated extensively, and I tried and tried dozens of variations and combinations. . . . The real work was being done in the Rules Committee and in those behind-the-scenes negotiations that really characterize the Senate and make it function.

"We did have it a time or two. We had the votes, but it was so close it would have depended on the absentees." Sen. Baker remembers that senators would threaten to filibuster if the issue came before the floor. "I was subject to that sort of political intimidation. . . . I had thought when I became majority leader, that would help me get TV in the Senate. And, as a matter of fact, it hurt." Today, though, he is pleased to see the Senate on TV. "I'm glad it finally did happen, though, because I think that's important . . . even though I was not in the Senate at the time it occurred."

Sen. Baker recalls that Sen. Robert Byrd was subject to similar political pressures and was "ambivalent" about Senate TV in 1981. As minority leader, Sen. Byrd had opposed the first measure to televise the Senate. His state, West Virginia, had a low rate of exposure to House coverage. He did not have C-SPAN in his home in Washington's Virginia suburbs or in his office. He says he had not watched C-SPAN's House telecasts until 1985, when he found the network by spinning the dial on a hotel room television set while traveling.

However, as television coverage of its proceedings began to win the House of Representatives a high level of public recognition, Sen. Byrd feared the possibility of "the foremost deliberative body in the world . . . fast becoming the invisible half of Congress." His own experience as a congressional leader in the television age was telling. For example, he relates the story about how, despite his nearly 30 years in the Senate, one of his own constituents in West Virginia introduced him to an audience as "Speaker of the House." Perhaps the daily television appearances of the white-haired Speaker Thomas "Tip" O'Neill confused that master of ceremonies as he introduced the similarly white-haired Sen. Byrd.

By 1985, majority leader Baker had left the Senate. His successor, Robert Dole, faced a full legislative agenda following the re-election of President Reagan, and decided to relegate Senate TV to the back burner. Sen. Byrd stepped into the vacuum and pushed for Senate television, offering a TV resolution at the opening of the 99th Congress in January 1985.

During the debate Sen. Byrd lived up to his reputation as a detail man and as an astute persuader. He made the issue a personal priority by working to soften the stances of longtime television opponent Sen. Russell Long (D-Louisiana) and by promoting Senate TV on the floor and in committee.

"I think it is about time we opened up this window to the American people," the senator declared in a floor speech in February 1986. "Why should they not see what goes on here? Why should they not hear what goes on here?" He made note of the attention the House had captured through television. "Whether we like it or not, the American public is forming lasting impressions about Congress from the image which reaches them through television. And the image of the Senate is not reaching them through television. . . . More people could be exposed to Senate debate in one evening through television than could visit our galleries in two decades." The senator's support and hard work were instrumental in bringing about a resolution for Senate TV that passed the Senate 67-21 that same month.

During the gradual melting of opposition to television cameras in the Senate, Sen. Dole maintained a low-key public stand on the issue. He began to focus more on it as Senate TV grew closer to fruition. Like Sens. Byrd and Baker, Dole was a seasoned politician, having served in Congress since 1960. As a close observer of congressional decision making, he chose to let the Senate move gradually toward a majority view, if not a consensus, about bringing in the cameras. A rush to a decision promoted by only a few senators could raise the suspicions of others and thereby cast the outcome in doubt. It would be far better for a vote on television in the Senate to succeed or fail on its own merits.

In debate over the issue on February 6, 1986, Sen. Dole urged that the Senate consider all aspects of TV coverage before bringing television to a vote. "Some senators want the rules changed before we have TV in the Senate. Some do not want any rules changed. Some do not want television. Some only want television. . . . I think we need to figure out where the majority of senators may come down before we start voting on the matter.

". . . I hope that if we do have television in the Senate, we can have some rules changes, so that the leadership will be able to exercise a little more flexibility in bringing matters to the floor without filibusters on a matter to proceed," he added.

On February 19, 1986, Sen. Dole called himself "very flexible" on the question of how the Senate would be covered. "I am prepared to do it any way we can." He said that he was "not certain whether gavel-to-gavel coverage is in the best interest of the Senate or the viewing public," and suggested moving Special Orders speeches to a time slot later in the day. "I hope that when it is all finished, we will have some reasonable rules changes."

By February 27, Sen. Dole said: "I hope we can have a huge margin in support of TV in the Senate. . . . I think it is going to be a good debate." He thanked Sen. Baker: "Without his longstanding commitment to televising Senate proceedings, today would never have come about." The majority leader voted with the 67 Democrats and Republicans who supported TV, but at a March 20 *Los Angeles Times* newsmaker breakfast telecast on C-SPAN, Sen. Dole said he'd "never had strong feelings one way or another." He did allow, however, that television ". . . may improve our discipline."

On June 2, 1986, majority leader Dole made the first televised speech on the floor of the U.S. Senate. He alluded to his "reservations," but announced, "We are going public. We will be watched by our friends and by people across the country. . . . Today we catch up with the 20th century. We're on TV now, and we're never going to pull the plug." After the initial test period, Sen. Dole spoke out in favor of the continuation of telecasts of the Senate.

Since Howard Baker first sought to put television on the Senate's agenda, the landscape of the Senate has shifted. Sen. Baker retired in 1985, later becoming White House chief of staff. Democratic victories in the 1986 senatorial elections caused minority leader Byrd and majority leader Dole to change places. Despite all the changes of the guard, the Senate marched on, and its televised proceedings are now available to 15 million homes. Sen. Baker, inspired by the notion that the American people desired access to the Senate via television, showed the way. Sen. Byrd accepted the idea, and then used his mastery of the Senate's traditions and rules to move it into the final stretch. And Sen. Dole? As he had told the *Los Angeles Times* reporters over coffee in March 1986, "I only did it for Howard Baker—he wanted us to see us on TV."   —*S.S., J.E., M.H.*

Messrs. Byrd, Dole and Baker can all watch C-SPAN in their Washington offices. At home in Sophia, West Virginia, Sen. Byrd can watch C-SPAN on Mountain State Cablevision; Sen. Dole can watch C-SPAN in his hometown of Russell, Kansas, on Falcon Cablevision.

"The Interpreter"

Philomena Benevides-Rogers

Washington, D.C.

Philomena Benevides-Rogers has always been very interested in, and sensitive to, other cultures. Born in the multi-ethnic community of Fall River, Massachusetts, to first-generation Portuguese-American parents, she learned early on to appreciate her heritage. Over the years she became increasingly adept at observing and comparing cultures and at understanding the subtle differences between them. Ms. Benevides-Rogers learned Portuguese as a child, and by the time she finished high school she was fluent in English and French as well. After college she went on to earn a master's degree in international relations from George Washington University.

Given Ms. Benevides-Rogers interest in other cultures, it's not surprising that she earns her living in international affairs. As a research associate at the Japan Center for International Finance, her job is to keep Japanese bankers up-to-date on American financial and political developments. But the 29-year-old analyst didn't get this job because she understood Japanese culture. "They didn't want an American who knew Asia," she explains, "they wanted an American who knew America." In this case, knowing America meant understanding politics, the Congress, and the current administration's perspective. Fortunately for Ms. Benevides-Rogers, her interest in other cultures is rivaled by only one thing: her interest in politics.

As a Ripon College undergraduate, she ran Wisconsin's Young Republicans organization. She's worked on numerous political campaigns including district attorney and Senate races in Massachusetts and the 1980 presidential campaign. (She first worked for Vice President Bush but later switched to the Carter-Mondale ticket.) She has been a congressional staff assistant and the director of research (and later, writer and assistant producer) for the "McLaughlin Group"—a nationally syndicated public affairs TV series, where it was her job to follow the activities of Congress. For all of these reasons, the Japanese organization hired Ms. Benevides-Rogers as its first and only American research associate.

JCIF represents 50 of Japan's leading financial institutions and has more than 200 member organizations. In 1984, Japanese bankers felt they were suffering from "an information gap"; the center was created to help alleviate that problem. Although it's closely aligned with Japan's Ministry of Finance, JCIF is not a lobbying organization, and it doesn't make policy decisions. "We're interested in the policy-making agenda of Congress," she says. The information gathered by Ms. Benevides-Rogers and her colleagues is used by Japanese financial institutions to assess American and Third World investments.

"I monitor legislation pending before Congress, and write weekly reports on trade and banking deregulation and reregulation. The stock market crash was very important to our people in Tokyo, and so was the changing of the guard at the Federal Reserve Board," Ms. Benevides-Rogers explains. She also writes an overall monthly report and an occasional special report, such as her recent 20-page report on the contra aid debate. In addition, she is responsible for following the presidential elections. This monitoring, analyzing, and writing takes time and resources. Ms. Benevides-Rogers was eager to save time, so she convinced JCIF to add C-SPAN to her research tools.

"It frees us from having to go up to Capitol Hill. We are not a very large office, so we don't have many expendable people to go to the hearings, which can take an entire day by the time you go to Capitol Hill, wait an hour or two to get in, listen to testimony, and then go back to the office and write a report." Her reports are generally needed that night: It's already the next day in Tokyo, so "it's better if you can do it all from the office," she says.

Although Ms. Benevides-Rogers speaks three languages and comes from a long line of multi-lingual people, she doesn't speak Japanese. So she enters her reports into the data base in English and they're translated in the Tokyo office. Her Japanese coworkers all speak English, but they do have a hard time understanding American traditions, like the political party system and the election process. "They find our system very confusing," she explains. "They have a democratic system, but it's rather controlled." She thinks it's especially hard for the Japanese to get used to the shift in priorities with each new American administration. "There's a lot more consistency and coherence in their policy, and it doesn't change as much—at least not as dramatically as it does in the U.S."

Those differences don't surprise Ms. Benevides-Rogers. "People speak different languages and there are a lot of differences between cultures; but after a while you start to see the similarities. I don't see the differences as much anymore. I see the similarities. And that tends to build bridges."   —P.K.

Ms. Benevides-Rogers monitors C-SPAN in her Washington, D.C., office by way of The Capitol Connection.

"The Channel Zapper"

Bruce Berman

Boston, Massachusetts

Bruce Berman, 32, calls his newspaper "the prince of the alternative press." The *Boston Phoenix,* one of the nation's oldest and largest independently run newspapers, can be irreverent, and can display moments of passion. With a circulation of 125,000, its tabloid format, and muckraking political stories, there are inevitable comparisons to another counterculture icon—the *Village Voice.*

Mr. Berman writes a political column for the *Phoenix* under the pen name "Spurious." "You can't necessarily believe any casual comment I make," he says. Pseudonym aside, he takes his job seriously. "I wear my politics on my sleeve. If the *Phoenix* didn't want a progressive Democrat with an ax to grind, I wouldn't be writing for them."

Mr. Berman says much of his information and inspiration comes from television. "Generally, what I do is watch TV," he declares. "I'm an inveterate channel changer." The columnist is also a "cable addict" whose home receives daily helpings of what he calls "the Rainbow Gold Bouquet" deluxe package of cable channels. The array of over 100 channels at Mr. Berman's fingertips gives him "the illusion of some control over my environment." Since even the atmosphere of the *Phoenix* office might be disrupted by "Spurious'" incessant channel-flipping, most of Mr. Berman's continuous viewing takes place in the rough-and-tumble atmosphere of his Boston flat. Cigarette in one hand, channel changer in the other, Mr. Berman holds the phone between his chin and his shoulder as the TV blares. Friends and *Phoenix* editors on unannounced visits ring the doorbell at any hour of the day.

Mr. Berman's two loves—skewering politicians and watching TV—come together handily in an age when television cameras record public officials' every move. As he forges his political beat from what he sees on TV, Mr. Berman finds a special use for the unedited, unanalyzed, complete political events he sees on C-SPAN. He likes to watch "good bites" on other networks, but "when C-SPAN's covering something, there's nothing between me and the event—just the technology, not someone's obnoxious opinions. It's just sitting there looking at me—no opinions and no 'spin.'" Mr. Berman is free to put his own uniquely spurious spin on what he witnesses on television.

The sight of the naked political process taking place onscreen has been known to add fuel to the flame of Mr. Berman's flaring cynicism. "When you're sitting at home and you see a guy out there pandering to a special interest group, giving in to a special interest, boy, is it clear." Of the Senate, he says, "The old saying that the 'Senate blows in the wind' may not be true, but undecided senators sure as hell have their fingers out the window." And in a sense he sees C-SPAN as aiming "a spotlight on some pretty dark corners where interesting things happen. Dark corners of politics in America, places where sometimes they can't stand the scrutiny—C-SPAN shines the light on them and sees what they're doing."

Working at home, says Mr. Berman, "is one of the pleasures of my life. It's one of the reasons I do the job. When I go to a press conference, I just can't kick and scream and yell at the figure who's speaking. When I'm home, I can say, 'Bull————,' really loud." Aside from precluding nasty public scenes, Mr. Berman's chair-bound ways save the budget-conscious *Phoenix* money. "If I said I wanted to go cover a [Rep. Jack] Kemp [R-New York] speech and it'll cost $1,800, they'd laugh. But if I wrote a piece on a Kemp speech on C-SPAN, they'll run it."

Mr. Berman used C-SPAN to do some investigative legwork in 1987. While working on a story about the FBI one evening, he looked up from his computer terminal into the eyes of then-FBI Director William Webster. Judge Webster was on a C-SPAN call-in program, taking viewers' questions. "This is too good to be true," Mr. Berman remembers thinking as he bolted for the telephone. Upon getting through to the program, the columnist asked Judge Webster about the FBI's interaction with the CIA and the National Security Council. He listened carefully to the answer, but concluded that if he "had been able to ask a follow-up question, the interview would have been more useful." Days later, however, a televised congressional hearing provided "unbelievably useful" information on his FBI story.

The 1987 Robert Bork confirmation hearings were of special interest to Mr. Berman, who listened to the sessions during the day on National Public Radio and watched C-SPAN's evening replays with friends. Was there any advantage in watching on television? "One thing we wouldn't have known if it wasn't for C-SPAN—that everybody was wearing Harvard ties at the Bork hearings. When you listen to the radio you miss these things—way too many Harvard ties."

Mr. Berman is grateful to the cable networks for covering politics in a time when broadcast networks are cutting back on political news or tailoring it to fit a rigid program format. "During a campaign gap, when network people aren't being sent out there to cover what's going on, C-SPAN's there. As a result, he says, "I'll forget a telephone bill, but I never, ever lose a cable bill."

During C-SPAN's interview with Mr. Berman, he shouted out to *Phoenix* editor Richard Gaines, who was waiting in his living room (and who had almost certainly popped in without calling first), "C-SPAN's made my columns a lot more interesting, hasn't it?" "Much," Mr. Gaines could be heard calling back. Because of television, "The bottom line is, the *Phoenix* is really happy because they always know where I am—not out spending their money." —*N.G.*

"Spurious" zaps TV channels on Cablevision Systems of Boston.

"The Ozark Caller"

Margaret Blair

Fayetteville, Arkansas

Margaret Blair, 50, of Fayetteville, Arkansas, may have more of an "in" with Washington bigwigs than the average inside-the-Beltway power broker. From her fieldstone house in the Ozarks she has talked to former Secretary of Defense Caspar Weinberger, Sen. Richard Lugar (R-Indiana), *Washington Times* editor Arnaud de Borchgrave, *New Republic* editor-in-chief Martin Peretz, and 30 journalists representing newspapers from around the world.

Television and radio call-in programs are Ms. Blair's vehicle for contacting these traditionally hard-to-reach Washington VIPs. Occasionally she calls the "Larry King Show" and a local religious radio show, but she says that the C-SPAN call-in program, which she calls once a month, is her favorite. And she would call more often if it weren't for the network's "30-day restriction," which is designed to allow more viewers a chance to participate. Ms. Blair says she prefers call-in programs with journalists, because "sometimes you have to strain too hard to read between the lines when the congressmen are on."

Margaret Blair lives each day with what she calls her "agenda of worries." Though constantly in flux, it usually includes about 30 issues—popular national concerns, matters that don't get enough press, and topics in which she has a personal interest. Among the issues are family planning, dangers of the nuclear winter, the health hazards of tobacco use, and the nation's educational system. For the past four years, she has been discussing these concerns with politicians and journalists on call-in programs.

Ms. Blair has a master's degree in education from the University of Arkansas. She taught school for many years and also worked as a registered nurse. Now she manages rental property. "The pay is better," she says. As a former eighth-grade science teacher, Ms. Blair says "the old schoolteacher part of me" is worried about the overemphasis on sports in America's schools. "Our children, as early as third grade, are not getting their values right," she insists. "They think they will all grow up to be professional athletes and make millions of dollars, so they don't do their homework."

At one time Ms. Blair worked as a nurse in the local Veterans Administration Hospital, and she was always appalled that they allowed patients to smoke. She's still concerned about the harmful effects of smoking, and she broached this subject with both Caspar Weinberger and Sen. Lugar on the call-in. She suggested to the senator that the government put a hefty tax on cigarettes to discourage smokers.

Ms. Blair has other news sources she taps so that she can keep up on her agenda of worries. For more than 20 years, she has been listening to short-wave radio. With a short-wave receiver in practically every room of her home, she listens to radio broadcasts from the BBC, CBC, Radio Moscow, and Voice of America. "The British devote a good deal of their programming to public affairs," she explains. "They have a good bit of arts programming. I guess it's a worldwide view, probably left over from their empire days. They're not as parochial as we tend to be.

"People tend to forget about short-wave receivers," she says. "The technology today is so dandy; digital systems—they're fairly inexpensive and you can carry them around." Ms. Blair learned about the digital systems from Arnaud de Borchgrave when she spoke to him twice on C-SPAN call-ins. Mr. de Borchgrave is one of her favorite guests. "He's so eloquent and gives so much interesting detail to his explanations," she notes. "The man works terribly hard. Apparently he sometimes sleeps at the *Washington Times* in a Murphy bed and listens to short-wave radios while he's there."

Although scanning the short-wave radio dial for distant signals has been a longtime hobby for her, she actually prefers televised public affairs programming. She regularly starts her day with CNN's business report at 5:30 A.M. (central time), and then switches to C-SPAN at 6:30 A.M. and watches the morning media call-in program at 7:45.

Exposure to journalists has been a primary way for her to expand her periodical reading list. After seeing a correspondent from the *Economist* on a C-SPAN call-in program, she subscribed to the publication. The same thing happened after she saw the *New Republic's* Martin Peretz. "I called in and talked with him, and was just so impressed with the magazine. So I decided to try it out." Ms. Blair says that sometime later C-SPAN had a guest from the conservative magazine *Spotlight*. And she thought, "Well, that's just the opposite pole, so I'll subscribe to that for a year."

Although Margaret Blair thinks of herself as "pretty much of a Democrat," she says that in this election, "I was going to give myself permission to vote for a Republican." But that was before the October 1987 stock market collapse. She didn't like the Republican Party's treatment of the crisis. Nevertheless, Ms. Blair's respect for policy makers is not based on party affiliation. She admires the conservative Mr. de Borchgrave for his hard work as much as she does the Texas liberal Democrat Rep. Henry Gonzalez. Even though he says "some far out things, he's fervent and passionate."

Listening to the morning call-in is also a way for her to learn more about her fellow Americans and their concerns. "A good many of them are informed, and a good many of them are upset," comments Ms. Blair. She had heard so many questions from callers on the controversial Trilateral Commission that she went to the library to check out the issue more thoroughly. She got the commission's telephone number from a book in the library and found out through a commission information officer that she could subscribe to its publication. After subscribing to the commission's newspaper for a year Ms. Blair says, "I'm more positively impressed with its goals."

Publications, says Margaret Blair, help supplement her

TV viewing. Together, she says they help "create a big picture" for her. "I get such a feeling of being right in the middle of policy making. Here we are, right in this little-sized community, and we get to peek in, through this window, and we get to see the power."   —P.K.

Margaret Blair watches C-SPAN call-in programs on Fayetteville's Warner Cable Communications Inc.

"The Legislating Dentist"

Walter Blevins

Morehead, Kentucky

Kentucky state legislator Walter Blevins represents a rural district in the eastern part of the state where people produce timber, coal, and tobacco. When he's not on the House floor in Frankfort, Kentucky, he's back home at his office in Morehead—filling cavities and performing root canals.

Maintaining a dental practice while serving as a legislator can be tough. "I've got to be in my office to make a living," he says. "It's not like running a shop where you can have someone else run the cash register." The Kentucky legislature meets in the early part of every other year for 60 days, adjourns for a 10-day recess, and reassembles for a two-day veto session. Committee hearings take place once or twice a week throughout the rest of the year. Dr. Blevins makes the journey to Frankfort—90 miles round trip—to attend each meeting.

Combining the two professions does have its advantages. "It's not often that people get a chance to sit down with their legislators," observes Dr. Blevins. "Therefore, patients come to me and kind of unload their concerns." Dentistry helps his legislative career because he gets to see a lot of people from diverse economic backgrounds.

The 37-year-old dentist represents one of the largest land areas in the state, but it also happens to be one of the poorest. Some 18 to 20 percent of his constituents are unemployed.

"Improved education, improved job opportunities, and better roads. I think these things run hand in hand to bring about a better life for the people in the area," he says.

Dr. Blevins uses C-SPAN as a resource for keeping abreast of national issues and as a model for honing his own legislative skills. He saw the U.S. House of Representatives tackle the problems of teen-age pregnancy, hazardous run-off, and toxic waste before they surfaced in the Kentucky legislature; and the experience helped to prepare him for the floor exchanges. "We are doing the same things, only on a smaller scale. I've led the charge on these issues, and I've listened to the House debates and have occasionally picked up ideas from other speakers that have been helpful in speeches and debate."

His colleagues in the Kentucky legislature also watch C-SPAN. "It generates discussion. Most of the members are pretty politically astute, so we can often discuss events and issues that are covered on C-SPAN." His wife Carla, a Democratic activist who sometimes helps out at the dentist's office, has become an avid C-SPAN viewer, too. "I've encouraged others to watch it," Dr. Blevins explains, "because a well-informed citizenry guarantees a good government. I always have it on at home. And a lot of people stop by the house, so they may see it and get hooked."

Morehead is the home of the district's cultural center, Morehead State University. Dr. Blevins attended undergraduate school there and served as president of the Young Democrats. "By 1981," Dr. Blevins recalls, "I saw some things that needed to be done here and I wanted to do them. I decided to put my name on the ballot and go out and work hard. I beat an incumbent who had been in office about 12 years."

He credits C-SPAN programming for helping him arrive at the decision to run for the statehouse. "It gave me at least a belief that it was worth a try—that whether I lost or won, I could bring some issues to the forefront and maybe make people aware that the political system does work. I'd done very little public speaking before that."

These days a lot of people get to see Dr. Blevins in action—Kentucky Educational Television broadcasts the state's House and Senate sessions and some committee meetings. Dr. Blevins feels that this public exposure of the lawmakers has strengthened the process of government. "Any time you put more information before the people, it makes for a better citizenry. I think that the caliber of the individuals elected to the House has been improved. The disruptive shenanigans of the pre-TV days are over," he says. "Because of television's scrutinizing eye it just takes better qualified people to fill those roles."

Dr. Blevins recently sponsored a bill to fund a community access channel to cover local government. But the funding proposal died in the Kentucky House, probably because it would have required a tax increase. He's sponsored other bills that have been successful, though, such as the New Car Lemon Law Bill, which protects automobile buyers, and a law that outlaws hazing on college campuses.

As vice chairman of the Appropriations and Revenue Committee, he's particularly proud of the role that he played in bringing about the construction of a medium-security prison in the town of West Liberty. He points to the prison as an example of successful diversification—something he feels is critical to economic well-being given the decline of the coal and tobacco industries. The prison is the state's biggest capital project in 10 years, and the district expects it to create 450 jobs. Dr. Blevins is also intent on earmarking more state funds to improve the education system and to fight illiteracy, although he warns that the federal government will have to contribute a share if that problem is to be overcome. "I want to do everything I can to help illiterate people lead more productive lives," he explains.

Dr. Blevins is a popular legislator—after waging a couple of tough campaigns, he won his last race with 70 percent of the vote. He attributes his success to the fact that "the things I've been talking about—roads, prisons, education—are starting to happen." And he might consider a bid for the U.S. Senate someday—although it all depends on finances and on how he does in future sessions. "I'm not a rich man. Perhaps I should have stayed a dentist longer before I got into politics."

Dr. Blevins believes that growing up in a small town made him realize that a politician can have great impact on people's lives. And that realization is at the heart of what

Walter Blevins sees as his mission as a state legislator: "Helping people—seeing them go to work, seeing roads opening up so people can get into my area—that's what I like best about being in the General Assembly. That's what makes it all worthwhile." —*P.K.*

Dr. Blevins subscribes to Centel Cable TV of Morehead, Kentucky.

"The High School Teacher"

Sandra Bradford

Standish, Maine

Southern coastal Maine is in a state of flux. Building and development are transforming the face of the Portland suburbs. Corporate professionals are moving into the area, bringing different priorities and values to neighborhoods where families have lived for generations. High-tech is reshaping the traditional farming and industrial economy.

Sandra Bradford, 40, sees the tension between the old and the new played out every day at Scarborough High School, where she teaches history and American government. Scarborough, a bedroom community of Portland, has, she says, "a large population of people who have been born and raised in Scarborough, and their roots are very deep there. Then you've got about half the population that is highly mobile and high-income—the professionals who move in to join many of the large businesses in the area. You have people who are coming in and putting a lot of pressure on the schools to provide special programs for almost an elitist population within the system. And there are people who are on Social Security and fixed incomes who are looking at their tax dollars. All those special things are going to cost a lot of money."

Ms. Bradford, a Maine native who grew up in South Portland, has been teaching at Scarborough High for 15 years. It was her first teaching position and she stayed, despite a

30-minute commute from her home in Standish, because "I really like the system and the people. We have a tremendous staff. They are a very warm and caring group of people."

Ms. Bradford explains that the 650 students at her school have developed a "class system or caste system," divided between what students call the "jocks" and the "burnouts": There are the students who take part in extracurricular activities and generally sign up for college preparatory courses; and then there are the career education students, who "usually get out at 12:00 or 1:00 and go to a job at Burger King or McDonald's to make car payments. These aren't the kids who are going on to college. These are kids who are preparing, in a vocational program, to go into the working world."

The school continually grapples with the question of how to treat these two groups equally. "We've sat down as a staff to assess our whole discipline system and whether we're treating everybody fairly." Ms. Bradford tries to make sure that she pays attention to students from both sides of the line. In 1986, she discovered a teaching tool that she uses to reach the jocks and burnouts alike: C-SPAN. "Government can be so deadly if you're just looking at a text," she says. "Every government text must weigh 25 pounds, minimum. Television makes it more real and alive."

Ms. Bradford often works televised portions of congressional hearings into classroom discussions. She first used the network's programming as material for a college preparatory course in American history. "They take six weeks at the end of the course to look at U.S. government." Her videotapes helped them "sense the complexity of the bill-making process and policy making."

Now students in Ms. Bradford's career education classes also watch C-SPAN, which was introduced in the classroom to address a practical problem: "It's very hard to get career education students to do anything outside the school day. It would be pointless for me to say, 'Go home and watch this tonight.' They just would not do that. As long as I did the work and brought it into class, they lapped it up."

It's a challenge to teach the career students, and Ms. Bradford worries at times about the tracking system that put them where they are. "I teach a lot of the career students, and for them, school is simply a bother. They've been slotted since their freshman year. This is something we've been looking at to judge whether it's the best way to go. We've gotten regimented and it's hard to get out of that mind-set."

Ms. Bradford has noticed that many of her students are taking a greater interest in national issues. They respond to "recognizable names, people who they have heard about, who are taking positions, and the issues. For example, if you talk about the Persian Gulf, a lot of my young men are going to be 18 in the near future and are thinking about registering for the draft. For them, that's a real issue." But, Ms. Bradford notes differences in perceptions between the college-prep contingent and the career-ed group. Many of the vocational-technical students had seen the 1987 Iran-contra hearings during summer vacation. "There was a tremendous sense of patriotic fervor, and yet I didn't sense that with my students who are going to college." The college-bound students, she says, "tend to be more esoteric about issues. But the career-ed students are more realistic about what their future's going to be, and whether they should enlist. They're not looking to Harvard."

Ms. Bradford says her career education students are starting to take an interest in politics. "Right now, they're all excited about competing in a state competition on the Constitution. These are kids who normally would not sit down and do this. But they really have gotten excited about this project and about government, and I think it's making a difference." Ms. Bradford says that some students even have taken up watching Congress in their free time.

Sandra Bradford wants to instill her own love of politics and history in her students. "I've always been a political animal," she says. Ms. Bradford got involved in local politics in high school and became more active at the University of Maine, where she studied history and education. She frequently takes part in local campaigns, stuffing envelopes and counting ballots. "I just love the political atmosphere," she says.

At Scarborough High, "you've got your kids who are involved in everything from sports to yearbook to glee club, and then you've got your kids who smoke in the bathroom and can't wait to get out of school." Ms. Bradford has found that television can convey the way government works to students across the board. Despite their differences, all her pupils are teen-agers who hate to lug that 25-pound history book. "I don't think I've had that textbook out of the closet this year. For the most part, I think kids are put off by things that give them hernias. Now when we talk about how a bill becomes a law, instead of just using the book I can bring in the visuals so the students can see the process." —S.S.

Ms. Bradford watches C-SPAN on United Video Cable.

"The Sample Voter"

Barbara Brian

Plaistow, New Hampshire

By March 1988, Barbara Brian had met and/or interviewed nine of 1988's major presidential candidates—one-on-one. And, sometime before the '88 conventions, she hoped to interview the other four. She's not a television reporter, or the League of Women Voters' debate producer. Ms. Brian, 69, is a twice-widowed retiree who lives in the tiny town of Plaistow, New Hampshire. She's an avid reader, writer, and artist-of-sorts who has two sons, five grandchildren, and a boyfriend. And in September 1987, the ABC affiliate in Boston, WCVB-TV, invited her to take part in its year-long "Five American Families" series.

In an effort to learn how people select their candidates, WCVB-TV chose five families from around the country to follow throughout the presidential campaign year. All of the voters were undecided about their preferred candidate; they represented different socioeconomic groups and political party preferences. The group consisted of a black family in Louisiana; a Hispanic couple in Colorado; an Iowa farming family; working-class newlyweds in California, and this 69-year-old grandmother from New Hampshire.

Barbara Brian came to our attention early in 1988 when she wrote to the network to describe her project. Watching C-SPAN programming, she claimed, had made her feel competent enough about the candidates to continue with this project. "Thanks for giving me the courage, at almost 70 years of age, to do this," she wrote.

"As I went through with this political thing," she explained, "I felt that I was a respected person, not just a senior citizen, which is a horrible description of an older person, I think."

At the outset, the Boston station interviewed all of the families on camera to see what they thought of the candidates. They followed up with one or two interviews each month with at least one of the families. They also made arrangements for the families to interview candidates who passed through their towns. And early in the year, they brought all five families and four of the candidates together via satellite for a special broadcast.

Until September 1987, Barbara Brian, who lives on a retiree's fixed income, kept busy with friends or hobbies. She says she was never interested enough in politics to follow issues or to get involved. These days she spends most of her time talking, reading, and watching politics. She's even gotten her friends and neighbors interested.

"I live in a senior citizen development," she says, "and I have educated all my neighbors to be political. We have a group that meets every afternoon now, and they want to know what's happening. It's made their lives better, I think."

Ms. Brian, who was chairwoman of the cable TV committee for the town of Plaistow, had never watched C-SPAN before her political debut. Once she was selected for this project, she says she "just logically moved" to the network. That's because she decided to follow the campaign trail intensely. She does it, she says, "so that I will ask the right questions and appear knowledgeable."

She has taken this project very much to heart. That may not have been what WCVB-TV was expecting, however, since originally none of the five families was especially politically inclined. She speculates that "they seem to be concerned that I know too much and the others know too little."

During the primary season, she tried to concentrate on one candidate each week. "I do all of my own research on a candidate," she explains. At one time, Ms. Brian was a reporter for the Lawrence *Eagle-Tribune*. That experience has come in handy. "I have three notebooks which I've kept since I knew I was going to be on television. I take lots of things—editorials, articles, my own feelings, and things I've heard—and put them in these notebooks. I put questions beside things in case I want to ask a candidate. So when I go, say for Kemp, I take my book down and note all the things I want to ask him."

All of this exposure has made Barbara Brian something of a celebrity. She gets calls from the different campaigns on a regular basis; one candidate, Sen. Bob Dole (R-Kansas), even called her himself. And she's been the subject of so many articles that, at this point, she's lost track.

But the celebrity status isn't really her style, she says. "It's really embarrassing. I'm not bashful, as you can tell, but I don't like to be thought of as a celebrity. I just want to be thought of as a person who is intelligent and should be respected." —M.C.

Barbara Brian follows presidential politics on C-SPAN by way of Rockingham County Cable.

"The News Designer"

Lewis Brierley

Columbia, South Carolina

Lewis Brierley, 56, has a flair for the dramatic, but it's not
the scintillation of a Shakespeare soliloquy or the pathos of a
stirring "Dynasty" episode that draws him in. Rather, it's the
emotional impact of the boxes, banners, and headlines of a
professionally designed newspaper. A beautiful bulldog edition feeds his appetite at breakfast. Since he was a child, when
he chose "drawing funny little cartoons" instead of playing
baseball, he has been moved by design and has devoted his life
to the aesthetic pursuit of the perfect Page One.

Prof. Brierley knows that the middle ground between a
paper's content and its display is elusive. As a graphic design
professor in the College of Journalism and Mass Communications at the University of South Carolina in Columbia, he has
labored to make this point to his pupils who, as journalism students, were more attuned to the editorial side of the paper than
to its overall look. The professor even tried to take his classes
down to the local paper so they could see the real thing—how
design grows out of daily editorial decisions. Unfortunately, the
small offices couldn't accommodate so many students.

One day in 1983, he stumbled upon a televised newspaper editorial meeting, part of C-SPAN's "Day in the Life of
USA Today." For him, it was an important moment, and it
resulted, more than all the examples in this book, in one of

the most direct, practical, hands-on uses of C-SPAN's programming.

"When I saw the 'Day in the Life' programs, I just about died, because it was exactly what I wanted to do with my students," he says. "I could take the students into a newspaper. Staff meetings seem to be where the design starts. I want the students to see the basic raw ingredients of how a paper's going to be designed. Through television, they had a seat at the table."

"Day in the Life" programs bring viewers into the newsrooms of big and small newspapers for editorial meetings, letting them see the day-to-day decisions of editing and publishing a newspaper. "I just cancelled class and stayed home all day and taped and edited right from the TV," he remembers. He rapidly incorporated the programs into his "Newspaper Design" class, finding a handy use for a coverage that *USA Today* editor John Quinn had feared would bore viewers. ("Most of us assumed that even our mothers wouldn't watch the 11-hour *video verité* presentation," Mr. Quinn had remarked.)

Through his consulting work with newspapers looking for new design ideas, Prof. Brierley had picked up on a trend developing in the industry. "One of the things I kept getting from people in the newspaper business," he says, "is that these people coming out of school now are not going to be just writers, but with computers and everything else going on, they're really going to be part of the design program." He created the newspaper design course with news and editorial students in mind. Last offered in the spring of 1986, it was a 14-week session, with two lecture hours and two lab hours each week, for graduate and undergraduate students. About 10 students enrolled each time he taught the course.

According to Prof. Brierley, his journalism students now have an edge over other students in weighing real-life considerations such as visual coherence and the reader's reaction to design. "I wanted to give them a feeling of reality. I want them to design things, but I want them to understand that in order to design something, whether it's graphics, a program, or writing, you have to be able to sell the concept, too. Design is content. They have to understand their public. If they're going to be designing something, who are they designing it for?" Designers must be aware of current markets and changing trends, but they must also make their papers reader-friendly:

"We're talking construction. When we talk about newspapers, we're talking consistency. There's a place for everything."

Prof. Brierley feels that what his students have seen on C-SPAN is a good model for personal interaction. "Unlike the way you see it portrayed in a B-movie, people aren't screaming at each other or tearing their hair out. The idea is to get the product out, and not necessarily ego." He showed his class "Day in the Life" footage when the students, as they designed a model newspaper, occasionally encountered some tense moments. He also has students watch the C-SPAN interviews with the editors to give them an idea of a paper's overall philosophy and principles.

Prof. Brierley says that newspaper design is constantly in flux, and that the latest development to affect it is television. Newspapers compete with television these days for advertising, and newspaper layouts have to be snappier to catch the eye. Stories have to be shorter. As an example, he mentions the *New York Tribune:* "It was completely redesigned in order to promote it better with the sales force. If TV hadn't come around, newspapers probably wouldn't ever have changed. We were quite content until we found out that there was something snapping at us. We got moving. You can't have 40 stories on the front page anymore." In an ironic blend of two media forms—C-SPAN, with its long, unedited coverage, and *USA Today,* with the news-bite-like stories and eye-catching design—Prof. Brierley found a useful tool for training his students.

Lewis Brierley still works as a design consultant for a few newspapers and clearly loves the newspaper world. He says that newspapers are "by their very nature, dramatic. Of all the different areas I've ever worked in, the newspaper is probably the most alive thing I've ever worked on, because it changes every day. You've got to get something in the morning and get it out that night. Television is a different kind of drama." He says that newspapers offer more solid coverage than television, or rather, most television. "I think the in-depth performance is what I like—just like C-SPAN's newspaper stuff. They could have cut the program down to an hour, but they didn't. They said, 'Here is life at a newspaper.'"   —S.S.

Prof. Brierley tapes C-SPAN for his students from Columbia Cable TV.

"The Colonel"

Howard Bronson

San Antonio, Texas

By his own admission, Howard Bronson of San Antonio, Texas, is hardly what one might call an activist. Yet, when his local cable company announced its decision to pre-empt a portion of C-SPAN's programming each week, this retired Air Force colonel led a battle that would put many respected lobbyists to shame.

Col. Bronson, 74, has been an avid viewer since the early 1980s. And his enthusiasm has yet to wane. He remembers the first time he "stumbled across C-SPAN" well: "The idea of watching the House of Representatives, especially gavel-to-gavel, was so revolutionary. I was astounded. And even though some of it is boring, the privilege of watching it is so great. I think it's just magnificent."

From the very beginning, he's enjoyed the uninterrupted coverage most of all. So, in December 1985, when he read in his local paper that his cable system was planning to pre-empt C-SPAN's gavel-to-gavel coverage for several hours a day, he was outraged. The system was pressed for channel space, and the plan to interrupt the House coverage was the cable company's solution. Howard Bronson didn't think that was much of a solution, and he decided to protest.

He had only 72 hours to make a difference. The plan was on the verge of going into effect, and once it happened it would be very difficult—if not impossible—to change. So, he called upon Prof. Bob Blanchard, an expert on Congress and the media and the chairman of the communications department at nearby Trinity University. The two of them joined forces, developed a strategy, and went to work. Their goal: To prove that a significant number of San Antonians wanted uninterrupted C-SPAN programming 24 hours a day.

Col. Bronson began by calling viewers in the area to ask for their support. "I did most of the work by phone," he recalls. "I didn't actually get a physical signature. But I got an assurance of one. I'd say, 'If I had a piece of paper in front of you, would you sign it?' I wanted to be able to tell Professor Blanchard that these people meant what they said. It was all confirmed later on. Professor Blanchard sent out a piece of paper to all of them." And they did sign. Within the 72-hour deadline, Howard Bronson delivered those names to the cable company.

This intensive campaign got immediate results. San Antonians got to keep their C-SPAN—uninterrupted. Officials at the cable system were so impressed by Howard Bronson's ability to mobilize their customers that they invited him to appear on their local program, "Cable Connections." The cable system hoped that Col. Bronson's appearance on the show would encourage other viewers to watch C-SPAN.

Howard Bronson and his wife, Olive, watch about 15 hours of C-SPAN a week, except when there's something of special interest on like the Iran-contra hearings or the Robert Bork nomination hearings. Then they watch more. They also subscribe to two San Antonio papers and the *Washington Times*. "I see a high correlation between what I see on C-SPAN and what I read in the papers the next day," he reports. Still, the retired Air Force colonel insists that it wouldn't be enough for him just to follow the news in the paper. "They appear to be more interested in entertainment." That's why he's drawn to C-SPAN. "These are dangerous times we live in, sort of watershed years. Congress is wrestling with these problems, either in committee or in the seminars that you cover, or in the House or Senate. It's fascinating. C-SPAN is the next best thing to being there."

Col. Bronson has always been interested in public affairs. Since retiring from the military in 1962, he's had more time to devote to that interest. He's even taken to writing his representatives and various policy makers. At this point he sends as many as 25 postcards each week, with about two-thirds supporting and one-third against something or other.

Before he started watching C-SPAN, he thought all politicians were "a bunch of lazy bums." But he's changed his mind about that. He's even changed his mind about Rep. Henry B. Gonzalez (D-Texas), his local congressman. "I'm against everything that he stands for 98 percent, but at least I admire him. I learned that the man has integrity. I was skeptical about him before, and now I respect him. I didn't learn that from the newspapers. C-SPAN taught me that because I was able to see him and take in the whole man, and do it over a period of time. Now there's a case where C-SPAN influenced my opinion. As a matter of fact, I wrote him a letter and told him so."

As one can see, Howard Bronson expresses himself when he thinks something deserves attention. For years he even bought special license plates that spelled out the name of his favorite network. He decided to stop last year when the fee went from $25 to $75. But now he's come up with something even better: an advertising light for the rear window of his car. Once it's hooked up it will spell out brightly for all the world to read: C-S-P-A-N.   —S.S.

Col. Howard Bronson is a subscriber of Rogers Cablesystems of Texas.

"The Golden Ear"

Lillian Brown

Omaha, Nebraska

When Sen. William Proxmire (D-Wisconsin) complained on the Senate floor that no one ever watches televised Senate proceedings, Lillian Brown, 70, responded, "I have news for you."

Lillian Brown watches the Senate, and the House, too. She wants to know who's shaking the tree in Washington, because she's convinced that even a "little old lady" from Omaha, Nebraska, can have an impact on the powers that be. She has seen the results: Her letter-writing campaigns have produced consistent responses from public officials.

So on a typical day in the Brown household, you'll find the television tuned to C-SPAN and a note pad in every room. While Ms. Brown goes about her daily duties, she'll take a note or two when she hears something that piques her interest. The notes go into files she's accumulated on politicians and issues that appeal to her. And when it comes time to bring the power brokers to task, she doesn't hesitate to pen an opinion.

A variety of issues, such as foreign affairs, the budget deficit, taxes, and farming, move Ms. Brown to contact national representatives. The airline industry has also been a longtime concern of hers. Her late husband had an office job with an airline for 31 years. When he retired in 1981 they formed a local retired airline employees group, the "Golden Ears," so called, says Ms. Brown, because the retired cornhuskers "keep their ears to the airline industry." Through the years the Golden Ears have come to rely on Ms. Brown for airline industry news as it happens in Washington. And, conveniently, Nebraska's Democratic Sen. James Exon sits on the Senate Aviation Subcommittee. His Omaha ear is just a local phone call away.

In fact, her voice is so well-known by the staff at the senator's office in Omaha that "when I call I don't even have to identify myself. They say, 'Oh, hi, Lillian.'" For the past few years she's been calling at least once a week.

Lillian Brown hasn't always been so outspoken. Her enthusiasm for politics was born after her husband died in 1982. Like many women of her generation, Ms. Brown dedicated more than 40 years of her life to her husband and daughter: "Outside of being a homemaker, I never really had any hobbies." The death of her husband sent her on a search for meaningful activity. "I didn't intend on spending my days playing cards or bingo. I didn't want to vegetate. Social activities weren't enough of a challenge."

Lillian Brown soon discovered that life has a funny way of giving you what you want, especially when you go looking for it. One day, she was flipping through the channels when she found C-SPAN, and "that finally turned on the lightbulb," she says. Since then, "my priority has been politics. That's what I invest in."

For Ms. Brown, the investment has paid generous dividends. "I've learned more about our political system since I've been watching C-SPAN than I've learned in my entire life. I have gotten interested in things I didn't know beans about—for instance, foreign affairs. I was aware of what was going on in the world, but I wasn't involved." She takes the lessons very seriously, watching the network with reference books at hand, such as the *U.S. Congress Handbook; Gavel to Gavel,* a guide to congressional proceedings; and the *Congressional Directory,* which lists information about the members. "If you're going to get into this, you have to have something to refer back to," says Ms. Brown.

Inspired by her Congress-watching to get an even closer look at the political process, Ms. Brown took advantage of free airline privileges and embarked on a trip to Washington, D.C., in 1986. "That was one of the highlights of my life. I felt like I was rubbing elbows with history, being able to visit the House and the Senate," she says.

Traveling alone and unacquainted with anyone in the area, Ms. Brown spent five days in Washington meeting with her senators, touring the Capitol, and watching debate in the House and Senate galleries. One special memory of her trip was a breakfast meeting hosted by the Nebraska delegation. At the request of the late Sen. Edward Zorinsky (D-Nebraska), Ms. Brown stood up and made assessments of a variety of issues, including the Iran-contra affair. "I spoke with strong conviction. I just got up and said what I felt. Quite honestly, I amazed myself." Her candid comments prompted Nebraska's Educational Television Network to interview her for "Washington Report to Nebraska," a weekly program highlighting the activity of the Nebraska legislators on Capitol Hill.

When Lillian Brown returned from her trip to the nation's capital, she resumed her studies and her self-styled activism with even more fervor. The trip seemed to reinforce her new-found conviction that even the voice of a "little old lady" should be heard. "I tell my family and friends, 'Don't let anybody ever tell you that your voice cannot be heard, because I have proven that it can.' And that can be very satisfying. I don't know how much difference I've made, but I certainly have voiced my opinion, whether they agree with me or not."   —S.S.

Lillian Brown watches C-SPAN's congressional telecasts on Cox Cable of Omaha.

"The Archivist"

Robert Browning

West Lafayette, Indiana

Throughout these pages are numerous references to television viewers who videotape C-SPAN for themselves, their friends, their students, or their children. But nowhere, not even at C-SPAN itself, had anyone set about the task of recording and cataloging all of the network's programming until Purdue University christened its Public Affairs Video Archives in September 1987.

Long renowned for its programs in engineering and agriculture, the 32,000-student Purdue University in West Lafayette, Indiana, is also a leader among Midwestern educational institutions in using communications. In addition to owning seven satellite dishes—one of which is a Ku-band satellite uplink—the university began offering graduate engineering degrees via television 20 years ago. It also operates Indiana's oldest radio station, WBAA.

Yet this fertile ground for a video archives needed an individual to plant the seed. The man who directs the monumental task of organizing hours of C-SPAN and C-SPAN II programming per year is Prof. Robert X Browning ("X" is his middle name), a 38-year-old native of Evansville, Indiana. "We're in a television age," he states, "an age where cameras are recording history, and that history needs to be preserved."

The professor's past consolidates a knowledge of cable

television, U.S. history, and politics. He holds a doctorate in political science from the University of Wisconsin at Madison, and joined the Purdue faculty in 1981. As an associate professor of political science, he has taught courses in American government, Indiana politics, and campaigns and elections. On the cable side of his life, Prof. Browning has a part-time career as host of a local-access program about the Indiana legislature, called "Statehouse Review," and he sits on the West Lafayette Citizens' Advisory Commission on Cable Television. The commission successfully pushed for televising City Council meetings on a regular basis.

He attributes much of his awareness of television's role in the political process to his father. "He is retired and spends a lot of time at home, and he's always telling his 'son the political scientist' to watch this or that on television. People in the community, particularly retirees, have led academics on the use of C-SPAN perhaps more than professors did at first."

The idea for the archives arose at a May 1986 meeting of several Purdue professors, including Prof. Browning. They had convened to brainstorm about ways to use C-SPAN programming in the classroom, but the group soon turned its focus to an educational archives. According to Prof. Browning, the group thought that an academic setting could provide an ideal place for the storage, cataloging, and use of the public affairs video record. Furthermore, it could make C-SPAN's history-on-video available to scholars, teachers, and journalists at minimal cost.

They took their idea to David Caputo, then head of the political science department and now dean of the university's School of Humanities, Social Sciences, and Education. In a modern way, Dean Caputo is intimately involved in politics: As a regional manager for News Election Service, he is responsible for collecting Midwest-region "key precinct" data from which subscribers to the service, for example, the commercial television networks and wire services, make their election projections. He, too, considered the archives proposal provocative.

But the idea remained just that until June 1987, when Prof. Caputo, as the newly appointed dean, gave the go-ahead for the project in one of his first decisions as head of the school. He asked Prof. Browning, with his background in politics and cable television, to serve as director.

Prof. Browning regarded the task of setting up the archives as more than a little daunting. "Starting anything with any university is a big job," Prof. Browning emphasizes. Fortunately, the pieces fell into place in three months. The head of Purdue's Center for Instructional Services offered that department's help handling the tapes; Prof. Browning ordered and received computer equipment, 12 video recorders, and 6,000 blank videotapes; and he hired a full-time archivist, a half-time secretary, and a half-time student assistant. The job of determining a method to index the thousands of public figures' names that would crop up in the course of a year kept him awake at night. But by September of 1987, the Purdue archives project was in business. Now the organizational tasks of the project have been superseded by the challenge of developing its classroom use.

"It's amazing to me," Prof. Browning notes, "just in the few months of taping we've done, the amount of material we have. A lot of things people might not use at first, but it will be very important to make sure that they are there for purposes we can't even imagine now."

For example, one professor remarked that 10 years ago he would not have thought of being able to show students actual proceedings of Congress. That professor now takes televised congressional sessions for granted; his new treat is to compare Congress with the Canadian House of Commons, televised from time to time on C-SPAN.

Furthermore, as the only source in the nation of readily available tapes of Congress, the archives has an enormous potential benefit for and responsibility to its educational constituents.

Purdue's video archives is open to the public for research purposes, but only teachers, or students authorized by a teacher, can buy duplicates of C-SPAN tapes. Prof. Browning notes that most commercial television networks sell copies of their programs for as high as $400 and restrict their uses, but the Purdue archives can make C-SPAN's material available to educators for just $30 per two hours of tape.

Prof. Browning hopes that journalists, writers, and ordinary citizens eventually will come to Purdue to make use of this archives. He sees something symbolic in the midwestern school's making a home for C-SPAN's unedited record of public affairs. "We are not a big private East Coast school. We are in the center of the United States. We are not dominated by any major media markets or a big press or something of the sort. It is symbolic in that C-SPAN reaches all over the United States and provides proceedings of government to the small cities. It's important the way technology, communications, and politics come together to help focus the talents and capabilities of this institution." —*R.C.*

The Purdue University campus receives C-SPAN off a satellite dish and through Greater Lafayette TV Cable.

"The Island Newscaster"

Lee Carle

St. Thomas, The Virgin Islands

In 1955, 23-year-old Lee Carle of Albany, New York, decided to take a job in radio news in the Virgin Islands. Perhaps he would have thought twice about forsaking a career in New York had he known of the conditions he was about to face.

After a seven-hour indirect flight, the Upstate New Yorker arrived in French Town, St. Thomas, wearing a brown tweed winter suit. "I walked into the studio and I could hear dogs and chickens outside. I put my suitcase down and said hello to a bare-chested young man at the radio control console. 'You're doing the 6:00 news tonight,' he said. And I asked, 'Really? Where's the teletype?' And he said, 'We don't have one.' He told me that the station gets its information from the *New York Times*. 'But it's two days old,' I protested. 'It doesn't matter,' the disc jockey said as he continued to track a record."

St. Thomas has changed since those days. Direct flights from the mainland are now available that take half the time they once did. WSTA radio no longer relies on yesterday's newspapers for news. In fact, satellite technology and cable television have dramatically changed the volume and time-liness of information that islanders receive. Mr. Carle, now 56, long ago traded in his brown tweed for cool cottons. And the shirtless young man at the control console, Ron de Lugo, is now the Virgin Islands' delegate to the U.S. House of Representatives. Mr. Carle still sees him from time to time when he watches the televised proceedings from the House floor by satellite.

St. Thomas is 72 miles east of Puerto Rico, today just a 2 1/2-hour flight from Miami. One would think that the three-island U.S. territory (St. Croix, St. Thomas, St. John) would have had access to up-to-date news from the mainland years ago. Quite the contrary: Although local radio stations have made use of live satellite feeds since that technology was in its infancy, television was another matter entirely. "Sending video signals was too costly," explains Mr. Carle. As a result, when television first came to the islands in the mid-'60s, "it was extremely limited," he says. Everything was tape-delayed, and the only live newscasts were local—"reading in front of the camera, that kind of thing." Up until 1984, "we even had Dan Rather one day late."

Now, with satellites and cable television, the 100,000 "Virgin Islanders are as informed as any American community of its same size," claims Mr. Carle. "No longer do our people have to wonder about the lifestyles, dress, and mores of those on the mainland. The whole thing is before them now; it's as if a window on the world has opened up. Young people in schools are talking about current events happening all over the world now, whereas before they could only do it from a news-paper or from an occasional program. And if a youngster here is studying politics in high school, he can simply turn on C-SPAN and see what's going on with his own Congress."

In a place where interest in religion and politics has always been strong, Mr. Carle believes C-SPAN finds a natural niche. "I think the Virgin Islands are growing up because of what is available on cable now, and I think C-SPAN is very much a part of that. The commercial networks would never report what Ron de Lugo said today on the floor of the House. I don't think the networks are that interested. By taking a look at Congress we sometimes get a head start on knowing which way it might vote on bills that involve the Virgin Islands."

Cable television may have helped Virgin Islanders come of age, but "oddly enough," notes Mr. Carle, "radio is still king in the Virgin Islands. People will listen to radio first, TV second, and read the newspaper third. I think it was ingrained in the early days." WSTA radio is St. Thomas' oldest station, and Mr. Carle says it has been the lifeblood of the community since it began broadcasting in 1950. For many years the station was the only voice of the islands, so in addition to providing news and entertainment, WSTA carried death and fire-alarm announcements and daily tips on where to buy the freshest fruits and vegetables.

WSTA radio is therefore something of a Virgin Islands institution, and so is Lee Carle. According to Ludrick Thomas, a young production assistant at WSTA, "Lee Carle is considered the most popular newscaster here in the Virgin Islands." But Lee Carle is quick to point out that it wasn't always so. In fact, his listeners were very skeptical about his initial broadcasts: "I was fresh out of New York, where the delivery and style was very fast and clipped. And I sat down and read the newscast in my New York style. People called up and said, 'What's wrong with him? Why is he talking so fast?' In those days nobody talked fast in the Virgin Islands. There was no reason to move fast. There was no reason to tell anybody anything very fast."

Lee Carle talks much more slowly these days, while the pace in the Virgin Islands has picked up somewhat. After 30 years, he's very much at home there. But as a former mainlander, Mr. Carle understands the tribulations of being thrown into another culture with no news from home. And that's inspired him to consider creating a television service that might help alleviate feelings of cultural withdrawal. He says he'd like to start a programming service from the Virgin Islands, a combination of C-SPAN and Black Entertainment Television, to send to Caribbean communities living up north—a sort of C-SPAN with an island beat.   —S.S.

Mr. Carle watches C-SPAN on Caribbean Communications.

Elaine Carlyle

Pittsburg, Kansas

Elaine Carlyle, 37, is a big fan of President Reagan. She also likes to watch sessions of the House of Representatives on C-SPAN for the humorous moments, the hot debates, and the day-to-day business. On a visit to Washington several years ago, the Pittsburg, Kansas, native was thrilled by a personal visit with Rep. Jim Wright (D-Texas), now speaker of the House.

Elaine couldn't say out loud why she's so interested in politics—she can only "talk with her eyes." Bound to a specially fitted wheelchair by cerebral palsy, she is unable to speak and barely able to move. Elaine has never even sat alone. Her parents, Allen and Doris Carlyle, now in their sixties, have taken care of her since birth. "We do everything for her," her mother says.

But Elaine, who is the Carlyles' only child, has worked out a special system of communication with her parents. She stares at objects and patiently waits as her parents ask her a series of questions to determine what she wants; she can make sounds of joy or displeasure; she has worked out signals that indicate "yes" and "no," and her parents have come to recognize that certain glances mean certain things. "I don't know how to describe it, but Elaine grabs words out of the air. Her big brown eyes are so expressive," says her mother. "We are so thankful that she is so mentally alert, because she can't do anything but communicate."

Two of the things that bring a sparkle to Elaine's eyes are the outdoors and C-SPAN. The Carlyle family likes to take its recreational vehicle to a lake about 25 minutes away from Pittsburg. From her chair-bed, Elaine enjoys taking in the moon, the stars, and the woodpeckers and whippoorwills; she is a bird lover and watcher whose piercing gaze once conveyed to her father that an ice cream cone box would make a perfect feeder for bluebirds. Camping cannot keep Elaine from her C-SPAN, though. The family RV has a small satellite dish mounted on top so Elaine won't have to miss anything while at the campground.

Educational resources were scarce for someone with Elaine's severe handicap. After a short period of home tutoring provided by the state, Elaine received most of her schooling from her parents and picked up information from TV. "Elaine could not go to school, so television has been her teacher as well as her entertainment. The TV is always on at our house," says Ms. Carlyle.

The Carlyles could tell that Elaine had taken a special liking to C-SPAN soon after they first began receiving the service in 1981. "The House of Representatives was really her favorite. She liked the battle of words. I'll tell you what she likes most— when the congressmen argued. The better the argument, the better she liked it." Elaine kept an eye out for Rep. Bob Walker (R-Pennsylvania): "When he took the floor or objected, that really interested her." Elaine would always let her parents know she wanted them to come look at what she was watching or when someone captured her interest, and it was clear that she got a kick out of watching then-majority leader Jim Wright in action.

"Jim Wright would quote poetry and I love poetry. I've read lots to Elaine and we both enjoy it so much. That's actually how we got to meet him," Ms. Carlyle recalls.

In 1981, Ms. Carlyle wrote a letter to C-SPAN thanking the network and mentioning her daughter's liking for Rep. Wright. Her letter was read on the air and forwarded to the congressman, who replied with a gracious note. In September of the same year, Elaine persuaded her family to visit the nation's capital: "She got so interested in Washington, D.C., she wanted to go there," her mother says. Together, the Carlyles observed the District panorama from the top of the 555-foot Washington Monument after taking Elaine's wheelchair up its elevator, and even rode the president's special elevator at the White House. While visiting the U.S. Capitol, the Carlyles casually mentioned their daughter's interest in C-SPAN—and Rep. Wright—to one of the tour guides. To their surprise, the tour guide arranged for them to meet the Texas congressman.

Elaine has "gotten after" her parents to frame her Washington mementos and photographs. A signed color photograph of the Reagans and a letter from them hang on the Carlyles' living room wall; Rep. Wright's letter to her is also framed. Elaine also urged her folks to videotape segments from C-SPAN and the nightly news, and the family library includes tapes of President Reagan in Camp David casual wear and of Doris Carlyle's letter being read on C-SPAN. After watching C-SPAN so much with Elaine, Ms. Carlyle, who was never much interested in politics, has done her share of getting after people herself, writing to the two Kansas senators and to her congressman on subjects like abortion and school prayer. One of her letters to a local newspaper urged the Senate to open up its chambers to television. That wish came true on June 2, 1986.   —M.C.

At home, Elaine Carlyle watches C-SPAN on Pittsburg Cable TV.

"The Coach"

Pete Carril

West Windsor, New Jersey

When the basketball season starts, Coach Pete Carril shows freshmen how to play a team game. At Princeton University, where there are no athletic scholarships and graduating athletes usually go on to boardrooms instead of the pro leagues, the team has to play together if it's going to win.

Pete Carril, the son of a Spanish immigrant, coached at some pretty tough Pennsylvania high schools from 1955 to 1967. His players were speedy, street-smart, and greedy for the ball. "Basketball has been dominated by kids from the lower classes, where life is kind of tough," says Mr. Carril. However, when he arrived at Princeton in 1967, he found a group of players very different from the ones he was accustomed to. A November 1987 *Esquire* magazine profile on the coach described the Ivy League material he had to work with: "He had inherited a team that couldn't run, couldn't jump, and wasn't fond of physical contact."

Given the team's limitations, Mr. Carril developed a strategy of play that emphasized defense, passing, and cooperation. That strategy has kept Princeton in the play-offs and boosted it to victory in several Ivy League championships.

When he was coaching high school basketball in Pennsylvania, Mr. Carril also taught social studies. He often took his students to the state capitol in Harrisburg to observe the legislature in session—an outing that he enjoyed as much as his students did, since he had an active interest in politics. He had several friends who were politicians. Joseph Yosco served as a state senator, and Mr. Carril worked on his campaigns and watched him make speeches on the state Senate floor. Another friend, Fred Rooney, went on to occupy a seat in the U.S. House of Representatives.

When he left Pennsylvania and headed for Princeton, New Jersey, he took his interest in politics with him. And he never lost it. That's what led him to C-SPAN in 1981 (a dedicated news fan, he pronounces most commercial television "crap"). And by that time he could see lots of familiar faces on the network—the frequent appearances of former Federal Reserve Chairman Paul Volcker, Treasury Secretary James Baker, Secretary of State George Shultz, Defense Secretary Frank Carlucci, and Sens. John Danforth (R-Missouri) and Paul Sarbanes (D-Maryland) make C-SPAN something of a Princeton alumni parade. "You get a look at the guys who are Princeton alumni and you get more interested," says Mr. Carril.

Coach Carril remembers one Princeton Tiger who went from the court to the Senate—Bill Bradley (D-New Jersey). These days the coach likes to watch the former ballplayer in action during the televised proceedings of the Senate, maneuvering legislation as he once maneuvered the game. "Senator Bradley was a team player known for playing without the ball. He believed in getting things done—and not necessarily getting recognition. He was very unselfish." Coach Carril recalls, "Those characteristics still show up in whatever he does. I always enjoy watching him get his point across."

Sen. Bradley seems to have equal admiration for Coach Carril. In the *Esquire* interview the senator said: "He teaches the fundamentals. He teaches a game full of substance. He gets a level of communication among his players that is not often achieved in basketball."

Much of Coach Carril's C-SPAN viewing takes place in the off-season, when the university team is not playing, practicing, or traveling. During the basketball season, he cuts down on his watching time, but still switches on after a long day of coaching. "What happens is, I have bad practices or good practices or good games or bad games, and I don't sleep that hot, and I'll be watching the thing all night long." He usually manages to squeeze in a couple of viewing hours before dozing off.

The coach considers C-SPAN a boon to retired people. "It must be great to get away from soap operas and stupid game shows. I imagine for them retirement is a heck of a lot more interesting this way." As for his own preferences, he likes the call-in programs with their presentation of diverse opinions. "Sometimes you're dismayed by the great range of knowledge to ignorance. Some of the questions, you can't believe anyone would ask a question like that—and then in the next breath it's something that's amazing in its depth of understanding. You get a broad spectrum of questions."

Senate floor action is another favorite of Mr. Carril's, although he sometimes finds that it goes against his personal philosophy of team play: "When they get into a little politicking, the country takes a beating." But when there's real debate, Pete Carril sits up and listens: "The tendency to take democracy for granted is always a danger. And so when you have this darn television network exclusively showing how the government works, that's exciting—that's something I think you should get a hold of." —C.M.

Coach Carril watches C-SPAN on Futurevision Cable Enterprises.

"The Television Pioneer"

Syd Cassyd

Los Angeles, California

Syd Cassyd, 80, couldn't have been any more involved with television if he had invented the cathode ray tube himself. He was there from the start, when television was little more than a scanning disc and a dream. But for Syd Cassyd, it was worth believing in, and sometimes even fighting for. Throughout more than five decades in the industry, he's done his fair share of battling for television. Some would say he's done more than his share; but that doesn't stop him.

Mr. Cassyd is, among other things, the founder of the National Academy of Television Arts and Sciences, which is perhaps best known for the Emmy awards it bestows each year. He says that he started the academy in 1946, just months after he arrived in Hollywood practically penniless and still in his Army uniform. Within a few days he'd landed a job as a laborer at Paramount Studios, which was working on several television experiments. That's when his interest in the fledgling technology was first aroused.

Over the years, Syd Cassyd has seen the television industry from inside and out. He was an editor for *Box Office* magazine. He's also been a producer, a filmmaker, a media consultant, a television critic, and an educator. He produced one of the Emmy Award shows, and he even won two Emmys himself.

Mr. Cassyd says his original vision for the academy was a

forum where industry people could debate different viewpoints. He also wanted to bring academics into this new industry. "The basic idea was to have a controversial thing," he explains. "Right now, with current academy rules, no member is allowed to get into politics or discuss politics. I think that's terrible." He wanted the academy—and ultimately the airwaves—to be filled with lively debate and exchange. Today, he says, "The academy is controlled by the powerful groups producing the junk on television."

Born in 1908 to a family that was heavily involved in both theater and politics, Mr. Cassyd developed an interest in film early. He got his first exposure to the developing technology of television in 1932: "A friend of mine was an engineer for the firm that eventually developed the television set." By that time, Mr. Cassyd had already become intrigued with the use of film as a "tool for information." A few years later he was making films himself under the auspices of the Educational Film Institute at New York University. And during the war he worked as a film editor, under Col. Frank Capra. By the time he arrived in Hollywood he'd been working in film for a number of years. All the while, he says, he was keeping his eye on the developing technology of television.

For Syd Cassyd, part of the allure of television was its unlimited potential. He believed that television could be used for the betterment of humankind: to enlighten, to instruct, and to inspire. That was before the realities of television as a business set in.

Syd Cassyd is the first to say that television hasn't lived up to his expectations; but he's seen glimmers of hope. He enjoys public television. And he enjoys C-SPAN, which he discovered when his daughter gave him a cable subscription as a birthday gift.

"She thought I deserved C-SPAN," he explains. "What C-SPAN is doing is what television should have been doing all along. I feel that C-SPAN is *the* effective instrument for carrying out the original intent of Congress, in that broadcasting should be in the public interest, convenience, and necessity."

Public interest is a concept that Mr. Cassyd claims to hold very dear. After all, he still remembers the early days of broadcasting, before the 1934 Broadcasting Act, when anyone could put a radio station on the air. Syd Cassyd believes that "broadcasting is a property of the people, like a public park or the Grand Canyon." Consequently, he spends much of his time fighting broadcast deregulation.

That commitment to something he believes in is part of what has made him a very vocal and sometimes, he concedes, controversial member of the broadcasting community. A heart condition has slowed Mr. Cassyd down somewhat, so he isn't as active as he used to be. He doesn't do much lecturing anymore at universities, and except for the reviews that he does of television shows, for magazines around the world, he has pretty much retired from his career as a journalist. But he's still an active member of the Hollywood Press Association, the Television Critics of America, and the Academy of Motion Picture Arts and Sciences, to name a few. He also votes for the cable industry's ACE awards. And every Monday morning, he and his wife lead discussions on constitutional law at the local American Civil Liberties Union.

"Call me anything," he says, "as long as you call me interested." —S.S.

Mr. Cassyd is a subscriber of American Cablesystems.

"The Congressional Dad"

Dick Cheney Sr.

Casper, Wyoming

In the few minutes before a live call-in begins, some guests—congressmen, senators, cabinet members—will ask if it's okay to make a quick telephone call. They slip out of the studio to phone family or friends and suggest that they tune in the program. Even after years in the public spotlight, many people still feel a basic desire for their family's approval.

One of Washington's many high-profile sons is Rep. Dick Cheney, Jr. (R-Wyoming). He was chief of staff to President Gerald Ford, and, in the course of his 10 years as Wyoming's congressman-at-large, he has moved quickly up the House leadership ladder. After only one term, Mr. Cheney was elected chairman of the House Republican Policy Committee. In 1987 he moved up a rung to the minority's third-ranking position: chairman of the House Republican Conference. He's often talked about as an eventual successor to Rep. Bob Michel (R-Illinois) as minority leader. Yet, when Rep. Cheney speaks before the House cameras, or appears on a call-in, even a man that official Washington is watching sometimes wonders if his father is at home watching, too.

His dad is Dick Cheney, Sr. He raised his family to believe that political awareness and voting are "more or less a regular obligation." As the son of a one-time Democratic county commissioner, the elder Mr. Cheney has always been amazed by people who don't bother to vote. He moved his family to Casper, Wyoming, in 1954, when Dick, Jr., one of three children, was 13 years old. Transferred there by the U.S. Department of Agriculture, the Nebraska native entered an economically depressed town. Nevertheless, despite several opportunities to work in Washington, D.C., he made Casper his home.

Twenty-three years later, when Gerald Ford left office in 1977, his outgoing chief of staff, Dick, Jr., came home to Casper to stay. He and his wife Lynne bought a home there. But the resignation of the incumbent Democratic congressman soon brought state Republican officials to their door. Dick Cheney, Jr., decided to run for Congress.

His father's familiarity with sparsely populated Wyoming (the last census reported 471,000 inhabitants) came in handy. "I was pretty well acquainted with the state," the senior Cheney recalls, "and there were people I could introduce to Dick. But as far as any participation, I told Dick that glad-handing and talking—that was up to him. I'd do the chauffeuring."

The elder Mr. Cheney proved a good chauffeur. Dick Cheney, Jr., won his first race for Congress handily. Today, his son's busy Washington life makes congressional telecasts an additional tool for keeping in touch with his family in Casper.

Setting up the Cheney house in 1954 didn't include a TV set initially. There wasn't really much to watch until the following year, when Casper became one of the first towns in the United States to have cable television. However, the system carried only one channel, which was on the air just four or five hours a day.

The TV picture has changed significantly in Casper since the '50s. Mr. and Mrs. Cheney now have 21 channels from which to choose, and their television set is on 10 to 12 hours per day. Their channel of choice is often C-SPAN, where they catch occasional glimpses of their son.

"Dick doesn't show up that much on the floor of the House," reports Mr. Cheney of his son. "Actually, in his Republican leadership role, the job he's got doesn't involve floor time as much as it does committee work." Nevertheless, other Wyoming constituents seem to catch glimpses of young Mr. Cheney from time to time (he was the ranking House Republican member on 1987's much-televised Iran-contra investigation committee, for example), and his father gets frequent feedback from friends and neighbors. "It's always a thrill to see your children get that attention. But, on the other hand, it happens enough that I learn to roll with the punches," he says.

As a result, Mr. Cheney doesn't go to the phone every time he has a comment for his son about something he's seen on the House floor. He explains that when watching his son on television he's "very careful not to be super critical."

The elder Mr. Cheney's reticence doesn't surprise his daughter-in-law Lynne. "He is not very talkative," she admits. "That's how Westerners are—we treasure our words. You won't get a whole lot out of us." As a member of the Commission on the Bicentennial of the Constitution and chairperson of the National Endowment for the Humanities, she, too, is a national figure with fairly high TV exposure, but says she receives infrequent feedback from her in-laws. "That's not how Wyoming people are. They wouldn't just call me up after they've seen it. The next time we see each other they'll mention it."

But the reticence works both ways, and calls home are infrequent as well. "I don't think they're different from any other kids," says Mr. Cheney of the high-profile Washingtonians. "Most parents comment that their kids never paid any attention to them, so why should they be any different?"

Besides, for the elder Mr. Cheney, the public affairs programming from Washington has become more than just a way to keep track of his son. Now that he's retired from the Department of Agriculture, he keeps track of legislation on health insurance and cost-of-living adjustments. He's an active member of the National Association of Retired Federal Employees.

Perhaps in Rep. Cheney's characterization of the C-SPAN audience is a subtle hint of awareness that his father is out there watching, too. "It is a knowledgeable audience," he says. "It is like radio call-in shows, in terms of having some folks out there who care deeply about things, and want to engage someone in debate and discussion." —K.M.

Mr. Cheney follows his congressional son by way of United Cable TV of Wyoming.

"The Congressional Correspondent"

Richard Cohen
McLean, Virginia

"I have spent more hours than I care to recall sitting in congressional galleries observing with fascination the peaks and, more often, the valleys of debate," wrote congressional correspondent Richard Cohen in his column in the *National Journal*.

Today, however, for journalists such as Mr. Cohen, televised House and Senate proceedings may offer an even better, if not more convenient, view than the galleries. "C-SPAN changed my life," he told his readers. "Through the magic of coaxial cable, I may never again enter the galleries to watch the House or Senate. In the comfort of my suburban living room, I can watch government in action at any hour of the day . . . . A simple flip of the wrist, rather than a trot down a long corridor, can take me from one gallery to the other."

Richard Cohen, 39, has been covering Congress for the *National Journal* since 1977. It's his job to sit in the press galleries of the House and Senate (or, when possible, at home in his living room) and watch. As a correspondent who covers an institution, Mr. Cohen says he has the "opportunity to sort of lean back and see what's going on." He looks for broad trends, for the movement of power, for up-and-coming members. The most interesting part about covering Congress, explains Mr. Cohen, "is getting with the members and finding out what drives them, what makes them tick, what they're responding to in terms of their constituents."

He keeps his finger on the pulse of American politics. He knows today's influence brokers and those who might one day become important. "The people who are elected to Congress are very competitive, and when they get into Congress, you know you've really got the stars. And in that group of stars, a few superstars will emerge. It's interesting to me how some emerge, why they emerge, and why others don't," muses Mr. Cohen.

Richard Cohen is one of 15 full-time reporters at the *National Journal*. First published in 1969, the *Journal* was originally founded to educate business professionals on policy development. However, the editors discovered that the weekly magazine fast developed a loyal following among government officials. Now its 5,000 subscribers include White House and congressional staffers, members of the House and Senate, Washington lobbyists, and corporate lawyers.

Following Congress is a seemingly perfect job for the self-confessed "legislative addict." As a teen-ager he dogged the heels of City Council members in his hometown of Northampton, Massachusetts. Congress, he says, is a continuing saga that is endlessly fascinating. He tracks the Jekyll-and-Hyde style of cooperation from both sides of the aisle. "One week both parties are saying they're going to work together on the budget to get the deficit down. The next week on the House floor they are at each other's throats, saying they don't trust each other. That's the ebb and flow."

He frequently contemplates the institution that has held his fascination for so long: "I think Congress reflects this country at large, the points of view that play themselves out in Congress. You don't get that in any other part of the government. That's healthy. It shows the broad, varied factions of this country."

Richard Cohen believes that televising the House and Senate proceedings has also been a boon for the nation at large: "It's good for the people to be closer to the interactions between the governed and those who do the governing. It's good to take these discussions out of the back rooms." He notes that the public's perception of the legislature has changed because "people now have a better understanding of what's going on.

They may not like it, but the point is they're closer to it, and that's good."

Nonetheless, he cautioned *National Journal* readers that "sometimes, the events can be dreadfully boring—both on-site and through the camera—but that, too, is worth knowing. Like the decisions on zoning permits made by my hometown council, action on regulatory laws or pork-barrel spending affects many people, and the galleries should be open to as many witnesses as possible."

While Mr. Cohen appreciates being able to keep an eye on Congress from his home in McLean, Virginia, "with my feet up on the couch and a soda," he does have "one beef" with C-SPAN. His few personal appearances on C-SPAN's call-in program, he says, "have shown the limits of my future in television. But, compared with the status or riches available to media heavies, being a C-SPAN junkie offers loftier rewards to those of us needing a regular political fix."   —*P.K.*

Richard Cohen occasionally covers Congress by watching Media General Cable of Fairfax.

"The Talkmaster"

Jack Cole

West Palm Beach, Florida

Radio talkmaster Jack Cole is the king of back talk. He has been hosting WJNO News Radio's afternoon talk show in West Palm Beach for over four years, and his engaging sense of humor can turn a Greek tragedy—a presidential hopeful's demise or the world debt crisis—into comedy.

"Captain Jack" broadcasts from "World Headquarters." What's World Headquarters? Well, of course, "it's the head-quarters of the world—top secret. And I run it," declares the captain. "We get crises that come in every day—the stock market, the Persian Gulf—and we just have to handle these." How did he handle the stock market crisis? "Very carefully—like porcupines make love."

The show has a large and loyal following in South Florida. WJNO Radio estimates up to 100,000 listeners tune in to the show each day, and the captain receives over 400 calls every two weeks for the call-in portion of his program. Jack Cole is affectionately referred to by Floridians as the "man they love to hate," and his listeners range from "Rose" in Century Village, who would send him chicken soup everyday if she could, to other regular listeners who call him a "commie." His WJNO colleagues describe him as "unpredictable and outrageous; Jack Cole is no ordinary talk show host." His credentials include a law degree from the University of Virginia, fluency in two foreign languages, and two Emmy awards for television news. The station says he "attacks politics, news items, and guests with equal fervor, but listeners need not fear; his bark is worse than his bite."

His philosophy of news and radio talk show success is simple: "My purpose is a combination of information and entertainment. If it's all information, nobody will listen, and if it's all entertainment, well, what's the point? Entertainment in an informative way, or information in an entertaining way—something like that." Mr. Cole is on the air live four hours a day, from 2 P.M. to 6 P.M. "discussing whatever is in the news that day, plus whatever is suitably wacko."

With four hours a day of live radio time to fill with entertaining news, the captain and his crew have to constantly keep up with the headlines. Besides reading several newspapers each day, he often uses material generated from his C-SPAN viewing. He tries to catch speeches from the National Press Club, stump speeches by presidential candidates, and university conferences. The ever-alert captain keeps his eye to C-SPAN for guests whom his producer can line up for radio interviews. Sometimes he'll see a member of Congress talking about an issue on the House floor, and he'll call him the next day and conduct a follow-up interview for his audience.

Washington politics—especially the campaign-trail theme—are good material for Mr. Cole's political punmanship. The captain says 1987 was a "banner year for funny presidential candidates." Disturbed that the media was working too hard to portray George Bush as a "wimp," he devised a radio campaign to help the presidential contender. He decided to challenge the vice president to three rounds of Olympic-rules boxing in the West Palm Beach municipal auditorium. He contracted Angelo Dundee as his manager and trainer, and a world champion kick boxer to promote the event. "We're still waiting to hear from George. His office told us they'll get back to us," notes Mr. Cole. He uses this type of call-in show stunt to highlight a point and draw in his listeners with an entertaining angle on the issue.

He also pokes fun at politicians on his radio show with Mark Russell-style "Snicker Tunes." In fact, the lyrical political satirist is a frequent guest on Mr. Cole's talk show, and they engage in duets making light of politicians' plights. He usually picks a tune that fits the mood of the theme he is trying to capture. For instance, about Sen. Robert Dole's presidential bid he wrote lyrics to the tune of Irving Berlin's "Anything You Can Do, I Can Do Better," which depicted marital infighting between the senator and his wife, former Transportation Secretary Elizabeth Dole:

> He says: If I run for president, you'll be beside me.
> She says: If I'm beside you, then I'm running too.
> No you're not. Yes I am. No you're not. Yes I am. . . .

> He says: I'm the Dole who belongs on the ticket.
> She says: Well, you can just stick it, it ought to be me.
> I'm the one. I will run. I'm the one. I will run. . . .

> He says: The weaker of the sexes.
> She says: I can carry Texas.
> He says: Isn't up to muster.

> She says: You mean like General Custer?
> He says: Can you motivate our boys?
> She says: Didn't nobody tell you 'bout Helen of Troy?

Captain Jack hasn't always been a laid-back Floridian sporting a sea captain's cap and a Maynard G. Krebs-style goatee. For most of the 1960s and '70s he was very much a part of the starched-shirt ranks of East Coast electronic journalists. He worked in Washington, D.C., as Metromedia's political correspondent, and later moderated a public affairs program for the network, called "Opinion Washington." Mr. Cole was also a TV news anchorman for the CBS affiliate in Boston. There he acquired the nickname "Boston's Bad Boy," because he had a reputation for picking on former Mayor Kevin White, whom he considered something of a "crook." Mr. Cole was awarded two Emmys for television news—one for moderating "Opinion Washington," and the other for a PBS documentary titled "Hot Shell," about illegal arms shipments.

However, even during less controversial years as a television anchor, Jack Cole was known—in fact even famous—for his irreverent approach to the news. He was once suspended from his Boston anchor job when he broke for a commercial by saying, "We'll be back in a moment with more *alleged* news." His intentional blooper generated wire copy all over the world. But the funniest thing about the story, recalls Mr. Cole, was when former NBC newsman Edwin Neuman did a piece about it on the "Today Show." Mr. Neuman said that every newsman had longed to make that comment at one time or another in his life, and then he turned to Tom Brokaw and said, "I'd like to do it right now." Mr. Brokaw gave the go ahead, and Mr. Neuman led into the commercial with "We'll be back in a minute with even less news." Mr. Cole pulled his television faux pas in 1978. The next year he left the TV news business for good.

Although the captain finds great humor in politics, he realizes it's not just all fun and games. For example, he encourages his listeners to watch C-SPAN so they can truly understand the issues he addresses. "C-SPAN has had an effect on the public," says the captain. "We are better able to make decisions on really raw data, without people interpolating and interpreting for us. And that's good."

Captain Jack was enthusiastic about C-SPAN's uncut coverage even before it was available on his cable system. In 1984 he called the local cable operator to ask when the system was going to carry C-SPAN. He didn't get much of an answer, so he decided to "put pressure on them." He devoted a program to a discussion with local cable operators about C-SPAN and conducted a poll of his audience that found 61 percent in favor of carrying the network. He was "struck by why a cable system would carry Jim and Tammy Faye Bakker, plus Jerry Falwell, plus Pat Robertson, plus the rest of the crowd, and no C-SPAN." Shortly after his self-styled media blitz, C-SPAN was added to the local cable fare.

Jack Cole believes that "an informed electorate is better than an ill-informed electorate because it's the ultimate decision maker. But whether watching Congress informs people or just drives them crazy and away from the system so that they are no longer voters is another question."   —*P.K.*

Captain Jack tunes in C-SPAN on Comcast Cablevision of West Palm Beach.

"The Fifty-first Stater"

Baltasar Corrada del Rio
San Juan, Puerto Rico

"Very often, late at night, I get home and turn on the television set and am pleased to see my old colleagues debating some important issue. So I stay up to watch," says Baltasar Corrada del Rio. For him, watching the Congress on C-SPAN is more than just informative; it's nostalgic. Mr. Corrada, now mayor of San Juan, represented Puerto Rico for eight years in the U.S. House of Representatives.

Baltasar Corrada served in Congress from 1977 to 1984 and had more constituents than any other member of the House. He represented all 3.2 million U.S. citizens of Puerto Rico, the largest of the four U.S. territories. He gave up the position to become the mayor of San Juan, Puerto Rico's capital and a city of 435,000 inhabitants.

Mayor Corrada, 53, had been in office a little more than a year when San Juan served as host city to the 54th annual U.S. Conference of Mayors. C-SPAN was there to televise the event and, during the conference, the network interviewed Mayor Corrada and Gov. Raphael Hernandez Colon. C-SPAN viewers had a chance to see quite a bit of the Caribbean island, something that Mayor Corrada says doesn't happen often enough. "Generally speaking, we are not too well covered in the U.S. mainland news."

Because of his years on Capitol Hill, Mayor Corrada

knew all about C-SPAN, and he wrote to encourage coverage of the mayors meeting: "Your telecast of the event would add immeasurably to mainland perceptions of modern-day Puerto Rico." Those perceptions are important to the mayor, because he'd like to "bring Puerto Rico closer to the United States, both politically and economically." In fact, he would very much like to see Puerto Rico become the 51st state. In 1986, he became president of the New Progressive Party, which supports statehood for Puerto Rico, and he is the party's 1988 candidate for governor.

The question of statehood has been a controversial topic in Puerto Rico since 1898, when the United States gained control of the territory in the Spanish-American War. Under the current commonwealth system, the island has certain advantages of association with the United States but still maintains its separateness. Essentially, Puerto Rico has its own laws, taxes, and representative government. Yet Puerto Ricans are American citizens, and the island is considered part of the United States when it comes to international trade, foreign policy, and war.

As a territory, Puerto Rico has representation in the U.S. Congress, but its elected delegate can't vote during House sessions. The delegate does have floor privileges and can vote in committee. Most Puerto Ricans are not seeking independence from the United States—the last two referenda on status are proof of that. But they're not all in favor of statehood, either. Some of them, particularly members of the current governor's Popular Democratic Party, are content with the existing commonwealth relationship.

More than 125,000 homes in Puerto Rico are wired to receive C-SPAN. Baltasar Corrada thinks that the network plays an important technological role in linking Puerto Rico with the mainland. "Because we are an island 900 miles from Miami, every time Puerto Rico gets closer to the mainland—for example, the fact that they are able to view proceedings and hearings from the U.S. House of Representatives—it brings about a much better understanding of how a great institution like Congress works."

Mayor Corrada is a native of Morovis, Puerto Rico. He received both his bachelor's and law degrees from the University of Puerto Rico. He practiced law with a large Puerto Rican firm and was active in island politics for years before running for Congress in 1976.

It was during his tenure as delegate that the House first went on television. "I was present at the creation," he recalls. "I surely supported it, as I believe that it is important for the American public to know what transpires in Congress every day."

House television has brought some changes, says Baltasar Corrada. "It used to be the practice that you would send a statement for publication in the *Congressional Record,* but not be personally present on the floor to deliver the speech." Now, he says, "when members really want to make an impact, they will go to the floor of the House and make that statement." He adds, "Members are better prepared now when they make their statements on the floor."

He also feels that the presence of television cameras has "brought about larger interest on the part of the members to participate in debates," something that's "more enlightening to the American public."

Nowadays, Baltasar Corrada stays busy as the mayor of San Juan while conducting his campaign for governor. However, he still keeps his eye on the House floor. "Frequently Congress talks about important legislation that may have an impact on federal programs in the city of San Juan," he explains. "And then there are the budget discussions, and appropriations for education, housing, employment, and training programs," not to mention just a touch of sentimental recollection.   —*P.S.*

Mayor Corrada can watch C-SPAN on Cable TV of Greater San Juan.

"The Flag Waver"

Gene S. Crockett

Irving, Texas

One would expect Gene Showers Crockett, a descendant of American frontiersman Davy Crockett, to be patriotic. And he is. "Being a Crockett, I was immersed in freedom in Texas history and American history," he says. "I'm a real history nut and flag waver for freedom." Indeed, Mr. Crockett of Irving, Texas, is so pro-America that he's quick to point out the last four digits of his home phone number are 1776, and the last four digits of his office number are 2776.

His mission in life is to live up to the Crockett family tradition: "I've made it my challenge to leave this world a better place than I found it." At 58 years old, Mr. Crockett says old "fuddy duddies" like him should "get off their duffers" and invest their time in the youth of America. "I love working with young people, because they're bright-eyed and bushy-tailed. They want to learn what's going on. The kids of today need heroes and heroines. To heck with these rock stars and all of these national football players," says Mr. Crockett.

As part of his crusade to get children on the right track, he has given some 17,000 Texas schoolchildren U.S. Constitution bicentennial materials that include special calendars and a four-page booklet of American symbols, "family fundamentals," and quotes from the Constitution. They read: "In dedication of a free America and freedom everywhere." Giving them out made him feel "like the pied piper," he says. "I feel as good as I'm sure Jesus did when he said, 'Suffer the little children to come unto me. . . .'"

For the past 15 years, he's produced over 20,000 calendars in three different sizes—wall, pocket, and notebook—for friends, customers, and kids. The 1987 edition, which noted the birthdays of famous Americans (Davy Crockett included) and had quotes from U.S. statesmen, also told readers to watch C-SPAN.

The educational calendars and handouts have amounted to a sizable financial investment for the electrical engineer: Mr. Crockett says he's spent over $20,000 on these printed pearls of wisdom. While it may have been nice to have a new car instead, he says "I've got to have a freer America. I'd rather spend my money on educating people. It's more fun to be knowledgeable than to be stupid. It takes money, though, and you've got to put your money where your mouth is."

In his quest to educate citizens about their government, G. S. Crockett, whose nickname is "Davey" (the "e" distinguishes him from the original), has also fashioned a personal campaign to get the word out about C-SPAN. He wears a button on his shirt pocket protector that reads: "C-SPAN, for People Who Think for Themselves." For more than a year "I've been wearing it everywhere I go, every place, except the shower and in bed," he says. "I'm just a walking advertisement for C-SPAN."

Not surprisingly, that button has attracted some attention. At one industry convention he attended as president of his electronics firm, Crockett Southwest, his colleagues couldn't help but notice. "They say, 'Hey Crockett! What's C-SPAN?' And I say, 'That means intelligence. It's for people who want to think for themselves.'" And, he reports that "our greatest hope for America—the little kids—all want to know what C-SPAN is."

For Mr. Crockett, C-SPAN is "like getting a Ph.D. in common sense and politics. I've felt doubly more informed about politics since I've watched C-SPAN." He calls the network his "right arm in getting to see what the people in Congress are all about."

So involved is Mr. Crockett in his Congress-watching that he has set up two televisions side by side. One is tuned to C-SPAN, and the other has C-SPAN II. "I've got two eyes, I've got two ears," he explains. "So I can watch both of them at the same time." He also has two VCRs ready for recording in case he wants to "pick someone's brains later on." He tunes in to the network more than 30 hours per week. "I should be doing business work and making money for Crockett Southwest," he admits, "but I am such a nut on my politics"—a suitable preoccupation for someone whose ancestor represented Tennessee in Congress and died as a freedom fighter at the Alamo.

Mr. Crockett estimates that by now he has 2,000 hours of C-SPAN programming on tape, mainly hearings and debates on the 1986 tax reform bill. High taxes stir the ire of businessman Crockett. "When government starts taking away your money to put into projects that you don't believe in, then you have to say, 'Hey, that's not right.' And then you start getting involved in politics."

In fact, it was after watching the evolution of the tax bill on C-SPAN that Mr. Crockett decided to take a trip to Washington, D.C., to discuss his dissatisfaction with the bill with members of Congress and their aides. "The only source I could really trust on the tax bill was C-SPAN, because I could listen to the guys in Congress giving their input. I could learn about the players and what they really felt," he says. "The commercial stations are just trying to sell beer and soap. C-SPAN sells America and freedom."

Gene Crockett's political convictions are as strident as his "dedication to a free America." "Probably about 10,000 people in Texas know that I'm an arch conservative," he jokes. They probably also know that embedded in his conservative philosophy is a libertarian ethic. The self-described "political animal" wants "government out of my hair." And he wants it out of the hair of his two children and three grandchildren, as well. No matter what their interests, he encourages tomorrow's voters to protect their liberties and get involved: "You're an individual, and you're a part of the system. And if you think the system is rotten, then you'd better change it." —S.S.

Mr. Crockett monitors both C-SPAN and C-SPAN II on Paragon Communications.

"The Wordsmith"

James Crosswhite
San Diego, California

"I watch C-SPAN because it gives voice to a nation. A voice from Florida responds to a voice from Iowa; a voice from Oregon comments on the exchange. I hear the voices raw, in dialect or regional accent. I descry the opinions of Americans in their fullness—the prejudice, the tolerance, the concrete perspectives of a farmer, a secretary, a construction worker, a nun. No sociologist or commentator or reporter classifies or evaluates or sifts these voices first. C-SPAN broadcasts them whole—voices whose roots still find nourishment in the centuries-old First Amendment."

This stirring language—a first-paragraph tribute to Americana—brought James Crosswhite to Washington, D.C. In 1984, the writing professor from the University of California at San Diego submitted the winning entry in a C-SPAN essay contest, earning a trip to the nation's capital and a visit to the network. During that trip, Mr. Crosswhite appeared on a live C-SPAN call-in program to voice his insights about Washington and the political process. Calls from viewers were friendly—even his sister phoned the program to congratulate him. Later, with his wife and four-year-old daughter, he toured the C-SPAN studios, the Capitol, and other Washington attractions.

Jim Crosswhite's essay was chosen from among over one

thousand entries to the "I watch C-SPAN because . . ." contest that helped mark the network's fifth anniversary. Network officials and an outside panel of judges that included former members of Congress selected his words as the most compelling description of C-SPAN's mission: "At a time when more decisions are reserved for experts, and when the very information for making reasonable decisions is available only to relatively small numbers of people, C-SPAN opens the discussion to an entire nation and draws the eyes and ears of a people to the deliberations at hand."

Prior to this trip, the then 32-year-old doctor of philosophy had never visited the nation's capital. He saw the city on the Potomac as an easygoing place. "Things in Washington aren't always done according to rules and schedules. There's a lot of personal relations among people, which is not like San Diego. It's more like Mexico City." He marveled that some offices on Capitol Hill still use quaint typewriters instead of computers to carry out office tasks.

On the other hand, his visit to the Hill gave him a better perspective on the job of a lawmaker. "Passing legislation would be harder than I thought. Now, I appreciate legislators because I realize what they're up against."

In his essay, Mr. Crosswhite said that he used C-SPAN's morning journalism call-in program "to measure the difference between what had happened and what is said to have happened." In an interview later, he elaborated on that theme: "It's important to learn a great deal about what actually happens and then compare that with how the newspapers report it the next day. That's invaluable. Papers decide what's important and what to exclude." By watching the network, he's been exposed to different points of view, and has a "better idea of people's reasoning" that leads them to reach their conclusions.

Jim Crosswhite is now the director of the U.C. San Diego's Warren Writing Program. He also teaches rhetoric classes, occasionally using congressional video to demonstrate to his students how members of Congress and scholars argue their points and how journalists interpret those points. He calls the exercise "a good way to stay informed about the decisions made by the elite."

Mr. Crosswhite believes that state governments' proceedings should be opened up to viewers as much as national government is. He would also like to see more national television coverage of California issues. "Some state issues have national implications," he says, citing a newly passed California law that he feels discriminates against children by allowing landlords to bar them from some dwellings. "Children have a right to decent housing."

In his own experience visiting C-SPAN and appearing on the call-in program, he saw an ironic fulfillment of Andy Warhol's oft-quoted prophecy: It was his chance to be "famous"—or at least a player in the national political debate—"for 15 minutes." However, he claims that call-ins offer other Americans the same chance every day, even if only for 15 seconds: "Callers have an audience for their views for however long the call-in host will let them go on." Viewers hear their peers' voices one at a time on the air, but those voices embody much more. As Mr. Crosswhite put it in the closing sentence of his essay: "In place of voicelessness come ringing hundreds of different voices, rooted in constitutional liberties which have become concrete, of all places, on television." —M.G.

Mr. Crosswhite is able to watch C-SPAN on Southwestern Cable TV.

"The Watchdog"

Kay Cutcher

Sioux City, Iowa

Kay Cutcher of Sioux City, Iowa, has a distinction that others
with a homespun passion for politics and devotion to C-SPAN
viewing don't have: Her steady eye on House and Senate proceedings has made her something of a celebrity. She's been
pursued by *People* magazine, *USA Today,* and the "Donahue"
show. And her forays into the public spotlight even culminated
with a backstage tête-à-tête with singer Julio Iglesias.

While Ms. Cutcher's notoriety came about almost over-
night, it was not undeserved. Her celebrity status was the by-
product of a good deal of hard work and intense monitoring of
the government in action. She takes her role so seriously that a
better portion of her day—and sometimes her entire day—is
spent in front of the television watching House or Senate proceedings. In fact, Kay Cutcher has even been known to drag
herself out of bed at 3 A.M. to watch an important debate. And
when she is forced to leave home during crucial floor action,
she tapes the events so that she can catch up on them later on.

Of course, watching television, in and of itself, never made
anybody famous. Kay Cutcher is one of the founding mothers
of a loosely knit group, dubbed the "Sioux City Watchdogs" by
the press, that tracks the actions of members of Congress. Up
until the summer of 1987, when the group split up and donated its treasury to the Oliver North Defense Fund, Ms.

Cutcher and her politically active friends were at work constantly. They wrote letters, sent telegrams, and made phone calls when they had a bone to pick with the powers that be. The Watchdogs, with a membership estimated at 100 to 150, apprised each other of daily legislative events by a "telephone tree" system. They called each other to make sure someone was always monitoring important legislative debates, and when an issue needed immediate attention they got the ball rolling with one member calling two others, and those two contacting two others, and so on. Occasionally the members got together for what could be called the Sioux City version of the "power lunch"—they gathered en masse for cold cuts, salad, and an afternoon Senate debate.

Before discovering C-SPAN, Ms. Cutcher, now 61, never had much interest in television, although she had always been active in politics. (She served 15 years, for example, as an officer of the local Republican Women's Club, first as treasurer, then as vice president.) In January 1981, Ms. Cutcher and her husband, Lane, traveled by bus to Washington, D.C., for the inauguration of President Reagan. The trip home was exhausting, leaving Ms. Cutcher with a high temperature and low spirits. While recuperating, she found herself flipping through the channels on her newly installed cable TV and, in the process, happening on C-SPAN. "I just got interested in the thing," she says, "and have been interested ever since."

Her "interest" quickly became a passion, and a morning ritual was established: The television was switched on early so she could get a handle on the day's legislative calendar. If something interesting was scheduled, Ms. Cutcher rearranged her day so that she could monitor floor proceedings. Then friends were notified about what the day held in store. Although the original core group of C-SPAN devotees only included members of the Republican Women's Club, the network of Congress-watchers eventually expanded to include a bipartisan collection of concerned citizens, some of them in other states. Day after day, Ms. Cutcher and the Iowa contingent studied the stars of the nation's new cable channel. Their motive was simple and straightforward: They wanted to stay on top of key issues and, in the process, help keep others informed.

In 1984, Kay Cutcher and another Sioux City C-SPAN enthusiast, Esther Larsen, were asked to co-author a guest column on *USA Today*'s editorial page. In that article, the two women described how their informal telephone network encouraged congressional scrutiny. "There is no need to worry about possible biased reporting concerning the U.S. House of Representatives," they wrote. "We can see and hear it firsthand. How wonderful. It's better than having a seat in the House gallery. . . . We know from the call-in shows that we see and hear that the American people are hungry for the truth— and that ever-increasing numbers are determined to find it," they concluded.

The column did not go unnoticed, and before long Ms. Cutcher and her group were the subject of newspaper articles and TV and radio segments. And, as is often the case, media coverage begat more media coverage. That's how Kay Cutcher was able to land an impressive memento for her Sioux City Watchdog scrapbook: She appeared with Rep. Robert Walker (R-Pennsylvania) and Rep. Dan Glickman (D-Kansas) on a "Donahue" show that explored C-SPAN's popularity.

In 1986, when the Senate opened its chamber to television, ABC News videotaped Ms. Cutcher and her friends watching the inaugural telecast of C-SPAN II. This event, in turn, generated a story about Ms. Cutcher in *People* magazine. "As Kay sees it," the story noted, "only Julio Iglesias—and perhaps her husband, Lane—are anywhere as scintillating as the U.S. Congress." As luck would have it, the week that story came out the Cutchers had tickets for a Julio Iglesias concert in Des Moines, and they were able to finagle hard-to-get backstage passes to see the singer. "All the time we were there," says Ms. Cutcher, "he kept saying, 'Thank you for mentioning me in *People* magazine.' I thought I would die."

Despite her celebrity status, Ms. Cutcher's routine hasn't changed. Although the Sioux City Watchdogs is no longer a formal organization, Kay Cutcher still monitors floor debate, she still phones friends with important legislative news, and she still contacts politicians when she's moved by an issue. Political involvement is a mainstay in Kay Cutcher's life, and she says that her C-SPAN viewing habits are a necessary component to keeping informed.

Lane Cutcher says of his wife: "She is so knowledgeable about what's going on that she makes me feel out of it." Television scheduling conflicts do come into play for the couple.

He likes to watch reruns of "Barney Miller" and, of course, she always prefers C-SPAN. But, as Ms. Cutcher told *People* magazine, she usually gives in to her husband's whims, but often doesn't end up missing too much: "I just wait for him to fall asleep, and then I switch back to C-SPAN."   —*M.C.*

Kay Cutcher subscribes to Sooland Cablecom.

"The Canadian"

Robert Desramaux
Ottawa, Ontario, Canada

Many Americans may not know that congressional telecasts have a slightly older Canadian cousin. In 1977, two years before the premier telecast of the U.S. House of Representatives, the Canadian House of Commons debuted live on two Ottawa cable systems. It was the first national legislature in the world to make its business available gavel-to-gavel to the voters on live television. And, by breaking ground early, the Canadian legislature ended up serving as a model for its southern neighbor.

The Parliament's television feed and the members' in-house TV network are overseen by Robert Desramaux, 40, an Ottawan who grew up in the border town of Windsor, Ontario. As the director of support and information systems for the House of Commons, he manages a staff of 325 and is responsible for the planning, development, and delivery of television services to members as well as the administration of the House. From 1968, when he graduated from the University of Windsor with a degree in political science and psychology, to 1981, when he joined the staff of the House of Commons, he held a variety of positions with Statistics Canada, the country's federal statistics agency.

Mr. Desramaux has, he says, "an affinity for things American." It may have been that inherent closeness to this country that inspired him to suggest the addition of C-SPAN telecasts to the Parliament's in-house cable system. Since 1985, Canadian legislators have been able to watch their American counterparts at work, on the floor and in committee.

Around the same time, C-SPAN added to its schedule occasional House of Commons telecasts, creating something of a satellite link between two nations sharing the longest undefended border in the world and tremendous economic, environmental, and security concerns. For Mr. Desramaux, a gentleman with a knack for understatement, the technological bridge is "a real plus."

The idea to bring the U.S. House to Parliament Hill occurred to him in the spring of 1985, when he ran into C-SPAN's then-marketing director Brian Gruber at a cable trade show. "It became apparent to me in the course of our conversation," Mr. Desramaux recalls, "that we were in the footprint [the area within which the signal can be received] of your satellite." He knew that "it would be a service that could be of real interest to members in our House because of the number of really key issues that affect both our countries." Their ability to watch American congressional telecasts, which he says struck the members as "the most normal thing in the world," occurred the following November.

"The vast majority" of members' offices, Mr. Desramaux reports, watch Congress from time to time. Their sophisticated in-house network, called OASIS, for Office Automation Service and Information Systems, is much more than a television system. It has 35 commercial cable television channels, plus C-SPAN, C-SPAN II, CNN, and four Canadian superstations, supplemented by "institutional video services." These include the three publicly available feeds of floor activity (English-only, French-only, and untranslated, which they refer to as the "floor sounds" feed); an electronic schedule of the day's proceedings in French and English; an electronic schedule of committee activity (committees, by the way, are not televised at present); flight arrival and departure information for Ottawa International Airport; an electronic news-clipping service; continuous-loop tapes of all the previous night's national news shows (edited to excise stories that are not of national political interest); a press conference channel; a House whip channel for nonconfidential messages to members from the party whips; a review channel that reruns certain high-demand programs at fixed times; and a "demand" video service: 15 channels that stand ready to cablecast prerecorded material at any time that's convenient to a member. It is through this feature that many members can watch U.S. House or Senate proceedings that they didn't catch live.

American audiences had their first full look at the Canadian Parliament in November 1985 with C-SPAN's initial telecast of the "Question Period." Unlike the U.S. Congress, the Canadian prime minister and his cabinet are required to take questions for 45 minutes each day from members of the opposition. "All we have are predictable presidential news conferences," a high school teacher from Tennessee wrote to C-SPAN after watching the Canadian Parliament. "I like the fact that the head of government has to come in and take his lumps."

"What your viewer has put his finger on," Mr. Desramaux points out, "is the fundamental difference between a parliamentary system of government and the form of government you have in the United States." In a parliamentary system the government stays in power only as long as it has the confidence of House members. Of the 282 members, the ruling Conservative Party had 208 in March 1988; the Liberal Party had 39; the New Democrats had 32; there was one Independent-Liberal; and two other independents. As Mr. Desramaux explains, "The number of instances where opposition members break ranks with their party, or members of the government party break ranks with theirs on a main issue are very insignificant."

The Canadian Senate, with 104 members, is largely an honorary institution. Senators are named by the prime minister. Their sessions are not televised.

American viewers may have a chance to watch another parliamentary system at work, however. C-SPAN anticipates carrying proceedings of the British House of Commons when it initiates a TV test period, probably in the fall of 1988.

The potential U.S. audience for a Question Period telecast is 38 million homes; only 5.7 million of Canada's 9 million households receive the House of Commons on cable television. "It's a little intimidating, I suppose, if you're a politician," to think of facing an audience that size, Mr. Desramaux observes. So, at the time of the initial U.S. telecasts of Parliament, he says, "we had this routine in place where we'd quickly try to call the House leaders" to tell them they were about to add a U.S. audience, and they would "spread the word around. Now that's being taken in stride." However, if the timing of the telecast coincides with an event of bilateral significance, like the U.S.-Canada trade agreement of 1987, Mr. Desramaux still takes time to apprise the members.

"Canadians," Mr. Desramaux says, "have always had sort of a peculiar ax to grind. We are in bed with this elephant on the continent, and while, as the mouse that sleeps with this elephant, we might be quite enamored of her, we don't want her to roll over. Maybe it's because of our relationship as a country, with that huge undefended border, the way we move freely back and forth, that we're just more conscious—or you're less conscious—of being a distinct society from us." Television can illuminate those differences.

But the medium can have the opposite influence, he believes, in a manner that is no less salutary.

Much has been written about the power of television to break down barriers, to make apparent that political differences, between towns, states, and nations, are in truth minute. "I certainly think that's a platitude that's true in any sphere of endeavor," Mr. Desramaux says. "Certainly in terms of government and legislation, the more we know about each other, the better we understand each other." —N.G.

The members of parliament can watch C-SPAN via Parliament Hill's OASIS system.

"The Moderator"

Phil Donahue

New York, New York

The man who hosts controversial TV talk shows on such subjects as AIDS, prostitution, and surrogate motherhood thinks C-SPAN is "the most exciting show in town." Phil Donahue, moderator of the ground-breaking morning hour, calls the network "a national keyhole to the inner Beltway" and says he keeps the network on all day at the office. "I'm the guy who sits there and watches the most boring stuff of all. You know, the guy at the podium with the big banner behind him at the American Association of something."

In March 1984, Mr. Donahue forsook juicier topics on one of his segments to invite Reps. Newt Gingrich (R-Georgia) and Dan Glickman (D-Kansas), and a C-SPAN official on the show for a discussion of television's effect on the legislative process. Members of the Sioux City Watchdogs, an Iowa-based cadre of "C-SPAN junkies," also joined the "Donahue" show.

For Phil Donahue, 51, C-SPAN opens government up to thorough scrutiny. "I can't imagine a better idea for the democratic process. I want to bring the cameras into the Supreme Court. If you can walk in as a citizen, what's wrong with the television citizen? There's no doubt in my mind that using this technology for this purpose can make the single most important contribution toward changing the drift away from serious examination of complicated issues.

"Television gives you a very detailed and informative picture of the way the two bodies work. I think it has the potential to make a stronger, greater contribution toward the well-being of our democracy than any other instrument."

Mr. Donahue has to stay on top of the news for his job, so he watches newscasts on ABC and NBC and takes in the "McNeil-Lehrer Newshour" ("in my opinion, the best newscast of them all"). He regularly reads the *Wall Street Journal,* the *Washington Post,* the *New York Times,* the *New York Daily News, Time, Newsweek,* and *People.* Mr. Donahue enjoys C-SPAN's examination of the print media in the morning journalists' roundtables, which compare front-page stories in newspapers all over the country: "I'm fascinated by where they're going editorially and who's getting on the op-ed page and who's making sense and who isn't." He believes that the network's invitations to correspondents from smaller papers add a welcome sense of perspective to the media at large. "I think the regular peek-a-boo at the nation's newspapers and what's on the front page in Washington versus Ogden, Utah, is an interesting idea," he says. "It lets editors, who can become pretty regal, know there's somebody outside their neighborhood watching what they're doing. There's very little media review left these days."

Phil Donahue, who often invites callers' comments during his own programs, is critical of C-SPAN's call-in format. "Remember, I'm a commercial animal with a very low tolerance for a windy, folksy question." Mr. Donahue takes pride in his efforts to make his talk show a democratic forum. So, even though he can "pop off" at will, he says, "I'm also subject to the boos of my own audience, which I've heard on more than one occasion."

Is Phil Donahue interested enough by politics to consider a run for office himself? In fact, he told C-SPAN viewers on a March 1987 call-in program: "I'd like to work for somebody I believe in. I'd like very much to be at the center of a campaign for office—either Congress or, may I exaggerate my own importance, the White House." But for now the television personality admits he's devoting great time and energy "to keeping the 'Donahue' show alive."

Other public affairs programming favorites of Mr. Donahue's include the seminars and association meetings that the network regularly telecasts. Like many Americans, Mr. Donahue says he was surprised at the number of nongovernment activities going on in Washington, D.C. "I wasn't really cognizant of the vast number of professionals who visit Washington to exchange ideas at meetings and seminars," he says. "Municipal associations, attorneys general, insurance underwriters, campaign strategists, pollsters. Every hotel's got something going."

Phil Donahue speaks with admiration of the audience that tunes in for long-form public affairs: "It certainly doesn't take a computer or a congressional survey to conclude that you have an audience that perhaps more than any other single channel can really be identified as a group of Americans who give a damn, and that's no small thing at a time in our nation's history when only half of us are voting, and when those of us who don't vote are complaining the most."

The idea of people "giving a damn" by staying informed about national issues, or by voting or running for office, gives Mr. Donahue a sense of hope. "Apathy, I think, is our biggest enemy at the moment. I really think it has the power to bring us down if we don't figure out a way to turn this around. I think that attitude has to be arrested. You can't do it alone, no one agency or institution can, but, boy, if anyone can make an enormous contribution toward the channeling of civic energy toward the democratic process, it's C-SPAN. To see these men and women, the 435 that I get to see regularly in the House, actually at work, I think enlarges the viewer's understanding of the issues. I am one American who is really pumped up by this drama." —E.Q.

Phil Donahue watches C-SPAN at his office on Manhattan Cable TV.

"The Ex-Trucker"

John Duncan

Phoenix, Arizona

John Duncan trucked frozen goods across the country for years. Always ambitious, he saved the money he made driving for other companies to buy his own rig—a big Kenworth cab over a tandem drive tractor. Despite that success he kept thinking he could do better. "I'd seen a lot of 60-year-old truck drivers who had very little to show for all their labor."

Eventually John Duncan decided to give up the security of his trucker's life, in exchange for the potential of a student's life. He enrolled in a nearby community college, and decided on courses in economics and politics. And today, the Phoenix resident is a full-time student at Arizona State University.

At 33, living the life of the full-time student hasn't been an easy adjustment. Money is tight, but John Duncan sees it as an investment in his future that "will pay off in the end." Through his political science courses at the community college, Mr. Duncan was introduced to C-SPAN. At first he was "simply curious," but his interest in the programming quickly "snowballed." Since he's a finance major, he keeps an eye out for C-SPAN's coverage of seminars and symposia held by groups like the American Enterprise Institute, the Heritage Foundation, and the Institute for Policy Studies—Washington-based organizations whose discussions help him understand domestic and international finance.

John Duncan, who is single and lives alone, takes school very seriously. With the exception of his jogging, he rarely lets anything interfere with his studies. Still, he jokes that his appetite for watching C-SPAN takes away from his studying, since he tunes in for a wide range of C-SPAN programming that is very often unrelated to his studies. But he's convinced that, while it may not add to his grade point average, watching C-SPAN certainly shapes his academic perceptions in the larger sense. It's all "part of being a student. Hearing what other people think and being able to tell them what you think. It's like an encyclopedia of knowledge. It's where I get lots of my ideas."

He attributes his fledgling cravings for politics almost entirely to the information he gets from C-SPAN. "As a truck driver, I had no interest in public policy," he recalls. "You'd be surprised how you can go through life without really caring about who makes the important decisions." But today he describes his interest in politics as "intense." He classifies himself as a conservative, and he's one who seeks out a variety of opinion magazines to supplement his understanding of national issues.

Now an avid viewer of House floor proceedings, Mr. Duncan appreciates elected officials more than he used to. "After watching, you know whom you're voting for, where before you were voting for someone whom you may have read about or seen for a few seconds on television." He credits television in the House with opening up government and demystifying the political process: "When you watch the House, you get a sense of the mechanics of it. You have a fantasy about it, but when the camera's there and you actually see the reality of what's going on, you see the weak points and you see the strong points—you almost want to run for representative."

Despite his new-found interest, John Duncan is sure that when he finishes school, politics will remain his avocation rather than his vocation. He's headed for a career in finance—perhaps as a researcher specializing in the fluctuations of securities prices. Even before he started college, business and finance appealed to him. While on the road, he'd read finance magazines to "kill time" and often perused books about economics while "waiting around for a load to come in."

In 1987, John Duncan took his own turn on television, as a participant in a Phoenix focus group that brought cable subscribers together to explore their views about C-SPAN. "It was an opportunity to give some feedback to C-SPAN," he says. Today, the former trucker is busy listening, reading, and learning about money, ideas, and the world. And C-SPAN is one of his teachers. "I've gone from uninformed and unconcerned to very opinionated and very involved. Now, that's a turnaround." —*M.H.*

When he's not studying, John Duncan watches C-SPAN on Dimension Cable.

"The Prisoner"

Russell Epperson

Moberly, Missouri

At a glance Russell Epperson of Moberly, Missouri, seems like your basic working-class American.

His daily schedule is routine. He rises early, at 4:00 A.M., to catch a couple of hours of public affairs television, manages a set of exercises, eats breakfast, and then gets on the bus for work, where he makes office furniture. He's home at 3:30 in the afternoon, and oftentimes stops off at the library to read the daily papers. After an early dinner, Mr. Epperson usually watches the news and retires early.

However, two factors set Russell Epperson apart from the average American Joe: He's a hound for public affairs and news, and he is a prisoner. In 1976, he was found guilty of three counts of first-degree murder. He is currently serving three consecutive life sentences at the Moberly Training Center for Men. "I guess there are some pretty basic differences in lifestyles," ponders Mr. Epperson. "At night I'm locked inside. I'm not allowed to go hunting and fishing, which I really enjoy. And every day I really miss contact with friends and relatives." And, of course, Russell Epperson, as an imprisoned felon, will never be able to vote.

Mr. Epperson says that his love of politics is unique among prisoners: "Not too many people here are interested in politics or public affairs." He watches C-SPAN and other public affairs programming in the small cell he shares with a room-mate (or "cellie," as they call each other) and spends at least two hours a day reading, which includes a couple of national newspapers, a few Missouri papers, and some weekly magazines. "I've always needed to know what's going on in the world," Mr. Epperson explains.

Cable television came to the Moberly prison over two years ago, when prison administrators purchased a satellite dish and made all the cells in the facility "cable ready." The television in Mr. Epperson's cell was purchased at the prison canteen, with the money books he earns at his job. In fact, the only material possessions prisoners can keep in their cells are the purchases they make at the canteen.

Mexico, Missouri, was Russell Epperson's home where he lived on a farm until he was 18. After high school he held a string of jobs, including feed mill operator, gas station attendant, and factory worker. "Before I was sentenced, I was trying to break into the farming industry," he remembers. But 11 years later he believes he would live life differently if he were free. He would go the small business route—"maybe a mail-order company of some kind."

He remembers President John F. Kennedy as the states-man who initially inspired his political curiosities. "I remember seeing his televised speeches. They were pretty moving. I remember his assassination—I was in eighth grade. What a terrible shame."

"When I was coming up through school, we were taught how the government operates, but now I see how it really works." He says that C-SPAN has him tuned in to the three-steps-forward-two-steps-back reality of how government proceeds. He notices the back-and-forth discussion that goes into making legislation. "I guess all the political infighting and bickering going on between grown men and women is necessary in the democratic process." The avid newspaper reader also says that watching the network's morning media call-in has brightened his view of journalists. "I used to see bias in all of them. Now, on C-SPAN, I see them sitting down and thoroughly discussing the issues."

Russell Epperson said he "never had any dealings with the law" before he was sentenced. He won't talk much about the crime that put him there, that thrust him into a world of bars, regulations, and other convicts. He claims he is innocent in more ways than one: "Before the trial, I had always thought justice prevailed. I was influenced by 'Perry Mason,' where right always came out in the end. That's not how it works." Mr. Epperson takes a dim view of the justice system. He says, "It's really not set up to let people out if they're reformed."

When he's not working at the furniture plant, reading, or watching public affairs television, Mr. Epperson may be studying for his classes. Now, at age 37, he is working on his associate of arts degree, and he's more than halfway to completion. The program entails "a little bit of everything," he explains. It lays the necessary groundwork for someone who may pursue a bachelor of arts degree. Though Moberly inmates can get training in electronics and auto repair, the prison does not offer a four-year degree. Mr. Epperson would have to be transferred to another facility in order to complete his undergraduate work. "That all depends on quite a lot of things in the future."

A letter he wrote to C-SPAN first brought Russell Epperson to the network's attention. In it, he mentioned the reason he has maintained an avid interest in public affairs, even though he will probably never again live outside prison walls or vote: "Just because a person has been convicted of a crime and locked in prison does not mean that he never thinks about the state of the world."   —M.H.

Russell Epperson is able to watch C-SPAN on a system operated by the Moberly Training Center.

"The Historian"

Harry Fletcher

Montgomery, Alabama

For Harry Fletcher, one of the keys to history is point of view. A writer's perspective informs and colors the writing of history. Interpretations of events vary with the experience and position of the interpreter. Mr. Fletcher, a historical scholar at the U.S. Air Force Historical Research Center in Montgomery, Alabama, examines historians' points of view as much as he analyzes what they say.

"All historians are biased," says Mr. Fletcher. "It's just a question of how much. I think when historians write things, especially if there's an emotional appeal, there's a tendency to bend things just a bit."

Mr. Fletcher, 62, enjoys the variety of interpreting and investigating tasks that come his way at the historical center, and says he wouldn't find that kind of variety elsewhere. The center is located at Maxwell Air Force Base, but is under the supervision of the Office of Air Force History at Bolling AFB near Washington, D.C. Harry Fletcher, a civilian employee, is a senior staffer at the historical center. Some 40 people, civilian and military, work at the facility. Sometimes their assignments have a personal touch: "We help servicemen find friends or things that they are looking for. We help people establish the fact that they were injured on the job."

On other occasions, Mr. Fletcher carries out research in

the field. When the Air Force found a World War II B-24 aircraft in the wilds of northern Canada, Mr. Fletcher went up to investigate. He traced the origins and uses of the undocumented airplane.

Mr. Fletcher's job requires him to use history to explain the present and to make recommendations for the future. "Our main purpose is to train today's Air Force. We help keep them apprised of what's been done in the past so that they don't do the same thing all over again. Sometimes the Air Force tries to reinvent the wheel. We try to prevent that if we can."

In his fascination with the effect of viewpoint on the recording of historical events, Mr. Fletcher looks at more than the Air Force official accounts. He bears in mind that historical accounts of events lie in the eye of their witnesses. "I started out translating the histories written by German officers about certain selective topics concerning German Air Force activities during the World War. The whole purpose was to find out how things look from the other side." Mr. Fletcher's studies were published for review by the Air War College and the Command Staff College.

Harry Fletcher and his wife Barbara moved to Montgomery in 1963, but still call themselves "transplanted Wisconsinites." Mr. Fletcher attended the University of Wisconsin, completing part of the requirements for a doctorate before moving south. Working as a military historian is interesting, he says, "and there are not a lot of historians who get paid as well as government-employed historians." Before moving, Harry Fletcher says he had become accustomed to good news reporting, and despite the promising job, he "felt a little isolated" in Alabama. Now, he says "we are coming out of that a little bit, but we still are a little bit provincial." Many of the center's historians had started watching C-SPAN in the early 1980s, and they urged Harry Fletcher to tune in so he could "find out what's going on in the world without tearing his hair out."

The network's no-analysis approach to public events and issues immediately appealed to the historian. "The best authorities are those who *are* the authorities," he says emphatically.

Mr. Fletcher says he and Barbara now watch "two to four hours a night." Barbara Fletcher often does crossword puzzles as they watch, but the historian "gets too wrapped up in what's being talked about to be diverted by something else." Sometimes he even takes notes. "As a historian, I'm supposed to keep up with everything that's going on."

One topic that generates a lot of discussion between Mr. Fletcher and his colleagues is military spending. During lunch, Mr. Fletcher and other senior staff discuss congressional hearings they have watched: "With Gramm-Rudman [the 1985 deficit reduction bill], everybody began to wonder where the cuts would fall, what your job situation was going to be. There's a lot of discussion among government employees now," he says.

It's not just learning about today's events, however, that makes Harry Fletcher so enthusiastic about the public affairs telecasts. It's his historian's eye to future generations.

"People don't write like they used to," he observes. "Presidents don't usually sit down and write down all their thoughts about a Cuban crisis or whatever. C-SPAN will make it possible for all sorts of important people to talk about these things. We'll have a record for posterity that will be marvelous. We'll have the whole story without undue coaching."

Observes historian Harry Fletcher: "I think history will have more accuracy because you'll now have something that can't be denied—you'll have videotape of it. If someone says, 'So-and-so favored such-and-such,' you'll be able to know whether he did or didn't." —P.K.

Mr. Fletcher watches C-SPAN on Montgomery's Storer Communications.

"The Recovering Lawyer"

Robert Fox
St. Paul, Minnesota

When Robert Fox of St. Paul, Minnesota, teaches a class on constitutional law or the civil rights movement, he doesn't hand his class a course syllabus crammed with copious due dates for required reading. Rather, he is mindful that while reading is a pleasure for some, it's the nemesis of others. "Thus, what I try to do is have as many things happening as possible, virtually all of the time," says Mr. Fox, who teaches at Metropolitan State University in the Twin Cities.

Metro State's approach is so unusual—and so effective—that it was written up in the Carnegie Commission on Policy Studies in Higher Education study as "one of the 25 curriculum innovations of the 20th century." It was also profiled in a book called *Open Learning,* a collection of case studies of 18 educational institutions around the world. The university was one of only three from the United States included in the book.

The upper division school, which opened its doors in 1972, offers its 5,000 students a bachelor of arts degree in a nontraditional setting. The university has only one required course, "Individualized Educational Planning," in which the students spend "a great deal of time thinking, reading, and arguing about what it means to be educated," explains Mr. Fox. His school's alternative approach cultivates an individual student's education process.

Robert Fox, who was named one of the school's charter faculty members in 1972, is a bit of an anachronism. His teaching philosophy, actually his general outlook on life, hearkens back to the '60s, when everybody was encouraged to "do their own thing." At age 44, he is a product of the civil rights and the anti-war movements. "That was a time—and to me it still is—when we needed to say, 'We are individuals. We are not corporate bodies.' Every person does not have to go through the exact same set of hoops, because each person is different. What is important is each person being empowered to make his own decision, being able to think through those things, rather than feeling helpless."

Mr. Fox, who calls himself a "reformed lawyer," teaches courses on introductory law, the history of the civil rights movement, and constitutional law. He also serves in an advisory capacity to the professors and guides the students in their course development.

In his attempts to deliver information to his students in the most effective ways, he has borrowed from C-SPAN's "America and the Courts" and "Inside the Constitution" series. He's fond of using footage from network programming that will shed light on weighty matters of jurisprudence. For instance, he used snippets of a 1987 conference on morality and the Constitution to explain the concepts of judicial activism and judicial restraint to his constitutional law classes.

"C-SPAN's programming presents an opportunity to see what is happening for those of us who aren't there. The network is participating in what I consider a transformation of American society and American learning," says Robert Fox. He cites C-SPAN's coverage of a 1987 meeting of the Federalist Society (a group of conservative legal experts) as a good example. "Previously, a couple hundred people would have attended. And then their articles would have been printed up, and some people would take the time to read them. But now we can say, 'Look, watch it on C-SPAN.'"

When someone asks, "Where's Daddy?" in the Fox household, a familiar chime from his six-year-old son rings, "Daddy's out in the kitchen watching the Constitution." With two televisions strategically positioned in the kitchen and in the front room, he can meander back and forth while he tunes in and out of more than 20 hours of C-SPAN programming a week. His interest in public affairs is more than professional: "I don't separate my professional life from personal life. I consider myself a complete unit. And I happen to be lucky enough to be doing what I am. And so, I don't go to work and do something different than what I do when I come home. It's all there."

But it hasn't always been quite all there for Robert Fox. The "recovering attorney" did what he "was supposed to do, according to the catalog," in his early years. Fresh from the University of Minnesota with a political science degree, he entered Duke University Law School in 1965. He described his law school study as a vocational program with almost no choices in curriculum. "Law school was just one course after another— never considering any broad questions of justice. I found it extremely frustrating," he says.

Immediately after graduating from law school he began working for an "old, established law firm" in the Twin Cities. "I spent virtually all of my time working with nonprofits and tax-exempt organizations, helping them figure out how they were going to give away their money. And the more time that I spent doing that, the more I wanted to be involved in doing something," recalls Mr. Fox. It wasn't so much that he was disillusioned with the practice of law, rather, he "wanted to be where the action was."

He discovered Metropolitan State University through his work at the law firm. The school's philosophy grabbed him immediately. "It was like suddenly something was speaking to me," remembers Robert Fox. Now he is teaching others to do their own thing.   —S.S.

Mr. Fox watches C-SPAN at home via Continental Cablevision.

"The Poetic Psychologist"

Helen Frank

Somers, New York

In the summer of 1987, the American public watched with great interest as the Congress conducted its investigation of the Iran-contra affair. The hearings generated editorials, news specials, commentaries, and debates. For Helen Frank, a retired psychotherapist from Somers, New York, the televised hearings spawned something altogether different, something she had been thinking about for a while—a poem about C-SPAN. Here's a part of what she wrote:

> As I sit and watch the show, I knit.
> Unable to waste time just viewing.
> Today the amendment to the budget
> Brought forth a spewing of invective.
> One "distinguished gentleman" called another
> A "young slasher," then was accused of misconstruing.
>
> Tempers rose at the mention of budget cuts,
> The weight of the deficit elicited scurrilous rebuts,
> Sharper than an ax was the reaction to a possible tax.
>
> I, like Madame La Farge, knitting while they chopped
> Thought cutting, slashing, and axing remarks
> Comparable to the action

Of the guillotine—budgets, bills, amendments
Severed like the heads that dropped.

As governments still euphemize
Violence with rhetoric
C-SPAN provides viewers with an opportunity to
    choose
Their own versions of the news.

"I just kept thinking how worthwhile C-SPAN really is and 'bingo,' I wrote the poem," she says.

Writing poetry is not something new for Dr. Frank; she has been penning poems for about a decade, and, more recently, has become a contributing writer to various senior citizen journals. She says that writing is a way of helping her understand what aging is all about. But an interest in politics, spawned by her accidental discovery of C-SPAN, was something new.

"My bag was always my work with my patients," she says. "I'm not the type to join a campaign. That's not to say I don't care. I always vote. And I'll write a letter if I think it will make a difference. I don't write just to mimic an opinion of someone else."

Dr. Frank says that her career pursuits predated the women's liberation movement by 25 years. After raising her four children, she decided she wanted a career, and she earned a doctorate in education from Columbia University. But in 1983 Dr. Frank gave up her practice, which centered on marriage and family counseling. "If you're accustomed to working, you have a kind of built-in calendar," she says. "It's the old business of the Protestant work ethic. When you're not working it's very hard building up your own self-esteem. It takes a lot of doing. You have to redefine your whole value system."

"Retirement is the opposite of how most people live their whole lives," she adds. "Suddenly, you have hours and hours of time on your hands, and what used to be free time becomes your whole life. It's not that I'm complaining; I've time now for a lot of things I didn't use to have time for, such as getting involved in senior groups. I read more. But I try not to spend my whole life in front of the TV. You don't have to get dressed, or communicate when you watch TV. That's not me. C-SPAN has occupied a bit of my time, and I like watching something stimulating where you can form an opinion on what you see."

In some ways, C-SPAN has helped Helen Frank fill the gaps left by retirement. She often watches C-SPAN in the morning; she particularly enjoys the media call-in programs because she is able to associate a face and personality with the reporter's pieces that she has been reading for years. However, C-SPAN is just part of the mix that now helps her keep up with events. She reads newspapers and magazines, and watches television news as well. In many instances, she says, the various media complement one another.

Dr. Frank believes that C-SPAN offers her something that other media don't—continuity. "You get absorbed," she says. "You don't have to lose track of your thoughts. In other words, if you sit down to watch a hearing or something, you know you're going to see it all." And that, says retired psychologist Helen Frank, "enhances my endemically argumentative nature and didactic tendencies." —*M.H.*

Dr. Frank is a subscriber to Westchester Cable TV.

"The Naval Professor"

Stephen Frantzich

Annapolis, Maryland

When political science professor Stephen Frantzich, 43, teaches government classes at the U.S. Naval Academy in Annapolis, Maryland, he keeps C-SPAN on for the whole class period with the sound down low. The presence of television in the class-room, he says lightheartedly, lets him know whether his lectures are engaging his listeners. "If none of the students is paying attention and they are all looking at C-SPAN, then the lecture is not a success." Another reason he keeps the network on is that its programming yields moments that can be used to illustrate points to the class. When something comes on the screen that bears out Prof. Frantzich's idea, he'll turn up the volume so the students can see and hear it. By his account, this happens about 10 times every term.

One of the early educators to recognize the potential of C-SPAN as a classroom aid, Prof. Frantzich has developed deliberate, sophisticated ways to use the material. He has organized footage into several educational tapes that examine Congress, showcasing its procedures, styles of debate, leadership, and relations with the media. He has made up lesson plans that incorporate C-SPAN as a teaching tool. And he has helped spread the word to other teachers, delivering lectures at seminars and publishing articles about the service in educational journals.

Prof. Frantzich is a longtime enthusiast of politics. He was a Minnesota state delegate while still in college, and holds a doctorate in political science from the University of Minnesota. A one-time visiting professor in the Philippines, he has published monographs on that country's politics. He has also written articles on technical innovations in Congress and a book about how citizens can write to their congressmen most effectively.

At the Naval Academy, professors are entrusted with teaching special students. "Midshipmen have greater responsibilities than just academic progress. It's like teaching students who all have full-time jobs. They are responsible to their companies, to athletic teams, and various other extracurricular groups." Students are under pressure to maintain an across-the-board academic average. According to Prof. Frantzich, the Naval Academy has increased its number of liberal arts admittees; higher numbers of students with strong verbal skills bring life to classroom discussions. And, as future naval officers, his students have a strong need to learn about their government.

In some respects, though, the midshipmen resemble other students in their age group. "We are teaching the 'Sesame Street' generation, which was weaned on visual pyrotechnics," says Prof. Frantzich. That's why he brings the video age into the classroom with a television set. That's also why he edited his tapes on Congress down to 20 minutes each. "Experience leads me to believe that tapes work best when they are short, narrowly focused, and to the point." Prof. Frantzich often stops the tapes in the middle during classroom sessions. "I make no apology for stopping the program, discussing the points made, and even replaying specific segments."

Prof. Frantzich has a specific formula for putting his educational tapes together. "I began by taping 10 hours of House proceedings over a one-week period. Then, with some general topics in mind, I carefully watched the raw tapes for good examples. It then became a case of choosing the best examples for inclusion in particular tapes." Prof. Frantzich concedes that his tapes may not have a "slick and polished look," but argues that "the visual component of some material is so important that substance overrides form."

Prof. Frantzich uses his tapes for classes at both the Naval Academy and at George Washington University.

His Naval Academy colleagues use them for courses on American government and international organization. The creator's own favorite video lesson compares actual footage from the House floor with the *Congressional Record,* and reports in *Congressional Quarterly,* newspapers, and the evening news. Prof. Frantzich has ideas for more tapes, and he hopes other educators will follow his lead and put together their own video versions of a typical day in Congress.

For perspective, Prof. Frantzich has his students watch unedited versions of Congress as well. "Congress is not all high drama," he says. "Students become bored with the slowness of the process, and that's good. They are seeing the reality of Congress—the rule, not the exception."

Stephen Frantzich readily makes his ideas available to other educators who want to introduce students to government on television. He gave C-SPAN a copy of his first lesson plans using video excerpts in 1984, long before the network had fully addressed its own usefulness as an educational entity. Since then he's helped spread the word to other educators.

By 1986, the network had established "C-SPAN in the Classroom," a project designed to exchange and develop ideas of how to teach with C-SPAN. The Benton Foundation, a Washington-based foundation that funds projects in government and communications, held a meeting of teachers from high schools, junior colleges, and universities to discuss C-SPAN's instructive potential. Prof. Frantzich joined the other educators for the strategy session.

That year, Prof. Frantzich and five other instructors were awarded Benton Foundation fellowships through the American Political Science Association to create lesson plans using network telecasts. A 1987 edition of the APSA educational journal *News for Teachers of Political Science* published the six courses for nationwide distribution. In his course, Prof. Frantzich noted that "while C-SPAN is a window on the congressional process, it retains all the limitations of a window. A window has no memory and one only sees things when one is looking through it."

In Stephen Frantzich's opinion, many students of political science consider the discipline "retrospective"; many of them "lack a feeling for how the tools of political science can be applied to the here and now." Watching congressional video can endow them with a sense that politics is real and alive. Prof. Frantzich sees his students taking a more active interest in government and showing more awareness. When he takes them on field trips to the U.S. Capitol, he says, they know what to expect. And, he notes, "There's a small but active segment" that comes back from vacation talking about things they have seen on the network.

These days, Stephen Frantzich jokes that it's hard to keep his students' attention just by lecturing. "I'm finding it hard to compete with anything so highly visual. I have a hard act to follow." Prof. Frantzich does not begrudge video's hold on his students, though. In fact, he sees television's "magnetism" as one of the keys to its use as a teaching tool: "People tend to gravitate toward it, and the video resources on the network are so extensive that its possibilities for classroom use are only limited by your level of energy and creativity."   —M.C.

The U.S. Naval Academy receives C-SPAN through an on-campus satellite dish.

"The Volunteer"

Ann Funck

Denver, Colorado

When Ann Funck truly believes in something, she doesn't hesitate to offer her services. At the height of the Vietnam War, the young Army nurse volunteered for a tour of duty in Southeast Asia. Today, she devotes considerable energy to grassroots lobbying on behalf of veterans of that war.

Ms. Funck, now 41, spent more than a year running a field hospital in Vietnam. The experience changed her life. "It took a while for me to reconcile what happened there," she says. But eventually her soul-searching led to political activism on behalf of her fellow veterans. She helped organize Vietnam Veterans for America, and served as president of the group's Colorado chapter for two years. Ms. Funck says the organization has earned a congressional charter, which enables the group to legally act on behalf of veterans with the Veterans Administration.

Working to effect change through political activism is rooted in Ann Funck's upbringing. She grew up in a political household: "I met Vice President Nixon when I was eight years old. Through my parents I've met every president since I can remember." She earned a degree in political science and later spent several years as a staffer in former Sen. Gary Hart's (D) Colorado office.

Over the years, she has amassed a videotape collection of many congressional hearings that C-SPAN has televised and uses those tapes in her veterans activities. "A lot of what happens through the veterans community is mandated by Congress," she explains, and notes that those videos have "critical importance" to the group's lobbying and educational efforts.

"If a new vet comes in and wants to know the background, wants to know what's going on, instead of my saying 'About two years ago Sen. Murkowski held hearings . . .' it's easier to say, 'Well, give me a half-hour, come in and watch this tape.'" She also uses the tapes at organization meetings to "spark debate to make people think, to stir up the issues." She considers the network a "great resource" for her work.

When we caught up with Ms. Funck she was on the road, organizing a veterans march on Washington, D.C. Groups of veterans were marching to the capital from as far away as Texas, seeking attention for veterans issues such as health care and MIAs. Ann Funck spent five months advancing the trek, seeking press coverage for the group in communities, large and small, that it passed through. "Think of the impact that those people can have in every little tiny town and large metropolitan community that they walk through—with press, radio, TV coverage, and governors coming out to greet them.

"Along the route, the group conducted a voter registration drive as part of a long-term plan to mobilize Vietnam veterans as a political force. "Veterans Vote '88," while not allied with any political party, was an effort to encourage veterans to become politically active, "to watch what's going on. If lawmakers are supportive to what you believe, encourage fellow veterans to vote them back into office; if they're not doing what we want them to do, vote them out." Ms. Funck told the veterans that "C-SPAN is a valuable tool for monitoring what your elected representatives are doing."

Ann Funck wasn't sure what she'd be doing once the march was over. Her airline pilot husband had been transferred to Dallas, and she had decided to leave Colorado to join him there. After all those months on the roads and highways, she said she had a lot of catching up to do. And she planned to watch a great deal of C-SPAN. Using her catch-up time to watch C-SPAN makes sense, since no matter what Ann Funck chooses to do next, "it's certain I'm going to be politically active." —R.C.

While in Denver, Ann Funck watched C-SPAN on Mile-Hi Cablevision.

Winnie Gill

Baton Rouge, Louisiana

Until six years ago, Baton Rouge housewife Winnie Gill, 65, never discussed politics with her husband, James Monroe Gill. It wasn't that she lacked interest in politics; rather, Ms. Gill felt she couldn't hold her own in debates with her "well-read" husband. For the past six years, however, Winnie Gill has been an eyewitness to the daily activities of Congress. Today, she says she can argue politics with anyone. And her husband of 44 years, couldn't be happier.

"He thinks it's great that I have such an interest in politics," she says. "He's been very supportive of me." Mr. Gill isn't the only one who's noticed his wife's newfound political acuity. Friends across the country are amazed by her knowledge of Congress, she says, and her grown children are impressed. Even the *Wall Street Journal* took note. A June 1984 story quoted Winnie Gill as saying, "When I watch the House of Representatives, I know many of them by name now. I want to know everything that's going on."

Knowing everything that's going on in Congress takes time. When her two children were grown and gone, Ms. Gill was left with plenty of unplanned hours. She had very little interest in watching television, but finding Congress on television one day stirred up an old interest in politics, "something that I had in me for as long as I can remember." Before long, she was "spending 40, 60, and even 100 hours a week watching C-SPAN." And, because she wanted to retain what she heard, Winnie Gill took notes, something she hadn't done since her college days at Louisiana Polytechnic Institute. "That's how I learned a lot," she recalls. "It was a way I could reinforce what I was gaining."

Winnie Gill says all her conversations used to revolve around the children or her husband's business, but "nothing that was mine." And while their mutual interests were very important to her, she didn't have "something that was basically coming from my interests. Nothing that was discussed was unique to me." Her growing interest in politics began to change that, giving her a renewed sense of confidence.

Forty-some years ago, Winnie Gill was fresh out of college, recently married, working as a secretary, and eager to give up her job just as soon as she and her oil executive husband started a family. First and foremost, she was her husband's wife. James Gill was a "young man who was very ambitious," she recalls. "He was working for a big company and back in those days a lot more was required of you as a wife—at least I was reared to believe a lot more was required of you."

In her early married years, she was a very busy and active woman. In addition to the social obligations associated with being the wife of a rising young executive, she was also very committed to community affairs. As an active member of the Junior League's speakers bureau, she gave talks on local issues to various civic organizations, occasionally even mobilizing them to take political action. She was also very active in the local Presbyterian church.

Like many women of her generation, Winnie Gill devoted much of her time, energy, and brain power to her husband and children. So, when the children grew up and left home, there was a void to fill. She found herself less stimulated by her outside activities. Eventually, she became less interested in just about everything. "This is certainly a very personal thing for me to say, but I was having a problem with depression in my life, and I was no longer as active and as able to get out." Even previously enjoyable pastimes became a chore. "Because of my problem with depression, reading was a difficult thing for me. It was difficult to keep my mind centered on something," recalls Ms. Gill.

Watching Congress debate issues, however, gradually "brought back an interest that I had always had in public affairs. It gave me something to really put my thoughts into," she recalls. "I guess this is one of the reasons that I started taking notes. I was so interested in all the men on the floor."

Winnie Gill hasn't needed to take notes since early 1986. She's been watching Congress so long now that she knows it inside and out. Sometimes still, she'll "pick up pieces of paper and jot things down—names and addresses, or books that sound interesting." She and James Monroe Gill, who's now retired, love to travel, but she hates to miss the House sessions. "I was telling my husband the other day," she says, "in the future when we travel I'm not only going to check the room reservations, I'm going to check whether they have cable TV with C-SPAN on the cable." Once, on a trip to Washington, the couple stopped by the network's studios for a tour and stayed to watch the production of a call-in program. And later, in 1984, when the network was on location in New Orleans to cover the campaigns, Winnie and James Gill drove in from Baton Rouge with a cake she had baked for the crew.

Ms. Gill wants her three grandchildren to start watching Congress too. They live in Nevada in an area without cable, so "the next time we visit I'm going to buy them a satellite dish," she says. As for Winnie Gill and her husband James, their dinner conversations continue to get livelier. "My husband calls himself a moderate, but I call him a liberal," she explains. "He says that I'm so conservative that it's terrible." She hopes to "move him more toward the political center." Short of realigning her husband's political philosophy, she'll settle for more debates and more Congress watching. "I can really say that it saved my life in many ways," she says. "I can really make that as a true statement." —M.C.

Winnie Gill keeps up with Congress on Cablevision of Baton Rouge.

"The Conservative Opportunist"

Newt Gingrich

Jonesboro, Georgia

For Rep. Newt Gingrich (R-Georgia), television has created a "grassroots Congress. . . . It creates the public capacity for any citizen anywhere in America to turn on a channel and sit in the living room and be a part of government." The attempt to reach this living-room constituency has led Rep. Gingrich into controversy. As a leader of a House GOP group called the Conservative Opportunity Society, Rep. Gingrich had been making fiery, partisan orations—clearly earmarked for television audiences—during Special Orders, the time reserved for speeches at the close of House business.

Rep. Gingrich concedes that some people considered him "an egocentric hot dog" when he began using Special Orders to get the COS message across. However, he considers that perception secondary to the importance of using television for cultivating the news media and getting a message across. "Television is the dominant medium in our society," he says. "The guys and gals in Congress who don't master it get killed."

Rep. Gingrich was attuned to the power of television early. "I grew up with Howdy Doody," he laughs. "I'm part of the television generation." The congressman, who holds a doctorate in history from Tulane University, spent several years as a history professor; a sense of the past tempers his awareness of the present. "It's important to understand that prior to the jet plane and to television, most people didn't understand government," says Rep. Gingrich. Instead, "most people tried to have a leader—either in Sunday school, the work place, or their political precinct—who understood government."

The advent of television, Rep. Gingrich says, subjected government to the scrutiny of more people and made the House of Representatives "a truly national body." He adds, "There are a lot of people out there who are fairly routine C-SPAN viewers. You have a cadre of activists and aficionados who are interested in government and politics. They have government brought into their living rooms conveniently."

It was this audience the COS had in mind when it began to reserve Special Orders time in 1983 and 1984: "When I do a Special Orders speech on the House floor, I know I will reach more people than I'd be able to talk to face-to-face all year," Mr. Gingrich explains.

COS members desired a more combative style and conservative agenda than that of the established Republican leadership. "We had created a very fine cadre of younger members who were giving the party a sort of fighting win, an ability to articulate values and debate on the floor, and in many ways take back the floor," he says.

According to Rep. Gingrich, COS members decided to use Special Orders as a platform for impassioned speeches on what they saw as the "spread of communism, the decline of the family, and the weakness of the Democratic leadership." The addresses were part of a two-pronged, long-term strategy to "awaken the American people." The speeches were directed primarily toward a television audience; the House of Representatives was often empty during Special Orders. However, the group knew that since the cameras stayed trained on the speakers at the podium, television viewers could not tell that COS speechmakers were gesturing before an empty room.

"We did more hours of directed television in '83 and '84 than probably any group that ever existed," says Rep. Gingrich. "In Special Orders, we reach the country, the reporters. In the fights on the floor in regular sessions, we create the drama that gets the press to watch, we create the votes that become decisive. In the Special Orders, we get the information out. The interaction of floor debate and Special Orders is what matters—it makes an impression on people. We always make sure we have a clear platform."

Special Orders did get people's attention. C-SPAN, which long ago made a commitment to its viewers to carry the House signal from start to finish, telecast the COS speeches live. Viewers began to write and call to revile or praise the speeches. The COS had hit a nerve.

Rep. Gingrich saw the COS' political tactics in a historical context. To him, the organization's use of Special Orders was an acknowledgment of the inevitable change that the modern age had brought about in government. "The age of the jet plane, the ICBM, and television networks together necessitate political decisions that were inconceivable in the 18th century. It means learning a new set of habits, a new culture, and learning the rhythm of vision and strategy and projects and tactics for the age of electronics."

Others did not share Rep. Gingrich's view. On May 10, 1984, Speaker O'Neill, who controlled House cameras, ordered them to sweep the House chamber during a Special Orders speech by COS member Rep. Robert Walker (R-Pennsylvania). C-SPAN viewers saw that Rep. Walker had been addressing a chamber full of vacant seats.

Several days later, an argument erupted on the floor of the House when Speaker O'Neill confronted Rep. Gingrich about another Special Orders speech the COS had delivered. In it, a group of Democrats were accused of making overtures toward communists; those named were not present for the speech. "You deliberately stood in the well of the House and took on these members when you knew that they would not be here," said Speaker O'Neill. "It's un-American. It's the lowest thing that I have ever seen in my 32 years in Congress." In a rare rebuff of a House leader, the parliamentarian ruled Speaker O'Neill out of order.

That episode between Speaker O'Neill and Congressman Gingrich generated significant media interest. "The stir we made in the House was a good moment," claims Rep. Gingrich. "I think Tip O'Neill made a fool of himself." Stories about the dispute made "all three television networks that night," which he says "didn't hurt. On the other hand, the House measures you over the years, not over minutes. I think that hard work, technical expertise, and good judgment are more important than any particular debating skill or moment in the House. I think the incident both increased by relative prestige and scarred me up some."

For the long term, Rep. Gingrich sees House television as a tonic for his fellow conservatives. "Television communicates morale. For example, people in the executive branch will watch their champions fight on a topic. That builds the morale of the people in the executive branch so they will take more risks." He also believes that House television helps spread the word on political positions: "I've had fairly senior Senate staffers on the Republican side say to me, 'I really enjoyed that series of speeches.' Not many years ago, we would have called a meeting to get these same people in a room just so that three of them could have heard what I was thinking. Nowadays they pick it up in passing, along with the rest of the people who watch."

Finally, Rep. Gingrich thinks that congressional telecasts give ordinary citizens the chance to watch government in action. "C-SPAN has created the opportunity for an audience to participate in a serious and systematic way in the House of Representatives. It allows, for those who care, the opportunity to see, live and unedited, the process of self-government in an extraordinarily complex society."

Of course, there is also a greater awareness of the electronic-age reach of Newt Gingrich. He tells the story of a man who got out of a car at a St. Louis shopping center and approached the Georgia congressman to say, "You're Newt Gingrich; I watch you on C-SPAN all the time." He says this incident just underlines his theory that "you can have an impact over time—that C-SPAN has an impact or Gingrich has an impact when people watch him on C-SPAN."   —*G.B.*

Constituents in Congressman Gingrich's hometown of Jonesboro can watch him on Wometco Cable TV of Clayton County.

"The Congressional Mom"

Gladys Glickman
Wichita, Kansas

Most mothers, even when their children are grown and have children of their own, can't resist the urge to keep close tabs on their offspring. Gladys Glickman of Wichita, Kansas, is no exception. Not too many mothers have the luxury of monitoring their children's comings and goings via national television. Gladys Glickman does.

Just about any day of the week, Ms. Glickman can tune in to C-SPAN to watch her son, Rep. Dan Glickman (D-Kansas), at work in the U.S. House of Representatives. And she's been doing just that for the past nine years. "I have to be honest with you," she says. "You get very interested in what your children are doing. My friends think it's wonderful. They say: 'Gladys, how does he know so much!' And I like to hear that."

Ms. Glickman is, not surprisingly, very proud of her congressional son. She says he's been a go-getter since the day he ran for president of his first-grade class. (He won.) And she's been rooting for him every step of the way. "I don't know how he does it," she says of his hectic lifestyle. "Maybe it's just because I'm his mother, but sometimes I worry about him. He just loves it, though. Like we always say, some love it, but others wouldn't get near it."

Ms. Glickman has been close to public affairs herself for almost 12 years now, ever since Dan first ran for a seat in the

House. Before that, she was interested in politics, but never got involved. "I never had a good reason to be involved," she says. "But, the more you do, the more interested you become." Now she follows Congress carefully, and when she and her husband, Milton, go to Washington, D.C., they visit their son's office. "I love to just go up there and sit, and see all the different people who come to talk to him." But she's not always on the sidelines. Ms. Glickman has been helping since the very first campaign. "I'll do anything," she says, "I'll lick envelopes, I'll address letters. The only thing I don't like to do is ask for money."

She does attend fund raisers, though, and that's where she's met many of her son's friends and colleagues. So now when she watches C-SPAN back in Kansas she has lots of familiar faces to look out for. She still remembers her thrill at seeing House TV for the first time: "Danny told me they were going to televise Congress, and that I should watch out for it. I thought it was awesome that here he is, in the House of Representatives, and I can watch what's going on."

Rep. Glickman, who represents Kansas' 4th Congressional District, says that his mom and other C-SPAN viewers are more likely to see him in his role as chairman of the House Agricultural Committee than on the House floor. "Hearings are great," he says, "because they really give you a chance to focus in on issues." When C-SPAN televises hearings, Dan Glickman's staff gets lots of mail from the folks back home in Kansas.

Rep. Glickman considers television "the key to success or failure, not just politically, but in terms of getting your message across." He adds that "C-SPAN gives me the opportunity to get my message out further." American technology is making the House of Representatives part of living-room conversation for hundreds of thousands of Americans."

In 1987, *Congressional Quarterly* featured Rep. Glickman's picture on the cover of its issue about politicians' use of local TV. It's a resource he uses: "Today I did a live 1:00 P.M. news shot for one local station, at 6:00 I'm doing one, and at 11:00 P.M. I'm doing another one." His staff notifies Kansas stations with Washington bureaus when Congress considers issues of local interest or when Mr. Glickman chairs a hearing. And, for stations without Washington bureaus, they make an effort to publicize C-SPAN's coverage so local news stations can take segments of footage and create their own news stories.

In 1984, when the "Donahue" show did a House TV segment, Democratic leaders asked Rep. Glickman to represent them on the show. He was asked to comment on "Camscam"— then-House Speaker Tip O'Neill's controversial decision to have cameras take full shots of the empty House chambers while Republican members made after-hours speeches. Rep. Glickman told the nationwide audience that the story was "much ado about nothing."

He was also one of the representatives who spoke out on behalf of wiring congressional offices to receive C-SPAN telecasts. In a November 1985 speech on the House floor he said, "Those of us who serve in this chamber, which is covered by C-SPAN, cannot have access to C-SPAN programs, all the hearings and meetings our constituents find so valuable. This member of the House thinks it's time to change that. It's ridiculous that I have to go home to Kansas to watch my colleagues meet in committee." In part because of Rep. Glickman, congressional offices today have C-SPAN.

Rep. Glickman doesn't just use TV to air his own views and positions. Like his mother, he uses it to keep track of Congress—although with more than one member in mind. A self-confessed "media junkie," he watches TV with the remote control in his hand, switching back and forth between network news programs and C-SPAN. "As a member of Congress, I find that C-SPAN makes it possible to catch things I missed because of schedule conflicts."

Gladys Glickman says she has a ringside seat at "history being made." However, Rep. Glickman concedes that when his parents watch "mostly they're looking for me. But after $11\frac{1}{2}$ years, they know most of the people they see. Whether it's Al Gore, or Dick Gephardt, or Paul Simon [Democratic lawmakers from Tennessee, Missouri, and Illinois, respectively], they know them all, and they get a real kick out of seeing them." —R.C.

Gladys Glickman watches her son Dan on AirCapital Cablevision.

"The Techno-politician"

Albert Gore Jr.

Carthage, Tennessee

Albert Gore (D-Tennessee) is one of many younger members of Congress who was interested and involved in the process of bringing television cameras into the House and Senate chambers. When Sen. Gore declared for the presidency in 1987, he was a new face on the political scene for many Americans. But to millions of C-SPAN viewers, he and others such as Rep. Jack Kemp (R-New York), Rep. Dick Gephardt (D-Missouri), and Sen. Paul Simon (D-Illinois), were familiar figures. Since 1979, they had been seen almost daily in televised sessions of the House or Senate.

On March 19, 1979, the first day that the House of Representatives' proceedings went on television, 31-year-old Rep. Albert Gore was the first congressman to make a speech. "Television will change this institution," he said. "The marriage of this medium and of our open debate have the potential, Mr. Speaker, to revitalize representative democracy. . . . I hope that the U.S. Senate will see this as a friendly challenge to open its proceedings."

Seven years later, the Senate took up the challenge. Its maiden telecast took place on June 2, 1986. This time, Mr. Gore, by then a U.S. senator, wasn't first—Sen. Robert Dole (R-Kansas) beat him to the punch. Second in line, Sen. Gore stepped up to congratulate his colleagues for joining the video age: "Today marks the first time when our legislative branch in its entirety will appear on that medium of communication through which most Americans get their information about what our government and what our country does."

Albert Gore, 40, grew up as the son of a U.S. senator and a child of the television age, and developed an interest in the media's effect on society. As a student, Mr. Gore wrote his college thesis on TV and the presidency, then the only branch of government extensively covered by television. In the late 1960s, he served as a Vietnam War correspondent for an Army journal. After leaving the armed forces, he worked as a reporter and editorial writer for the *Nashville Tennessean* until deciding to run for Congress.

When Mr. Gore arrived in Congress in 1977, members had been debating the idea of going on television for several years. He joined those voices in favor of the idea. In October of that year, a resolution establishing broadcast coverage passed the house, but the first telecast wasn't to occur until March 1979. In the year-and-a-half interim, some members were anxious to get the ball rolling. Albert Gore was one of those members.

"I took the 50 freshmen members in to see Speaker O'Neill," recalls Sen. Gore. "As their spokesman, I said, 'We have a formal request, Mr. Speaker. We would like to see the House of Representatives opened up to coverage on live radio.'" Technically, it was an easy step. The House chamber already had microphones for its internal public-address system. He remembers that the speaker first demurred. But "one week later, the switch went on." On June 12, 1978, the audio portion of House floor deliberations was made available to accredited news organizations.

Albert Gore was the first congressman on the floor that day. "I commend Speaker O'Neill for the decision he announced last week to allow radio coverage of our proceedings," he said. "I want to continue to work with the speaker in solving the problems of television coverage. The public will benefit from this change, and so will the House, for we will be able to communicate more directly than ever before with the people we were elected to represent."

Rep. Gore carried his enthusiasm for televised democracy to the other side of Capitol Hill. After his election to the U.S.

Senate in 1984, he joined a number of senators who were already working to bring cameras into the chamber. It was a much-debated proposal; the Senate Rules Committee had been holding hearings on the topic since 1980. "I asked to be assigned to the Senate Rules Committee primarily to pursue this issue," said Sen. Gore.

To further the plan, Sen. Gore had an idea from his days in the House: "I'm going to recommend that we open the Senate to live radio coverage. I'm hoping that the theory will still hold, that senators will become comfortable with the idea that their words are going to be broadcast, and that at some future time we can add the picture. . . ."

Although there was some support for the concept, Senate television opponents were strong and entrenched; measures to televise the legislative body had stalled several times. With the backing of Democratic leader Robert Byrd (West Virginia), Sen. Gore and others launched a campaign to persuade Senate television opponents to test broadcasts of Senate proceedings.

Some senators suggested that broadcast coverage be limited to special debates. Sen. Gore disagreed, countering that turning the cameras off would "arouse cynicism and suspicion among the American people." The freshman senator appealed to more skeptical colleagues not to fear changes in the rules, urging them to consider complete coverage as "an experiment with change, to see whether or not we can encourage a better pattern of behavior in the Senate. . . ."

On February 27, 1986, after six years of debate, the Senate voted to allow immediate radio coverage of its deliberations and agreed to test television coverage with a closed-circuit feed to Senate offices. By March 3, an audio feed was available to news organizations. Over the next few months, cameras and lights were installed in the tradition-bound Senate chamber. A closed-circuit test began in May. Satisfied with the results, lawmakers allowed TV news organizations access to Senate floor debates on June 2, 1986, for a six-week test of national exposure.

To a *USA Today* reporter, Sen. Gore predicted, "Once things settle down, the cameras will be taken for granted." He quipped that he foresaw "better and shorter speeches. Long speeches don't go over well on TV except in places like Cuba, where you can't watch anything else."

On July 29, 1986, in the debate on final passage of the Senate television resolution, Sen. Gore joined other senators who spoke out on behalf of making the experiment permanent. By a vote of 78 to 21, the Senate agreed. Somewhere on the Senate floor, Albert Gore must have been thinking that his theory about radio breaking the ice had once again held true. —L.M.

When in Washington, Sen. Gore can watch C-SPAN at home through Cable TV Arlington; in Tennessee, he can watch on Carthage Cable TV Co.

Joe Grandmaison

Rye, New Hampshire

New Hampshire Democratic Party Chairman Joe Grandmaison understands that some people resent the influence his state has on the presidential nominating process through its first-in-the-nation primary. He also understands how seriously people of New Hampshire take that responsibility.

"We don't necessarily expect everyone to agree that we should hold the first primary, but it's important from our point of view that people at least walk away impressed with the fact that we try to do it well," he says.

In April 1987, New Hampshire Democrats elected Joe Grandmaison to a two-year term as state party chairman. That put him at the helm of the party during the state's 1988 primary. For a man used to running individual campaigns, the chairman's role in the primary was a new one: "Obviously, party chairmen are active in politics. We know who we like and who we don't like, who we favor and who we don't favor. But we try to make darn certain that every candidate feels that they're being treated fairly." However, he adds, "It ain't easy."

In addition to accommodating the candidates' needs, as a party official Mr. Grandmaison must attend to an influx of media professionals who come to New Hampshire every four years. In 1988, officials estimated that approximately 2,000 credentialed reporters went there to report the primary results.

For the past 26 years Joe Grandmaison's career has involved a mixed bag of politics and media. This 44-year-old New Hampshirite has worked as a government relations and media consultant, a college instructor, and a television talk show host. He has also been a congressional candidate, a campaign manager, and a federal appointee. He seems to be enjoying the fruits of his labor. "You know, I keep thinking the past couple of years have been really great because I've been able to do little pieces of everything I've wanted to do," muses Joe Grandmaison.

Over the years, Mr. Grandmaison says he's seen many changes in presidential campaign strategies, including an increase in the amount of money spent on the campaigns, an emphasis on negative advertising, and a decrease in "retail" politics. "In 1972 we fervently believed you had to shake every single hand in order to get that vote," he says.

Mr. Grandmaison has watched many hours of C-SPAN's "Election '88" programming. The Boston stations, he says, were concentrating on Gov. Michael Dukakis (D-Massachusetts), and the New Hampshire chairman needed to know more about all of the Democratic contenders. Too much emphasis on one candidate "doesn't allow you to get a good feel of the other campaigns if what you are trying to do is put them all in some kind of context," he explains.

Joe Grandmaison has been watching cable programming since 1981, when he convinced his local system to wire his remote beachfront neighborhood. "I live on the ocean and was interested in getting cable for two reasons: You can't keep an antenna on the roof because of ocean winds, and I wanted to get C-SPAN."

Mr. Grandmaison watches the network to help him relax. "I use television to help me come down, and many of the so-called entertainment shows are not entertaining. I think the public affairs programming you all do is much more entertaining," says Mr. Grandmaison. Beyond appreciating the network's entertainment value, however, the Democratic chairman uses C-SPAN to keep up with political and public affairs events from outside New Hampshire.

He's also no stranger to television himself. In addition to the many interviews he was asked to do during primary season, Mr. Grandmaison co-hosts a weekly public affairs show that airs on the local ABC affiliate.

Joe Grandmaison ventured into New Hampshire politics in 1962 at the age of 18. He first received national attention in 1972 as director of former Sen. George McGovern's unexpectedly strong New Hampshire finish. Since then, he's managed candidates and campaigns in "half a dozen" states. He was a candidate himself in 1976, unsuccessfully challenging a five-term House incumbent. Shortly thereafter, President Jimmy Carter appointed him as co-chairman of the New England Regional Commission, an economic development authority.

National attention may subside, but the job of New Hampshire's party chairman isn't over after the primary. "More than anything else, my role is to prepare us for a successful November '88, with particular attention to the state races. New Hampshire is not a state in which Democrats would normally expect to be successful in the general election," says the man who calls himself "a Democrat by birth, but equally by conviction." —*M.C.*

Joe Grandmaison follows presidential politics on C-SPAN through Continental Cablevision of New Hampshire.

"The Writer"

Ellen Greenberg

Dobbs Ferry, New York

Ellen Greenberg was baffled. Once again, the freelance writer and editor was spending her lunch break tuned in to C-SPAN, but much of what she was hearing sounded like sheer gobbledygook. "The problem was I didn't know what was going on," she recalls. "I wasn't involved in politics. I hadn't paid much attention and I didn't understand the language. I didn't know what the members of Congress were doing or who was who."

Ellen Greenberg reacted by doing what most editors would have done: She went to the library in search of answers. Unfortunately, she came home empty-handed. "The more I wanted to know," she says, "the less I could find."

What she was looking for was a book that explained the meaning of both the legislators' words and the actions taken in the chamber. What exactly is a "continuing resolution," for example, and why do they move the mace around in the House chamber? "What I wanted was a fast answer," she recalls. "If they said 'floor debate,' I wanted to know what those two words meant put together. I didn't want to know all the different kinds of debate. Or 'votes by electronic device.' I didn't care about all the other kinds of votes; I wanted to know what that one meant."

Part of the problem she encountered was that the material

she was looking for wasn't available in one location. Getting answers required considerable research and numerous requests to the House and Senate parliamentarians for information on rules.

But, as she proceeded, she kept notes. And more notes. And slightly more than a year later, despite several interruptions (including the Senate's decision to televise its proceedings), Ms. Greenberg's notes became a book. *The House and Senate Explained: A TV Viewer's Fingertip Guide* details the often Byzantine procedures of the House and Senate and provides a key to understanding arcane legislative language. In her effort to make the book's subject matter more understandable, she even tapped the services of a longtime friend, Boston psychotherapist Marsha Medalie, to illustrate the copy with cartoons and diagrams.

"It didn't really start out to be a book," Ms. Greenberg explains. "At first it was a guide for myself. I envisioned it as just a couple of Xeroxed pieces of paper. But it got more and more interesting, and as the material became increasingly difficult to find, it dawned on me that other people might want to know this, too.

"I didn't want to learn the material, I wanted to know the answer. And that's what I tried to do with the book. That's why it's arranged alphabetically, like a dictionary. You can ask, 'Hey, what does this word mean?' You're not going to stop and study it and learn it—you're just going to know enough so that you can get on with your watching."

She and her husband, Martin, produced the book through their own small publishing house, The Streamside Company. Most of Streamside's business consists of mail order, direct mail marketing, and textbook editing; the congressional TV guide was the first book it had ever published. They decided against using an established publishing house, says Ms. Greenberg, because "we didn't want the book to get lost in the shuffle. More traditional publishers would have overlooked certain avenues of distribution. This way we never get remainders," she jests.

In writing her book, Ellen Greenberg deliberately set out to offer C-SPAN viewers a user-friendly guide to what is actually happening on the screen: "It's not a civics lesson. It's designed especially to assist the viewer who is already watching the television coverage."

Ms. Greenberg discovered C-SPAN by accident one day while she was flipping channels at her home in Dobbs Ferry, in New York's suburban Westchester County. The televised proceedings immediately reminded her of the McCarthy hearings, which had taken place while she was a student at New York's Queens College. "We used to cut school to listen to those hearings," she says. "Our professors were being canned right and left, so it was of immediate interest." Even though C-SPAN does televise congressional hearings, they were not what really caught Ellen Greenberg's attention. "What hooked me was the House," she says matter-of-factly, adding that she has developed a liking for her own representative, Benjamin Gilman (R).

To those who think of C-SPAN as "that funny channel where people are always talking and the seats are always empty," Ms. Greenberg likes to point out that C-SPAN sometimes pulsates with moments of genuine action. "Sometimes when we're discussing my book, people will ask, 'Is it boring watching Congress?' I'm a sports nut, so I say, 'I think anyone who likes sports should be able to put up with Congress. You're really waiting for that one moment when something big happens.' It's the same kind of thing."

The book—and Ellen Greenberg's interest in writing it—has sparked considerable attention, drawing numerous radio talk show invitations and a mention in the *Wall Street Journal*. The local Westchester-Rockland newspapers have carried stories about it, and some cable companies are promoting it to their subscribers. "Sales have been surprisingly good," notes Ms. Greenberg. "Politicians have used it as a fundraising gift. School libraries have picked it up. And high school teachers are starting to use it in their courses. Everyone likes it—that's what surprises me. We've gotten terrific feedback." But, more important, it brings her a sense of personal satisfaction when she thinks of the people the book has reached: "The letters and orders come from all over the country, from little towns that I've never heard of and some that aren't even on large maps of the United States."

All of these people are watching and taking part in "this wonderful thing that we call democracy" and for that Ellen

Greenberg is very grateful. She sums up her feelings in the dedication page of her book: "With thanks to the wizards of today," she writes, "who make our government visible. And to the wizards of yesterday, who created it in the first place."   —K.M.

Ellen Greenberg tunes in to Congress on UA-Columbia Cablevision of Westchester.

"The C-SPAN Junkie"

Gary Greene

Holland, Michigan

"If I'm going to watch TV, I want to learn something." Self-educated Gary Greene shows an insatiable zeal for learning—he watches C-SPAN 35 to 40 hours per week, except during the fall. That's apple-picking season—an important industry for central Michigan—when Mr. Greene puts in 14-hour days at the helm of his small trucking company in semirural Holland, Michigan.

Mr. Greene, 52, likes to joke that he took 10 years to complete an eighth-grade education, but claims that the hours spent watching C-SPAN now enable him "to debate national issues with the best of them." In the past year alone, this self-confessed "C-SPAN junkie" has tuned in to the Bork confirmation hearings, the Iran-contra investigation, journalists' roundtables, National Press Club speeches, and innumerable House and Senate floor sessions. He augments his public affairs viewing with ready reference books he's purchased such as the *Almanac of American Politics, U.S. Congress Handbook,* and *Gavel to Gavel,* the guide to congressional telecasts. "I'm an enthusiastic kind of guy, and when I'm interested in something, I give it my full attention," he says. He's not joking about his enthusiasm. Mr. Greene has a satellite dish for picking up C-SPAN telecasts, which bears a huge, picture-perfect C-SPAN logo that he painted on himself.

Mr. Greene and C-SPAN go back a long way. He came across the network about six years ago, when it was being carried on South Ottawa Cablevision. When the system dropped C-SPAN, Mr. Greene was "upset as hell" and made his displeasure known in a series of letters and visits to the cable company. South Ottawa ignored his pleas to return C-SPAN to the viewers in his area. So, Gary Greene took matters into his own hands and installed a satellite dish in his own backyard to pull C-SPAN's signal out of the air. (A footnote to the story: Centel Cable later purchased South Ottawa Cablevision and carries C-SPAN full-time.)

Mr. Greene's satellite dish is the biggest item in the collection of memorabilia he calls the "C-SPAN museum." He maintains the library of congressional reference books obtained through C-SPAN. He also has a C-SPAN clock, C-SPAN mugs, and innumerable C-SPAN pens and pencils. He keeps C-SPAN buttons, wearing one on his hat for the benefit of people he meets. "Of course I have to go into a dissertation to explain it to them," he says. Mr. Greene prizes a special C-SPAN album, filled with pictures of the time he visited a C-SPAN crew on location and got a close-up, behind-the-scenes look at his favorite television network.

In July 1987, C-SPAN was covering the National Governors' Association conference in Traverse City, Michigan. Mr. Greene and his wife, Betty, drove two hours to meet the crew. They stayed in the same hotel as the C-SPANners, sporting special visitors' passes that Mr. Greene had created for the occasion. He spent time at the studio and inspected the TV technology. Hungry crew members still have fond memories of Ms. Greene. She baked 21 trays of cookies especially for them.

"My friends probably think I'm a bit of a nut about C-SPAN," concedes Mr. Greene. But he sees nothing eccentric in the wealth of insight C-SPAN has to offer. "It's educational, for one thing, and it's interesting. I don't necessarily want to be entertained, I want to be educated. I want to know what's going on." Mr. Greene says that watching the network has helped form his political opinions, and his increased awareness has spurred him to action. He phones the C-SPAN call-in program from time to time, usually to remark on Michigan issues or laws pertaining to the trucking business. He also writes to state and national representatives and stores his letters and their replies in a C-SPAN album.

In the absence of an apple avalanche, Mr. Greene usually tunes in to C-SPAN while working at his desk in the trucking company's small office adjacent to the house he and Betty share. "You don't necessarily have to watch it, you can just listen." But he prefers to keep an eye on the programs; he claims that he can learn more about politicians by looking at their facial expressions and observing them in their own environment. By diligently watching C-SPAN 35 to 40 hours per week, Mr. Greene has developed a feel for the politics that places him, to say the least, far ahead of your average eighth grader, not to mention your average college graduate. "C-SPAN has changed the political process," he says. "Politicians are more aware that they are being listened to and watched, perhaps making them more careful about what they say." —S.M.S.

Gary Greene has his own backyard satellite dish.

"The Desert Editor"

Brian Greenspun
Las Vegas, Nevada

In the past 200 years, there have been only 14 federal impeachment trials. Only five of those trials have resulted in convictions. The last occurred in the fall of 1986. The defendant, Federal District Judge Harry Claiborne, who had already been convicted of two counts of felony income tax evasion, stood trial before the Senate.

His impeachment trial—the first in almost 50 years— did not attract widespread national attention. But in Nevada, where Judge Claiborne lived and worked, it was a big story. At its peak, it was the only story.

"People had been reading about it for two or three years," explains Brian Greenspun, president and associate editor of the *Las Vegas Sun*. His family-owned newspaper took a strong stand in support of Judge Claiborne. During the trial, he said that people "were glued to their TV sets at work, and at night when the hearings were on. That's all people talked about." To help its readers follow the complex procedure, the *Las Vegas Sun* produced a 20-page special supplement on the impeachment.

These historic proceedings had one special aspect: It was the first time in history that the entire impeachment process was televised nationally. Although the impeachment was virtually ignored by the major television networks, C-SPAN covered the U.S. House as it drafted and approved the articles of impeachment; the hearings of the special Senate committee created to investigate the impeachment charges of the House; and Judge Claiborne's trial live from the Senate chamber.

Brian Greenspun, who is also vice president of Las Vegas' Community Cable TV, was pleased that his readers could watch the trial. "We wrote about the Claiborne story every day, and we had boxes on the front page, telling our readers that they could watch the hearings live." Mr. Greenspun is first and foremost a newspaper man, but recognizes that television also has its advantages.

"Being able to watch something on television adds a dimension that newspaper and magazine accounts don't allow for," he says. "Being able to sit in your living room and look into someone's eyes—whether it's Bork, or Biden, or Claiborne, or Hatch—and listen to them while they're asking or answering questions, it makes you feel like you're sitting in the hearing room yourself. And what you can see and hear a lot of times has a greater impact emotionally than what you read."

Brian Greenspun, 41, was born and raised in Las Vegas. He spent seven years in Washington, D.C., during his Georgetown University years and in the early part of his career. He also has a law degree, and he worked for several years for Nevada's Clark County Public Defender's office. Even today he's active as an alternate juvenile and municipal court judge. The newspaper business, however, remains his first love.

The Greenspun family has had a presence in Las Vegas for many years. Mr. Greenspun's father, Hank, started the *Las Vegas Sun* in 1950 and is still publisher today. The family also owns the local cable company. "Ever since we've gotten cable—87,000 subscribers now—the number of people you run into during the day who have an opinion or can talk intelligently about what's going on in Washington has grown dramatically. I believe it has broadened the base of people who will involve themselves in the democratic process."

"We are a nation of television watchers," he says. "People have grown up watching television. There are only a certain number of people who really read newspapers. A lot of them subscribe, and glance through them, but there are only a certain number of people who read them religiously. There are many more people who watch television. So I think it cuts deeper into the electorate, in terms of the number of people it impacts."

Nevada's Harry Claiborne was the first federal judge to face removal from office following a felony conviction. When impeached, he was already serving time in a federal penitentiary. Since judges receive lifetime appointments, Harry Claiborne continued to collect his $78,700 salary while behind bars. Not until the U.S. Senate found him guilty of "high crimes and misdemeanors" would he be officially removed from his post.

On July 22, 1986, C-SPAN viewers in Nevada and elsewhere watched as the House voted 406–0 to impeach Judge Harry Claiborne and approved four articles of impeachment. A special nine-member House committee, headed by Rep. Bill Hughes (D-New Jersey) was selected to present the case against Harry Claiborne to the Senate. One month later, C-SPAN II viewers watched as the evidence of Judge Claiborne's case was presented to the full Senate.

On October 9, 1986, Judge Harry Claiborne was convicted by the Senate on three of the articles of impeachment the House had brought against him. He was acquitted of the fourth. Harry Claiborne, no longer a federal judge, returned to his Alabama federal prison to serve out his sentence.

Mr. Greenspun writes opinion columns for the *Las Vegas Sun*. He gauged the impact of this televised trial, in part, by the change in public attitudes. "I listened to people's opinions change all over the country. Prior to the hearings it was a 'hang the judge, he's no good' type of attitude. But, when you listened to the call-in shows, people were saying 'Hey, he got a raw deal.' Whether it was true or not, it was based on people watching the hearings and involving themselves in the process, which I think is very healthy for this country."   —*S.S.*

Mr. Greenspun watches C-SPAN on Community Cable TV, part of the Prime Cable organization.

"The Good Neighbor"

Paul Griffith

Black Mountain, North Carolina

When Paul Griffith of Black Mountain, North Carolina, heard
senators arguing about whether to allow television to cover
the Senate, he got angry. Then he wrote a few letters. When a
reporter from the *Wall Street Journal* called to ask him what he
thought about television in the Senate, the 79-year-old retired
engineer replied, "A lot of those old senators are really fuddy
duddies" for not wanting TV cameras.

The next day, Mr. Griffith's remarks were printed in a
front-page *Journal* article. Then-majority leader Howard Baker
(R-Tennessee) read the story aloud on the Senate floor. That
was just one exciting incident that occurred during Paul
Griffith's more than eight years of C-SPAN viewing. In the
intervening years, he has collected hundreds of tapes, viewed
countless programs, and even established a special C-SPAN
viewing area in the Black Mountain library.

Paul Griffith made Black Mountain his home 14 years
ago, after retiring from 30 years of civil service as an electrical
engineer at Fort Monmouth, New Jersey. Some see retirement
as a time to take things easy. Not so Mr. Griffith, who takes
civic duties seriously. He has been honored by the local Kiwanis
chapter for his work in the mountain retirement town—he's
helped to remap the town, arranged for the incorporation of the
Kiwanis Club thrift store, and served on the sewerage and water

quality boards. He has used his engineering skills to set up sound systems for local citizens' groups. He is the legislative chairman of the local chapter of the National Association of Retired Federal Employees, and publishes its weekly newsletter. (One issue offered guidelines for writing members of Congress.)

Mr. Griffith watches public affairs programming to stay informed on current debate over issues close to home, such as catastrophic health care insurance and cost-of-living increases for federal retirees. He often uses what he sees on C-SPAN in the NARFE newsletter: "It's crucial to my job. Where else could information be obtained from men or women of national stature in their specialities? I get a very broad continuing education from experts in our nation's capital."

He discovered C-SPAN in 1980 and was immediately "fascinated. I'm a retired engineer and engineers want to know how things work. C-SPAN is my way of finding out how the government works." That year he made audio tapes of a hearing on federal annuities and distributed them to several state NARFE chapters. Thus began a long tradition of taping what he heard on C-SPAN and giving the material to groups he felt might be interested. Three days of a hearing on genetic engineering went to local biology professors, and area retirees received a number of tapes on long-term health care. Mr. Griffith has willed his entire collection of some 500 tapes to Warren Wilson College in the hopes that it will prove of historical interest.

Mr. Griffith has brought more than C-SPAN tapes to Black Mountain—he's brought C-SPAN, too. At his own expense, he donated a specially adjusted television set to create a C-SPAN viewing area in the local library. He later added six headphones with long cords. His next gift, he says, will be high-tech cordless headphones to allow greater movement around the library. "The outstanding use for this is to provide a source by which Washington may be viewed and heard directly, without having the information filtered and cut by the news media," he says. His attitude about use of the "C-SPAN Corner" is practical: "There are many good books in the library that are never read," he told a local newspaper. "This could be like that."

Mr. Griffith's interest is founded on his belief that "It's important to see your congressman and get to know him and what he's doing." Mr. Griffith once told the *Asheville East* newspaper, "There are so many of us who sit back in the boondocks and say, 'Those doggone congressmen, they don't deserve to make over $60,000 a year.' But after hearing all the information that they must filter through, you realize there are no clear-cut decisions. I don't see how they make decisions when there's so much conflicting information."

Sometimes, though, he finds Congress "just plain hilarious," such as when Mr. Griffith watched Rep. Pat Schroeder (D-Colorado) introduce a floor amendment prohibiting the use of government funds for cuff links, helicopter rides to Camp David, and barbecues. On another occasion, he remembers Rep. Bud Shuster (R-Pennsylvania) taunting the Democrats with a bandaged lame rubber duck named Donald Democrat.

As he gets older, Mr. Griffith finds himself relaxing a bit more in the beautiful mountaintop setting afforded by Black Mountain. He is an amateur ham radio operator who was honored recently for having his amateur license for 60 years. He also keeps busy as a member of the Institute of Electrical and Electronic Engineers, which also presented him with an award for sustained service. However, his interest in politics is still strong: "A good citizen must have an appreciation of politics, for without politics, our greatest national heritage would never have happened." —*R.L.*

Thanks to Paul Griffith, patrons of Black Mountain Public Library can watch C-SPAN on Sammons Communications.

"The Cable Marketer"

Brian Gruber

Albuquerque, New Mexico

In 1983 a "C-SPAN Review" was held in the San Francisco Bay area to acquaint cable operators and their marketing staffs with the young network. During the presentation a young man from the audience spoke up, "I sold cable door-to-door, and I used C-SPAN to make sales to a segment of the community that thought it was unfashionable to watch movies and sports."

Brian Gruber, then 27, was the young cable salesman who spoke up. His honesty pitch landed him a sale he wasn't really looking for—a job offer as C-SPAN's marketing director.

Mr. Gruber's story is important in the list of "who watches C-SPAN" because, unlike any other viewer profiled in this book, he has watched the network as a cable marketer, a C-SPAN insider, a home viewer who got hooked in the early years, and a man with an avid interest in politics and the communications industry.

Mr. Gruber's testimonial was unusual. Although many cable operators understand C-SPAN's public service value, few thought of the network as a sales tool. Brian Gruber's inventive cold-call sales experience proved to him that not every cable customer wants MTV.

"C-SPAN was a way to catch certain people's attention. I used C-SPAN to illustrate how different, unique, and valuable cable television was," explains Mr. Gruber. He saw that

C-SPAN could provide a "way for cable operators to reach upscale, educated TV viewers who are concerned about the impact of television, people who are gatekeepers of information and public opinion in the community."

C-SPAN was ready to expand its marketing staff and wanted someone to help the department grow. After some initial hesitation about breaking loyalties at Tele-Communications Inc. in San Mateo, California, Mr. Gruber left his marketing manager job to come East. He says he took the C-SPAN marketing position for two reasons: "It was an incredibly exciting challenge for me to take this service, reposition it, aggressively sell it, and change the perception of why C-SPAN should be carried by cable operators." And, "consistent with my philosophies and ideas, C-SPAN was one of the few truly unique examples of cable television providing something really different."

During Brian Gruber's three-year tenure, the marketing department grew from a two-person staff to six people. And the network's approach to marketing went from "responsive" to "aggressive": Marketing staffers no longer waited for cable operators to call and ask for the service. They finally had the staff to begin making pitches to the industry. In pursuit of new C-SPAN affiliates, Mr. Gruber traveled to almost every state, hoping to educate cable operators about the benefits of C-SPAN to their business and the community. The expanded marketing staff added five million subscribers to C-SPAN's rolls. It wasn't an easy job. Despite Mr. Gruber's success and enthusiasm for selling the network, he was often frustrated by the seeming ambivalence of hard-to-reach cable operators.

Today he's on the receiving end of those sales calls. As director of marketing for Jones Intercable in Albuquerque, New Mexico, he now understands that the operators weren't really being aloof. His job now is to keep the system's 68,000 customers happy and to continually expand the cable customer base in this southwestern city of 340,000 people. Deluged with the day-to-day problems of running a cable system, he says, "It's very difficult for me to think solely about promoting C-SPAN, because the amount of work I have just running the marketing end of the business is awesome."

At age 32, Brian Gruber has already worked in cable television for over 10 years at every possible angle, both behind and in front of the camera. In addition to his various marketing positions, he served as on-air host for C-SPAN call-ins and as producer of a local access cable program. During his years at Queens College in New York, "a very hard realistic judgment" turned him away from an acting career to the rapidly growing cable industry—"a place where a young man could make his mark in a short amount of years." He says, "Quite frankly, the responsibilities of the job I have now and of the job I had at C-SPAN, are simply not available to newcomers in long-established industries. For someone with initiative and enthusiasm, who is willing to work hard and has good ideas, the cable industry is a place to move ahead quickly."

Another aspect of the cable industry appealed to him as well. The Brooklyn-bred boy, whose political activism was shaped in an era "when it was almost taken for granted that radical social change was needed," saw cable television as a way to serve the public interest. He was critical of broadcast television, which he felt was mostly in the business of "selling eyeballs to advertisers. I saw cable as a way to break up the real monopoly power of the networks and do things like quality news and public affairs, children's programming, cultural programming. It was a way to give viewers more options," he says.

"I've always had a personal feeling that I wanted to make a contribution to society. I wanted to do something meaningful. Here in Albuquerque, I can have a real impact on people's lives when I make programming decisions, when we do community service work, and when we try to introduce more public affairs, cultural, and education programming into the community."

When his workload allows, he is still thoughtful about his responsibilities as a mass communications executive. Occasionally, his rose-colored perspective takes on a jaded quality on the days that are filled with customer complaints such as "You messed up my bill!" "You disconnected me!" or "I can't get through on the phone lines." However, once in a while, amidst the slew of problems, a cable subscriber will enthusiastically tell Brian Gruber, "And, by the way, I used to watch you on C-SPAN's call-in show." —N.G.

Brian Gruber hopes many people in Albuquerque will join him in watching C-SPAN on Jones Intercable.

"The First Friend"

William "Bud" Harris

Cherry Hill, New Jersey

"I have a mission to get every cable company in the country to carry C-SPAN, and I don't care what people think about it." William "Bud" Harris took on his first cable challenge back in 1982 in his hometown of Cherry Hill, New Jersey, but his efforts eventually exceeded New Jersey's borders. "Friends of C-SPAN," an ad hoc group that Mr. Harris formed that same year, has successfully encouraged cable operators in communities across the nation to continue carrying the network on their systems.

Bud Harris has become passionate about C-SPAN over the years, but his efforts on behalf of the network are carried out in a modest fashion. He uses every available forum to state his support for C-SPAN, and he sticks to it. Mr. Harris' zeal goes beyond his interest in public affairs. Having watched the network since its infancy, he feels somewhat paternal about its growth. "As a matter of fact, I used to phone the call-in shows. It was so informal that when I'd call I'd say, 'Hi, there, can I offer you a drink?' It was not as serious as it is now."

In C-SPAN, the retired insurance executive felt he had found something above ordinary TV. Watching the House or congressional hearings, "you could really get an in-depth picture of an issue, instead of a 30-second bite on the evening news. I just found that very absorbing."

His C-SPAN viewing, however, was subject to an unplanned interruption. The cable company serving Cherry Hill took the network off without warning. "They didn't think there was much interest in C-SPAN," he says. Mr. Harris contacted the company and asked that C-SPAN be restored. "I made the usual calls to the cable system," he remembers, "and got nowhere."

Frustrated at the lack of local response, Bud Harris decided to appeal directly to the cable system's parent company, the powerful *New York Times.* The *Times,* he reasoned, calls itself "the newspaper of record"—of course, he thought, it would lend its support to C-SPAN, which Mr. Harris describes as "the television channel of record." Mr. Harris decided to start his appeal at the top, with publisher Arthur Ochs Sulzberger.

Not surprisingly, Bud Harris' call to Mr. Sulzberger was transferred until he found a sympathetic senior vice president. The *New York Times* executive began to correspond with Bud Harris about C-SPAN, eventually agreeing to intercede with the Cherry Hill cable system.

In addition, a local newspaper, the Camden *Courier Post,* wrote what he considered a comprehensive story about the campaign, and the story generated supportive letters to the editor. In hindsight, he credits that one piece as "having a lot to do with resolving the situation."

The system restored C-SPAN, but in the process created a government channel where C-SPAN programming was interspersed with city council meetings and local access programming. This arrangement did not satisfy Bud Harris. "In the middle of a very intense congressional hearing," he remembers, "they would cut to the school board of a community that I don't even live in. It was just absolutely infuriating."

His passions aroused, Bud Harris widened the circle of his campaign for C-SPAN to include the mayor and the city council. Bud Harris persevered with his one-man campaign for C-SPAN, certain today that he had become a *persona non grata* in the cable system's eyes. Finally, after "a lot of hassling back and forth," Mr. Harris' efforts paid off. C-SPAN was restored full-time to Cherry Hill cable subscribers.

Despite being caught up with his own C-SPAN cause, Bud Harris responded to other viewers' calls for help. In early

1982, C-SPAN moved to a new satellite, which caused it to lose more than 400 cable affiliates. The loss of subscribers for the fledgling network was staggering. C-SPAN call-in programs passed the word along as C-SPAN viewers called in daily to complain that the network had disappeared from their television screens.

Listening in Cherry Hill, Bud Harris figured it was time to organize the "grassroots." "Friends of C-SPAN" was formed when Mr. Harris phoned a C-SPAN program just prior to the network's satellite switch to offer his support to other C-SPAN fans. "I must have gotten *300* or *400* letters. It was amazing to me, the degree of passion among the devotees of C-SPAN." Mr. Harris responded to each C-SPAN viewer. He—and others—began to write to cable systems, asking them to make the process of government available for the American people's review and participation.

Mr. Harris even bought a word processor so he could write letters in earnest. One was to television producer and former cable system owner Norman Lear. Mr. Lear owned 19 systems in Kansas that dropped C-SPAN after the 1982 satellite switch. Mr. Lear, who hadn't been aware that his cable operations manager had dropped the network, assured Mr. Harris that his systems would find a place for C-SPAN.

"This was a crusade," he says now. "And why shouldn't it be a crusade? I don't care what you read or watch on TV, you couldn't get the information that you can get from C-SPAN."

The effort began to reap rewards. Faced with organized consumer demand, cable systems began to make room for C-SPAN. Little by little, C-SPAN began to regain the subscribers it had lost, and then some. With a little help from C-SPAN's friends, Bud Harris played a role in helping the network through a difficult period. Today, thanks to cable industry support, the network is seen in 38 million homes.

Mr. Harris looks back on that time in the early '80s with a sense of perspective. His relations with the Cherry Hill cable company have long since mended. "They're very nice people. It's just that at the time they didn't agree with me." He says he realizes that the company was trying its best to serve 55 different New Jersey communities with just one system. He concedes that "it was difficult for them."

Bud Harris is still a cable subscriber. He describes himself as "fat and content," and is not eager to get involved in other cable carriage causes.

But every once in a while, Bud Harris can't resist sitting down at his computer to pound out letters for C-SPAN. "I've always lived by the rule that if you believe deeply enough in something, you cannot just sit back and do nothing about it. I know that if you want to get something accomplished you can get it accomplished if you work hard enough at it."   —K.M.

Bud Harris is a longtime subscriber of New York Times *Cable TV.*

"The Collector"

Larry Hart

Inglewood, California

Larry Hart, 36, has a collection of 3,000 45 rpm pop records. He also has President Nixon's resignation, the Apollo II moon landing announcement, and dozens of old-time radio call-letter jingles recorded on reel-to-reel tape. And he estimates that he owns tapes of some 14,000 hours of public affairs programming, much of it taken from C-SPAN.

Mr. Hart enjoys the ability to follow events from beginning to end: "There's always something breaking and you always have to follow it hour by hour. You can follow it like a sporting event, up to a point." And he should know. This lifelong radio buff went through a sports mania phase some years ago, taping dozens of no-hitter baseball games.

His interest in baseball gradually began to fade after he had listened to most of his New York teams win championships. "It just didn't have the same thrill anymore," says Mr. Hart. Although he had been taping news events sporadically for several years, his interest in public affairs really blossomed during the 1979 Iran hostage crisis: "I went crazy recording all the different specials." Mr. Hart recognizes that he has a pattern of "things kind of cyclically going in and out of my life." And it might come to pass that his sports-like enthusiasm for news will wane. But right now public affairs, especially foreign affairs, is, he says, the "big thrill" for him. "With news I think there'll always be something I haven't seen before," speculates Larry Hart.

The avid archivist can't watch the network—he was born blind. Collecting audio tapes has been a passion ever since he got his first tape recorder in 1965. "I don't regret anything," he says of his blindness. "A lot of people used to ask me, 'Don't you wish you could see?' I just tell them, since I've never seen, I don't really miss it."

And when it comes to certain kinds of programming, blindness is not a barrier. "Obviously a debate is an audio thing," he says. "Sure there are certain visual cues that I miss, but I don't think I miss much that would really get in the way of making a decision." He does, of course, miss out on House and Senate vote tallies and the on-screen graphics that explain parliamentary action. That problem first brought Mr. Hart to C-SPAN's attention.

In 1987, Mr. Hart and one of his old college professors, Michael Biel of Kentucky's Morehead State University, wrote to the network asking for changes that would make the programming easier for blind people to follow. C-SPAN was able to adopt some of their suggestions and is still looking into other ways of addressing the needs of handicapped viewers.

C-SPAN isn't the only show on Mr. Hart's daily schedule. He monitors the broadcast networks and CNN, sometimes all at the same time. His bedroom contains four TV receivers, two reel-to-reel tape machines, a 12-channel mixing board (which allows him to select which input he wants to record), a couple of FM tuners capable of picking up stations as far away as Jacksonville, Florida, and several sources for non-FM radio signals. With the flick of a switch or two, Mr. Hart can cut from program to program, taping various segments one at a time or simultaneously. These days, he says he goes "hog wild looking for every network analysis." He and Prof. Biel are on the phone several times a month to discuss news angles on various stories.

Larry Hart, who works as an equipment maintenance technician at the GTE facility near his Inglewood, California, home, has created a special world for himself. And the materials he has collected for his own use may prove to be of lasting value for others. Through his consistent effort and enthusiasm he has managed to stay on top of sports, music, and current events, while amassing a huge archive in the process.

These days Mr. Hart infrequently listens to anything without taping it. His collection is now so big that he admits he can rarely go back and listen to what he has put on tape. And he figures he has a five-year backlog of material to catalog. He has considered making his collection available to the public, but it's not a simple matter. For one thing, he realizes that video and cassette tapes are supplanting reel-to-reel tape in common use. He's also concerned about preserving his tapes. "If they're in a public place, anybody could just borrow one, and it might never be brought back. I don't mind that the public could have access to them, but I want it to be done carefully, because I know what it's like to want something and not be able to have it." If a friend wants a copy of a tape, however, Mr. Hart gladly provides.

"If, God forbid, my time is up, my collection will go to some private collectors who are members of an old radio society—that's the way I have it lined up right now," says Mr. Hart. But he's still young. Already he has close to 2,500 reel-to-reel tapes stored in his one-bedroom apartment, and continues to fill 50 reels every 90 days, or 200 reels a year, or over 3,000 more by the time he's 50. Larry Hart may be forced to make other archiving plans before his "time is up," otherwise he may be listening to C-SPAN from the front stoop of his apartment building, while his tapes rest comfortably inside.   —S.S.

Larry Hart tapes C-SPAN programming from American Cablesystems of California.

"The Wall Street Editorialist"

Dan Henninger

Ridgewood, New Jersey

Dan Henninger, 42, has a lot riding on his opinions. Every day, several million people pick up his newspaper to read what Dan Henninger thinks is important. And the curious part is, hardly anyone knows his name.

As chief editorial writer for the *Wall Street Journal,* Mr. Henninger's opinions appear in the paper under the heading "Review & Outlook." He writes editorials himself and manages the daily editorial-writing process. It's a job he loves. "When I wasn't doing this I couldn't imagine writing anonymously. But once I started, it didn't bother me in the least. I get to write an opinion piece on a major public issue at least twice a week for this newspaper. The fact of the matter is, that kind of real estate is really rare in journalism now. There just aren't as many outlets as there once were, and there haven't been for a long time. It's a pretty extraordinary forum to have."

Clearly, there are major differences between being a reporter, whose job it is to observe and report the news as objectively as possible, and being an editorial writer, whose job it is to present a point of view. "It's an opinion page and we express opinions very aggressively. The idea is to influence policy or to elicit a response, to get people thinking about some of these issues." But Mr. Henninger says that doesn't mean that an editorial writer is free to abandon journalistic integrity: "You try to be fair. One of the main responsibilities is being aware of what the various points of view are that are involved in the issue, and getting the facts right. It's an imperfect process, there's no question about it. But if you keep those priorities in line, by and large, the process will work properly."

In their effort to keep those priorities in line, Mr. Henniger and his editorial writers look to a wide variety of information resources. Much of it, like the Dow Jones News Retrieval Service, is computerized, which enables them to find information quickly. In addition to the usual sources, the *Journal* also has a media center where its editorial staff can tune in to important events on television.

"C-SPAN has enlarged my access to important and useful information, and it definitely contributes to the process that we go through in trying to formulate opinions about what in fact is going on there in Washington. What you're getting from C-SPAN is primary source material. If it complements something you're writing about, it is just enormously useful to be able to sit there and hear one of the key participants describe in his own words exactly what he thinks about an issue," says Mr. Henninger.

The *Wall Street Journal* has seven editorial writers in New York, all of whom watch C-SPAN on a regular basis, particularly when a big issue is being discussed or an important hearing is underway. If it's an issue they've been following, they take notes or tape it. Mr. Henninger prefers to watch in his Ridgewood, New Jersey, home. "Some people listen to the radio when they are getting dressed in the morning. I watch C-SPAN."

Every morning, the editorial process begins with a meeting in Mr. Henninger's office. Those editorial writers who aren't busy writing join in on a discussion—guided by editor Robert Bartley—about the topics for the next morning's paper. "We meet and talk about what's going on, and begin to shape a point of view." They go their separate ways to start writing, and by late afternoon, four to seven editorials are sent to Mr. Henninger, who must choose two. "It's my job to work with the writers to get the editorial in shape for publication." And even though people do tend to develop specialties, "We're not set up to have one person who writes exclusively about foreign policy or economics, or solely about Washington or Congress. You are expected to be able to write about a pretty wide range of subjects for this page."

Fortunately, Dan Henninger has always had rather eclectic interests dating back to his college days. A Cleveland native, he graduated from Georgetown University in 1968 with a bachelor's degree in foreign service. He chose that major not so much because he wanted to pursue a career in diplomacy, but because he "ended up with what amounted to a minor in political science, economics, English, and history." The years he spent in Washington, D.C. (1964 to 1977), had a great impact on him. "That was really an extraordinary period of time to be in that city at that age." Today, Dan Henninger finds Washington less interesting than it used to be, but he still considers it a fascinating place.

"A person can make up his own mind about whether he thinks the political process in Washington is functioning properly based on what he sees on C-SPAN. Cumulatively, you're getting a pretty good view of what makes Washington tick even though you don't get behind the scenes. So, for the person who's really interested in public affairs and politics, it sure is an education. I don't see how you can't benefit from watching it."

Mr. Henninger has been a journalist since 1968, when he landed his first job as a copy boy for the *New Republic*. He joined Dow Jones in 1971, writing for its weekly, the *National Observer*. When the *Observer* closed its doors in 1977, he moved to the Dow Jones flagship publication, the *Wall Street Journal*.

Every so often, readers will see C-SPAN mentioned in the *Journal* editorials. Credit Dan Henninger for those mentions. "The original source deserves some credit for having generated the news," he explains. "The other reason we might do it is if we know C-SPAN is going to cover an event. We'll draw attention to that fact because we feel, quite frankly, that people ought to see for themselves exactly what arguments are being made around an issue—say, funding for the contras. We want our readers to decide for themselves whether the opposition is correct to refuse aid. We want people to see the face of some of these arguments. It can serve as a complement to one of the points we are trying to make in the editorials. And so it's part of the process." —*P.K.*

At home, Dan Henninger watches C-SPAN on UA-Columbia Cablevision.

Bruce Hoertel

C-SPAN chairmen: (left to right)
Jack Frazee, Ed Allen, Jim Whitson, Gene Schneider, Bob Rosencrans, and John Saeman in the Assembly Room of Independence Hall, Philadelphia, Pennsylvania, April 1987, to mark the two-hundredth anniversary of the U.S. Constitution.

James C. Wright,
Speaker of the U.S. House of Representatives,
first called C-SPAN "America's Town Hall."

Roy Allen
The Typical Viewer
Savannah, Georgia

Tuckerman Babcock
The Legislative Aide
Wasilla, Alaska

Richard Armey
The Challenger
Denton, Texas

Clark Calvert, Fayetteville, Arkansas

Margaret Blair
The Ozark Caller
Fayetteville, Arkansas

C-SPAN Update

Robert Dole
The Leader
Russell, Kansas

Howard Baker
The Leader
Huntsville, Tennessee
White House Chief of Staff
Former Senate Majority Leader

Robert Byrd
The Leader
Sophia, West Virginia
pictured with former C-SPAN president Paul FitzPatrick (left)

C-SPAN Update

Michael Romanos

Bruce Berman
The Channel Zapper
Boston, Massachusetts

Philomena Benevides-Rogers
The Interpreter
Washington, D.C.

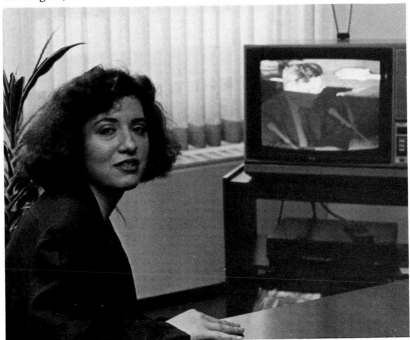

Wooley

Lewis Brierley
The News Designer
Columbia, South Carolina

Walter Blevins
The Legislating Dentist
Morehead, Kentucky

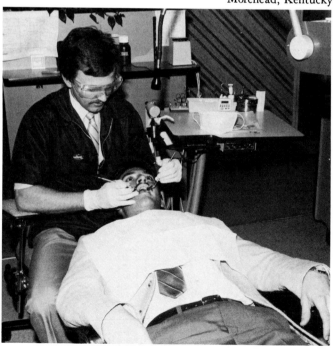

Rockingham County Newspapers

Barbara Brian
The Sample Voter
Plaistow, New Hampshire
pictured with 1988 presidential candidate Jack Kemp

C-SPAN *Update*

C-SPAN *Update*

Robert Browning
The Archivist
West Lafayette, Indiana

Howard Bronson
The Colonel
San Antonio, Texas

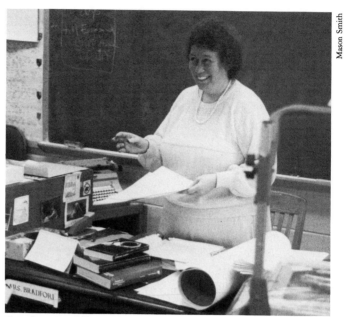

Mason Smith

Sandra Bradford
The High School Teacher
Standish, Maine

Lillian Brown
The Golden Ear
Omaha, Nebraska

Fred Veleba, Omaha World Herald

Charles J. Divine

Pete Carril
The Coach
West Windsor, New Jersey

Lee Carle
The Island Newscaster
St. Thomas, The Virgin Islands

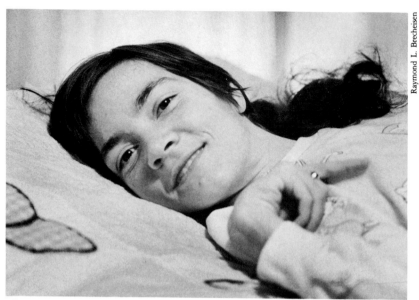

Raymond L. Brecheisen

Elaine Carlyle
The Special Viewer
Pittsburg, Kansas

Syd Cassyd
The Television Pioneer
Los Angeles, California

Lionel Rolfe

Davidoff Studies

Jack Cole
The Talkmaster
West Palm Beach, Florida

Zbigniew Bzdak

Dick Cheney Sr.
The Congressional Dad
Casper, Wyoming

Richard Cohen
The Congressional Correspondent
McLean, Virginia

Gene S. Crockett
The Flag Waver
Irving, Texas

Baltasar Corrada del Rio
The Fifty-first Stater
San Juan, Puerto Rico

James Crosswhite
The Wordsmith
San Diego, California
pictured with daughter Hillary

Phil Donahue
The Moderator
New York, New York

Robert Desramaux
The Canadian
Ottawa, Ontario, Canada

Kay Cutcher
The Watchdog
Sioux City, Iowa
pictured with Julio Iglesias and husband Lane (right)

John Duncan
The Ex-Trucker
Phoenix, Arizona

Russell Epperson
The Prisoner
Moberly, Missouri

Bob Murray

Mickey Welsh, The Alabama Journal

Harry Fletcher
The Historian
Montgomery, Alabama

Robert Fox
The Recovering Lawyer
St. Paul, Minnesota

Jeff Christensen

Stephen Frantzich
The Naval Professor
Annapolis, Maryland

Ann Funck
The Volunteer
Denver, Colorado

Mel McIntire

C-SPAN *Update*

Winnie Gill
The Retired Housewife
Baton Rouge, Louisiana

Newt Gingrich
The Conservative Opportunist
Jonesboro, Georgia

Nicholas Renda

Helen Frank
The Poetic Psychologist
Somers, New York

John Freeman

Gladys Glickman
The Congressional Mom
Wichita, Kansas

Albert Gore Jr.
The Techno-politician
Carthage, Tennessee

Joe Grandmaison
The Party Chair
Rye, New Hampshire

Ellen Greenberg
The Writer
Dobbs Ferry, New York

Nicholas Renda

Drew Torres

Gary Greene
The C-SPAN Junkie
Holland, Michigan

Brian Greenspun
The Desert Editor
Las Vegas, Nevada

Cary Herz

The Wall Street Journal

Brian Gruber
The Cable Marketer
Albuquerque, New Mexico

Dan Henninger
The Wall Street Editorialist
Ridgewood, New Jersey

Maggie Palmer Lauterer

Paul Griffith
The Good Neighbor
Black Mountain, North Carolina

Shirley O'Neill

William "Bud" Harris
The First Friend
Cherry Hill, New Jersey

Larry Hart
The Collector
Inglewood, California

Brent Nicastro

James Hood
The Civil Rights Pioneer
Madison, Wisconsin

Ruth Janger
The Close Up Matriarch
Oklahoma City, Oklahoma
pictured with husband Harry

Paul Hellstern

Photo provided by CTAM

Nicholas Johnson
The Commissioner
Iowa City, Iowa

Edward Kienholz, Nancy Reddin Kienholz
The Artists
Hope, Idaho

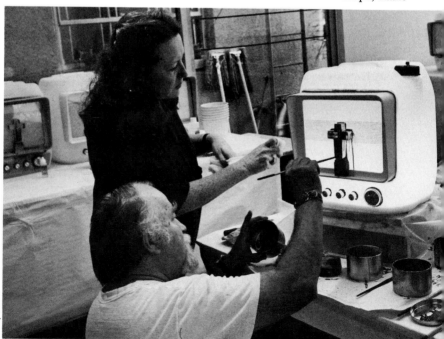

Sidney Felsen

C-SPAN *Update*

Nackey Loeb
The Union Leader
Manchester, New Hampshire

Michael Kelley
The Capitol Connector
Fairfax, Virginia

Mike Schmidt

Keith Knautz
The Page
Glendale Heights, Illinois

Katherine Loew
The Leaguer
Honolulu, Hawaii

Bruce Asato

Suzanne Lauer
The Feminist
Decatur, Georgia

Libby Beckham

Larry Caruso

Stephen J. Liesen
The Letter Writer
Wyandotte, Michigan

Patrick Lynn
The Anchorman
Bismarck, North Dakota

Tony Maidenburg
The Small-Town Mayor
Marion, Indiana

Patricia Anderson, Jr.

Manny Lucoff
The Communications Professor
Tampa, Florida

Michele Cardon

Aimee Maxfield
The Teen-age Politico
Marietta, Georgia

Bob McBarton
The Guest Columnist
Redondo Beach, California

Mark S. Murphy

Michael McGough
The Area Man
Pittsburgh, Pennsylvania

Jack Nelson
The Bureau Chief
Bethesda, Maryland

The Los Angeles Times

Bob Michel
The Minority Leader
Peoria, Illinois
talks to C-SPAN's Connie Doebele

C-SPAN *Update*

Marian Norby
The Monitor
Arlington, Virginia

Robert O'Brien
The County Administrator
Dover, Delaware

William Proxmire
The Golden Fleecer
Madison, Wisconsin

Stephen Szydlowski

NANCY ANN
CONVALESCENT
HOME

Raymond O'Dette
The Caregiver
Foster, Rhode Island

C-SPAN *Update*

Mike Peters
The Cartoonist
Beavercreek, Ohio
pictured with C-SPAN's Carl Rutan (right)

Thomas P. "Tip" O'Neill
The Speaker
Harwichport, Massachusetts

The Washington Post

John Putka
The Priest
Cincinnati, Ohio

T. R. Reid
The Camscammer
Denver, Colorado

Wayne Arnst

Joyce Robinson
The Rancher
Great Falls, Montana

Bill Fitz-Patrick

President Reagan talks with Close Up students in the Old Executive Office Building.

USA Today

Barbara Reynolds
The Role Model
Washington, D.C.

Brent Riley
The Crusader
Logan, Utah

Jeff Christensen

Tom Rose
The Doctor
Stillwater, Minnesota

C-SPAN *Update*

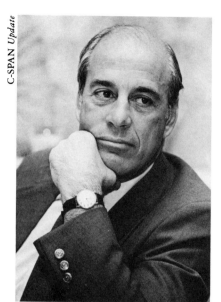

Bob Rosencrans
The Risk-Taker
Greenwich, Connecticut

Ken Gunter
The Risk-Taker
San Angelo, Texas

Dean Miller

Shirley Rossi
The Mountain Belle
Pueblo, Colorado

Sally Salmon
The Presidential Questioner
Jackson, Mississippi

Ray Schwartz
The Conference Caller
Dover, New Jersey

Stan Singer
The Legislative Addict
Harrisburg, Pennsylvania

C-SPAN Update

John Sununu
The Governor
Salem, New Hampshire
pictured with C-SPAN's Susan Swain

Joe Bauer

John Stolarek
The Lone Star Reporter
McAllen, Texas

Ken Uston
The Gambler
San Francisco, California

Shani Taha
The Independent Thinker
Seattle, Washington

Nelda Thompson
The Runner Up,
Applegate, Oregon
pictured with grandson Mike Kellington

C-SPAN *Update*

Jane White
The Neighborhood Organizer
Scottsdale, Arizona

Nancy Engebretson

Tom Winslow
The Park Ranger
Philadelphia, Pennsylvania

C-SPAN *Update*

Lawrence White
The Eternal Optimist
Culver, Indiana

Washington Post Photo

David Yepsen
The Caucus Pundit
Des Moines, Iowa

Kendall Wild
The Localizer
Rutland, Vermont

Joe Yerkes
The Special Educator
Jacksonville, Florida

Lee Wing
The Stateside Producer
Durham, North Carolina

OPEN/net

Andrew Young
The Big-City Mayor
Atlanta, Georgia

Frank Zappa
The Political Rocker
Los Angeles, California

Sergio Albonico

Margaret Doyle is one of 28 C-SPAN field crew members who help produce over 4,000 hours of first-run programming each year for the network.

Tony Gross is one of 26 C-SPAN master control operators who monitor the 24-hour-a-day television signals for both C-SPAN and C-SPAN II.

C-SPAN BOOK STAFF

(beginning with front row, left to right)

- Mary Holley, Martha Gallahue, Suzanne Stahl, Jenna Eudaley, Rosemary Harold
- Kathleen Brown, Lea Anne Long, Eileen Quinn, Sheila Quinlin, Carrie Lamson, Maura Clancey, Mark West, Caroline Ely
- Rosemarie Colao, Paul Sinclair, Nan Gibson, Robin Garber, Susan Swain, Lori McFarling, Kathy Murphy, Susan Lamontagne, Chris Maloney
- Bruce Collins, Ruth Kane, Terri Sorensen, Michelle Lynch, Jana Dabrowski, Pat Watson, Brian Lamb
- Peter Kiley, Greg Barker, Rob Lee

"The Civil Rights Pioneer"

James Hood
Madison, Wisconsin

For the better part of two days in April 1987, James Hood sat transfixed in front of his television set in Madison, Wisconsin. C-SPAN's live telecast of "Covering the South: A National Symposium on the Media and the Civil Rights Movement," had him glued to his seat. The symposium, sponsored by the University of Mississippi, brought together more than 60 veteran reporters, public officials, and key decision makers. All of them had had a role in the civil rights movement. So had James Hood.

The symposium marked the 25th anniversary of the university's admission of black students. Those were turbulent times. And James Hood, 45, remembers them well. He was one of the first two black students to enter the University of Alabama.

Today, as chairman of the public safety services program at Madison Area Technical College, James Hood is responsible for overseeing the training of future police officers, firefighters, and emergency medics. He also works as a management consultant and teaches a course called "Current Affairs." Mr. Hood occasionally monitors C-SPAN for events he can show to his class. But, as it happened he wasn't even aware that the symposium was taking place, until a friend called to tell him to tune in. When he did, he saw the familiar face of John Doar, an integral part of his college experiences.

As head of the Justice Department's Civil Rights Division from 1960 to 1967, John Doar was responsible for young James Hood's safety when he entered the University of Alabama. But "I hadn't seen him in 20 years," Mr. Hood explained. So, for the first time in his many years of watching C-SPAN, James Hood picked up the phone to call. It took him more than an hour to get through to the program, but he hung in there. "I wanted to say how much I appreciated John and the role that he played in helping us to get through that. He went well beyond what his responsibility was as a government official. He would call me on a regular basis to see how things were going, and to see if I needed to talk."

The two had a lively reunion on the air, and James Hood offered the audience an account of how he had first come to be at the university. At the age of 19, Mr. Hood had set out to prove wrong an assertion by University of North Carolina professor W. C. George that blacks were inferior because of smaller brain size. After consulting with Andrew Young, (then administrative assistant to Dr. Martin Luther King, Jr., now Democratic mayor of Atlanta), Mr. Hood, an active member of the Student Nonviolent Coordinating Council (SNCC), applied for admission to the all-white University of Alabama. One court injunction and a presidential order later, James Hood was ready to begin.

On the day Mr. Hood was scheduled to enroll, Gov. George Wallace stood in the doorway of the university's admissions office to bar the black students. At President Kennedy's command, the National Guard stood by, too, to ensure the students' admittance. The governor backed down.

Enrolling in the university, Mr. Hood explained, was only half the battle. For James Hood, life as a student was anything but typical. "My roommates were two U.S. marshals," he recalls. "I lived in the dorm right across the street from the cafeteria, but I couldn't just walk over there. I had to take a car [driven by U.S. marshals] and go almost a mile around the campus."

C-SPAN televised 15 hours of the "Covering the South" symposium from Oxford. The opportunity to see that sort of in-depth exploration is what James Hood appreciates most about the network and why he uses it in his "Current Affairs" classroom. He and his students discuss topical news or subjects that will generate debate. "We get a great deal of mileage out of C-SPAN in these kinds of projects." In fact, Mr. Hood reports that at Madison's student center, C-SPAN, rather than daytime soap operas, is the fixture on the student lounge television set. "I think C-SPAN has been forcing some of my students to look beyond their local community concerns and into national and international affairs that they probably would not have done otherwise."

"Covering the South" prompted James Hood to remember and re-evaluate his own experiences during the civil rights movement. "Some of the things that happened at that time didn't seem important," he says. "They were just part of the scenario. But when they're put in terms of how the movement was historically projected, you get a different feeling about them."

He especially enjoyed listening to the panels with journalists such as Jack Nelson, John Chancellor, and David Halberstam. "One of the things I did during those years was to keep news clippings. You see the name of the person who wrote those articles and then, all of a sudden, 20 years later you get the chance to see the person live and to hear some of his statements about that particular subject."

While a cable TV program can bring back the sights and sounds of those few days in 1962, James Hood has carried its lessons with him every day since. "One of the things I learned very early on was that black people couldn't afford to carry hatred around with them for the rest of their lives, because you were not going to develop to your maximum. You need to take advantage of the opportunities, prepare yourself so that when the opportunity presents itself to show that you are qualified to do the job—you've got accomplishments, industriousness, integrity, honor. Those are the things that I learned as part of the civil rights movement, and those are the things that I try to pass on to my students. You don't get things simply because you're black and simply because you've been deprived. You get things because you work for them. And if you work hard enough and prove yourself, people tend to forget about what color you are." —*P.K.*

Mr. Hood watches C-SPAN on Complete Channel TV.

"The Close Up Matriarch"

Ruth Janger

Oklahoma City, Oklahoma

"I love Washington," says Oklahoman Ruth Janger. "I would love to make it my second home." Not only does Ms. Janger use television for vicarious trips to the capital, it allows her to check in on an organization she helped her two sons start. Today, Ms. Janger's son Steve is president of the Close Up Foundation, whose seminars and conferences with students and top policy makers have been telecast on C-SPAN since 1979.

The nonprofit, nonpartisan foundation was founded in 1970. Its main mission is to bring high school students from all over the country to Washington for an in-depth look at government. When students come to the capital for a week-long stay, they meet public servants and national leaders for question-and-answer sessions, visit government agencies and offices, and become familiar with Washington history through sightseeing tours. Over 235,000 students and their teachers are Close Up "graduates." C-SPAN has televised many of Close Up's teleconferences and meetings, including the five sessions that put high school students face-to-face with President Reagan between 1983 and 1986.

"I think education is a wonderful thing," says Ms. Janger. "When these young people become voting citizens and responsible family people, their thinking will have been changed in some way due to Close Up. The program is striving for more awareness in politics and for understanding."

Ms. Janger spent her youth in Oklahoma and married Harry Janger in 1934. She and her husband worked for his family's produce company, raising as many as 300,000 chickens on the outskirts of Oklahoma City. Although the Jangers were busy running one of Oklahoma's leading produce farms and didn't go to college, they imbued their four children—Steve, Chipsey, Sara Lee, and Sharon—with the importance of getting a good education. In the course of their university studies, Chipsey and Steve each spent a year at the Sorbonne in Paris, France.

Ms. Janger traces her sons' interest in public affairs and education to that experience: "They saw what happens to young people when they are exposed to various cultures and government, and they were very much interested in the government process and of making our young people aware of what was happening on a national level, so all of that became a natural concept."

After several jobs in Washington, D.C., and a few stints in Europe, Steve and Chipsey Janger started a program that took high school students to Europe for four-week courses at European universities. The travel logistics became a little overwhelming, their mother recalls, so they decided to scale down their efforts somewhat. "They wanted to maintain and work with the education of young people, so Chipsey, Steve, and Steve's wife Kathie set up the Close Up Foundation with the idea of bringing young people to Washington for a week of government learning and study. From that, the whole concept snowballed."

According to Ms. Janger, Close Up got off to a "rocky" start, selecting most of its students from Oklahoma and looking for cut-rate air fares. Funding from private foundations and government sources energized the project, though, and Close Up began to bring more and more students to the capital. In 1972, Congress appropriated money for Close Up's fellowship program, allowing less fortunate students to join in. This grant was an important boost in the program's scope.

Today, the 26,000 plus students who visit Washington each year come from all over the United States. And Close Up's international program brings in students from as far away as Malaysia. Handicapped students are also encouraged to participate, with close to 3,000 of them coming to Washington each year. Some students are selected by their teachers to take part in the program. Others join Close Up simply because they want to.

Ms. Janger remembers when Close Up made an agreement with C-SPAN in 1980: Close Up would provide cameras and other equipment in return for C-SPAN's providing a wider audience for Close Up programs on television. Close Up was by then an established educational institution on the Washington scene; the fledgling C-SPAN had a staff of four. Even though C-SPAN had a low profile in the early years, Ms. Janger was pleased with the marriage. "We were jubilant and thrilled. I think television has greatly enhanced Close Up. The very fact that you can sit in your living room and watch children from every state in the union and from foreign countries who become aware of what is going on in the United States and in our government—you know that they, too, will be the future leaders. You see these bright young minds and the questions that they come up with and the questions that they can answer. It's mind-boggling.

"I think some of the questions these young people present are even more sophisticated than the ones posed by people who watch the news constantly. They are thinking and they are not afraid to jump in and ask the questions that might be embarrassing to somebody. It's amazing and wonderful."

Naturally, Ms. Janger keeps an eye out for her son, who moderates some of the Close Up programs. "I am just like a true mother. I'll pick up the phone and call my friends who I know are interested in C-SPAN and tell them that Steve has a program or that C-SPAN has a program today. They are all very interested in Close Up here; they all enjoy watching it."

Ms. Janger says that watching Close Up on television has stimulated her appetite and that of her friends for other C-SPAN programming. "Not only do we watch when Close Up is on, but we tune in frequently to watch C-SPAN to see what's happening and what's going on. It has given us more of an awareness of government on a national level—it is a good government program." Ms. Janger and her husband watch the network a few times a week, when they aren't watching Oklahoma football games. "We're avid football fans," she says.

Some of Ms. Janger's fondest memories of Close Up telecasts were when President Reagan took questions from high school students in face-to-face meetings in the Old Executive Building. The meetings were followed by call-in programs in the network studio with the program's students. "I couldn't believe when President Reagan called in to the show," says Ms. Janger. "We were watching with a group of friends because Steve alerted us that it was going to be on."

Ruth Janger says that at the beginning she never expected Close Up to become the educational force that it has. "Now, I've seen it progress and the sky's the limit. Steve is still just as excited about what he is doing and still comes up with new concepts. It's a vital part of his life.

"Students come back from Close Up with such excitement and awareness that *they* can make a change. This is one of the things that Close Up stresses—that if, even as one person, they get involved, they too can have an impact on government. Through organizations, in numbers, they have force. They are aware that if they get together with other young people, they can make a difference," observes the mother of the Close Up founders. —*J.D.*

Ruth Janger watches C-SPAN's Close Up telecasts on Cox Cable Oklahoma City.

"The Commissioner"

Nicholas Johnson

Iowa City, Iowa

According to Nicholas Johnson, the people should seize television and make it their own. "We have programmed people to think, 'Don't touch that dial,'" says the former Federal Communications commissioner. "'Sit there—television is something that's done to you.' . . . For all our talk about democracy, we really don't provide people much training and opportunity to become involved and express themselves, whether it's with a letter to the editor or with video material they prepare for a local television station or for cable."

The 54-year-old communications lawyer and teacher has long advocated wider public participation in television. As early as 1970, he wrote *How to Talk Back to Your TV Set,* a book that lambasted commercial TV and proposed ways that citizens could play a greater part in deciding what came on their screens. Mr. Johnson's outspokenness and his desire for change made him something of a controversial figure in Washington, D.C., during his term as an FCC commissioner from 1966 to 1973. Cable television was then in its nascent stage, and Mr. Johnson wanted to give it a chance to grow. He argued against the broadcast networks' monopoly over television and pushed for the growth of cable, hoping that the novel medium would give the people an outlet for their ideas and creativity.

"A part of my drive as a commissioner in fighting for

cable, and particularly fighting for public access channels on cable, was the belief that if the channels were made available, people would use them," he says. "The great thing that cable can offer a community is genuine local service. It's a great opportunity for people to express themselves or use TV in ways to serve a cause." The passivity bred by regular television dies hard, though. "You have a lot of untraining to do first to convince people that this is something they really can and should use."

Mr. Johnson left Washington in 1980 to return to his family home in Iowa City, where he teaches communications law at the University of Iowa. He says that his dream of communities grasping the opportunity provided by public access has not yet been realized: "I really feel as if I've been beating my head against the wall trying to get church groups, unions, and other organizations to use it." But for Mr. Johnson, a national cable network offers something that can also help democracy flourish, and that network is C-SPAN.

"One of the things that C-SPAN offers the cable industry is the opportunity to have a local dialogue between your congressman in Washington and school children back in the district," he says. "Members of Congress are hearing from their local constituents on C-SPAN. Given what lobbying costs the cable industry or any other industry these days, the whole operation pays for itself just in terms of political representation."

C-SPAN, in Mr. Johnson's view, brings the national scene to local screens. It's a transition made possible in the modern world of communications, and it benefits Mr. Johnson, who is "involved in politics at every level. I try to practice what I preach about communications enabling you to live anywhere you choose. I can go through this litany of how I hosted a network television show, have a radio commentary sent by uplink and satellite all over the country, and feed my column by computer to New York—all from Iowa City. With C-SPAN, I have a sense that I'm keeping up with what's going on in Washington better than if I were actually in Washington. It enables me to follow on a 24-hour basis the kind of things that are going on there and brings it right into my home. It's similar to the way you sometimes get a better seat watching football games on your television than if you were in the stands."

It's important for Mr. Johnson to have that ringside seat.

Politics and media dominate his intellectual and professional life. In addition to teaching courses in mass communications law and law of electronic media at the Iowa College of Law, Mr. Johnson teaches a course by computer at the Western Behavioral Sciences Institute in La Jolla, California. He ran for Congress in Iowa's 3rd District in 1974, and has been serving on the Democratic Party's Harriman Communications Center Board in Washington.

Mr. Johnson was host and contributing editor for the PBS television program "The New Tech Times" from 1983 to 1984. An amateur radio operator, he has been a radio commentator for National Public Radio and writes a syndicated column called "Communications Watch." He served for six years on the Iowa City Cable Commission.

"I'm a real news junkie," says Mr. Johnson. "I've got short-wave radio going, National Public Radio going, and the *New York Times*." C-SPAN has competition for Mr. Johnson's attention, but he says that he monitors the network "with one ear open" while grading papers. "I will linger over floor debates if the person talking is a congressman I know, and then it's just a personal thing—I'm just interested in how old Joe's doing and whether he looks pretty good and he seems to have the best of the argument or whatever." Mr. Johnson also tunes in to hearings or call-in programs when "C-SPAN takes you to the center of the action, like the Bork or contra hearings."

When Mr. Johnson teaches his Iowa classes, he'll often use brief excerpts of videotape to illustrate a point or lighten up the classroom atmosphere. "One of the great hazards of law school is that all feelings are driven from the students and they just become automatons capable of tight analysis and no more. So one of the things I try to do is bring some more feeling into it. I'd use piped-in music if I could," he laughs. "We've got the whole law school wired for computers and television. We've got 30 miles of cable in here," says the former Federal Communications commissioner, "and C-SPAN's one good way to use it." —*T.S.*

Nick Johnson stays in touch with Washington through Hawkeye Cablevision.

Michael Kelley
Fairfax, Virginia

Michael Kelley's life is a mix of Chaucer and high technology—he's a professor of medieval literature with a longtime second career in communications. The red-bearded baritone delivers lectures on the poems and legends of the Middle Ages at George Mason University, delving into the dusty but still vital traditions of antiquity.

He has a master's degree in speech and drama and a doctorate in English, but Mike Kelley has also pursued more modern methods of communication: "Radio is in my blood," he says. The Washington, D.C., native was a ham operator as a kid. For him, the technology was "the magical part." He started working at radio stations while still in college and he has been a radio news director, and a bluegrass disc jockey. He once worked as a press secretary to former Maryland Rep. Clarence Long (D). In 1979, President Carter appointed Prof. Kelley to the board of the Corporation for Public Broadcasting. But one of Mike Kelley's finest hours in communications took place when he found a way to bring live televised House floor proceedings to the movers and shakers of Washington—a capital city without cable.

Congress on television beat out the Arthurian tales in taking up Prof. Kelley's time in 1980. The communications industry was growing, and so was George Mason University.

This northern Virginia state school with a student population of 18,000 was attracting well-known scholars and making other deliberate moves to heighten its profile. Aware of Prof. Kelley's experience in radio and TV, the university president asked him to take a year off from teaching and look into ways the school could "enter and serve the telecommunications industry as a major player."

Armed with a shoestring budget and boundless enthusiasm, Michael Kelley looked for ways to build the university's telecommunications program. In time, he found patrons to donate a satellite dish, television cameras, and other television equipment. He even convinced Lady Bird Johnson to donate an entire AM radio station to the school.

His biggest communications brainchild, however, came about through a series of circumstances. Washington, D.C., was not yet wired for cable television. Washingtonians, inhabitants of one of the world's major power centers, could not watch the House proceedings or congressional hearings available to millions of others through C-SPAN.

Richard Neustadt, a domestic policy assistant to President Carter and a friend of Prof. Kelley's, remarked upon this irony over breakfast one morning. "You know, it makes me mad that a housewife in Kansas City could sit there and iron clothes in the middle of the day and watch the House of Representatives in session, and the president of the free world has to send somebody down to call him on the phone to let him know what's happening on the House floor."

Apparently, this lack of a local TV eye on the political process was beginning to upset some lawmakers as well. Leafing through *Broadcasting* magazine in July 1981, Prof. Kelley spotted a report in which the chairman of the Speaker's Advisory Committee on Broadcasting proposed that Congress broadcast itself by setting up its own low-power television station for the Washington-area audience.

"Hey, that isn't a good idea," Prof. Kelley recalls thinking. "I didn't like the idea of the government operating its own TV station." In his opinion, the establishment of a "Congress channel" might encourage other branches to set up their own. Through C-SPAN, the basic service was already there. What was missing was a way to connect the city with

C-SPAN's congressional telecasts. Mike Kelley decided that George Mason University would create that link.

He came up with a plan to send C-SPAN into the District of Columbia by microwave, using a special frequency called ITFS, which the Federal Communications Commission had reserved for educational use. He drew up the proposal and asked for the commission's okay.

In September 1981, the FCC granted Michael Kelley permission to send C-SPAN over his university's ITFS bandwave. Prof. Kelley set up a small microwave television station in Arlington. In just three months, the service, christened "The Capitol Connection," was ready to bring the Congress to Washington.

The nonprofit Capitol Connection wires offices and some apartment buildings to receive C-SPAN. It's aimed at a select clientele—lobbyists, journalists, and politicians, who are most likely to want to watch Congress. Orders began pouring in after a *Washington Post* article profiled the service in its business section. "Once people knew about us, it snowballed," says Prof. Kelley. The Senate's decision to let itself be televised led to another order avalanche in 1986.

The Capitol Connection has wired approximately 900 office buildings to receive C-SPAN and other programming services. Its client list looks like a "who's who" of Washington insiders. The offices of Fortune 500 companies such as Ford, General Motors, and Chrysler keep an eye on televised trade and technology. Lobbying groups watch for new developments in legislation. Campaign offices, embassies, law firms, and governors' offices also get The Capitol Connection. Prof. Kelley's clients have told him, "This is really going to change the way we do business here in town."

One of Mike Kelley's most notable clients is the White House, which was equipped with The Capitol Connection in 1982. The Capitol Connection employees were not allowed onto the premises. They handed off their antennas at the White House gate to staff members, who positioned the receivers on top of the Executive Office Building and wired the White House offices and residence. Over the years, President Reagan has taken advantage of the hookup. "If anything goes wrong," says Mike Kelley, "if there's any little problem with

C-SPAN, the White House is the first call we get." He was even asked to install an antenna at Bethesda Naval Hospital so President Reagan could keep an eye on Congress there, too. "We're helping to educate the executive branch about the legislative branch," declares Prof. Kelley.

Cable television is now coming to the District of Columbia, but Prof. Kelley is confident that the service will retain its office-building clientele, which is located in areas unlikely to be wired for cable.

In turn, revenues from The Capitol Connection have helped the school's telecommunications department grow. Eight years ago, the school had no mass media courses. Today, it is about to launch a master's program in telecommunications.

Will Mike Kelley, 47, ever reconcile his medieval and modern interests? "It's a schizophrenic kind of thing. It's two different worlds. I really can't talk about the television thing in any classes—I don't even mention it. Outside, I don't talk about medieval stuff too often. I think that whatever God gave me in terms of a talent for literary criticism is probably the same thing that relates to my ability to figure systems out with microwaves." —S.S.

Michael Kelley is able to watch C-SPAN at home on Media General Cable of Fairfax.

Edward Kienholz
Nancy Reddin Kienholz
Hope, Idaho

Artists Edward Kienholz and Nancy Reddin Kienholz are just waiting for the Supreme Court to slip, to make a decision that they really disagree with. Then they're going to bring out the "Caddy Court." Says Edward Kienholz: "We'll send it someplace, almost as a protest."

The Caddy Court is a driveable sculpture that the couple created using the Supreme Court as its subject matter. They took a Cadillac stretch limousine, cut it in half, and welded a 1966 Dodge van body in the middle. Inside are figures representing the nine justices—stuffed animal heads that are falling apart. ("For the past 10 years we've been taking stuffed deer, buffalo, boar, and coyote heads and leaving them out on the porch while we go to Europe," explains Mr. Kienholz. "When we come back, all the stuffings are coming out.")

The Caddy Court, he explains, demonstrates one way in which current events are incorporated into their art. It responds to the fact that "the Supreme Court is an extremely strong influence on all of our lives. Yet until the Bork hearings, it was remote to people, unless you were a constitutional scholar. At first the artwork looks like a joke, then you start thinking about it, and it gets to be a very important kind of social statement about the conditions of living today."

Inspiration for the piece came in part from watching

the 1986 hearings on the nomination of Justice William Rehnquist to chief justice of the United States. "We would listen to Rehnquist talking about the Supreme Court while we were working, almost like ambient music in the background. You get into the spirit, and you're taking in information all the time. It's pretty abstract. I mean, we don't say, 'Hey, we're going to make some art from it.'"

Known for his sometimes disturbing three-dimensional art forms, which often evoke strong social comments, Mr. Kienholz has had his artwork displayed in galleries around the United States and in Europe. A *Washington Post* review of Edward Kienholz by Paul Richard says that Mr. Kienholz' new works are made of "timbers, parts of elephants, pistols and stuffed bats, of fields of gray metal, mirrors, lenses, lights. These sculptures, although elegant, cast a spell so eerie that the real world itself seems to pale in their presence."

To create his works, Mr. Kienholz has become a seasoned "garbageologist." For more than three decades he has been combing back alleys and dumpsters salvaging America's disposable culture, giving it a second life as art. "All the little tragedies are evident in junk," he says. As a master electrician, carpenter, welder, and clothier, Mr. Kienholz takes the sows' ears of yesteryear and turns them into silky social commentary: "Kienholz is a pamphleteer. His work is highly specific, precisely planned visual literature," says the *Post*'s Mr. Richard.

Edward Kienholz officially began collaboration with his wife Nancy Reddin in 1979 with the signing of both names to all their artwork. However, a 1984 issue of *Art News* claims that his wife's "contributions over the past decades have been enormous." The bi-continental couple spend six months of the year in Hope, Idaho (population 63), where they create sculptures and run their gallery: the Faith and Charity in Hope Gallery. The other six months are spent working in West Berlin. The subject matter of previous major pieces includes illegal abortion, saloons where people go and just kill time, heavy petting in the back seat of a car, and various commentaries on television and the news media.

C-SPAN, which they receive via satellite dish in the isolated northern Idaho community, has come to be integrated into their workday. They play C-SPAN all day long in their studio on a black-and-white television set, "for esthetic reasons," says

Mr. Kienholz. "C-SPAN is like background noise, but it's also a source of general information. We learn a lot from that noise." He says his unusual viewing habits probably date back to the years when he could only afford a five-dollar TV with a burnt-out picture tube and only the audio intact. Mr. Kienholz has listened to many of the old movies, but has never seen them.

"In a way we're television addicts," admits Nancy Reddin Kienholz. "Nevertheless, we feel like the television industry has taken over control of our news. And we think the news in America is not the best. Once we created a group of TVs called the "Same Old Shoe" because it doesn't make any difference whether you're watching ABC, NBC, or CBS. It's all the same thing."

Mr. Kienholz says he's "long had a love-hate relationship with American TV. I sit dummy-style in front of that marvelous communication tool and find my years slipping by and my mind turning to slush from the 95 percent trash being beamed my way. To try and understand my ongoing stupidity and perhaps to express some kind of critical objectivity, I find that I keep making TV sets out of anything that vaguely resembles a TV apparatus—oil containers, blocks of concrete, surplus jerry cans, etc."

Television figures prominently in another piece, too, called "Unique TVs," which consists of sets that have sound but no pictures. The sound is taken from background music recordings and tells a story of sorts, without pictures or words. For example, one can hear a cowboy riding a horse, cows lowing, a rinky-dink piano playing in the saloon, and so on. "You begin to invent your own story. It's the weirdest damn thing you ever saw," says Mr. Kienholz.

The Kienholzes discovered that people will sit and look at that piece even though it is more radio than television. "We're all so programmed," suggests Ms. Kienholz.

At the same time, it's the kind of work that gets people scratching their heads, wondering where the art is.

"I don't know if it's art," says Mr. Kienholz. "And I don't give a damn."   —S.S.

The Kienholzes receive C-SPAN on a backyard satellite dish.

Keith Knautz

Glendale Heights, Illinois

Keith Knautz, 17, of Glendale Heights, Illinois, considers himself a typical teen-ager. However, what makes him "un-normal" as he says, is his enthusiasm for government; while his peers are watching "Miami Vice" or "The Cosby Show," he has the "urge to watch C-SPAN."

C-SPAN first learned of young Mr. Knautz when the *Wheaton* (Illinois) *Daily Journal* wrote a July 1987, feature story about his 18-week stint as a congressional page, and an unconventional (for a teen-ager, that is) interest in current events that draws him to C-SPAN. His interest in politics had been brewing before his semester in Washington, D.C., but it was enhanced by his work in the nation's capital. As for his desire to participate in the page program: "It was a change of pace and it was something that, once I thought about it, it automatically sort of clicked in my head. I love social studies, so that would be something to learn and experience."

Working on the House floor obviously made a big impression on Mr. Knautz, because he talks enthusiastically about one day moving full-time into the political arena. "I'd like to be a congressman. I've seen what they do and I feel it to be very important. It would be my way of helping," he says. For him, "all the laws they pass are very important, or they wouldn't spend time on them. They help run the country, and that's a big job, and that to me is very impressive." But for right now, he is filling out his applications for college. And he thinks law school will be in order after college.

Mr. Knautz told the *Daily Journal,* "pages don't get to stop. We get 45 minutes for lunch, that's all. Other than that, you're running all the time." The page program, designed for juniors in high school, combines school studies with page duties. School starts at 6:45 A.M. and lasts until 10 A.M. Then the work for members of Congress begins. Each day the pages take back seats on the House floor waiting for congressmen, clerks, and even reporters to beckon them, most likely to deliver legislative documents. The pages are required to dress in uniform—blue blazers, white shirt, gray slacks, and black shoes. They perform their duties until the speaker gavels the day's session to an end. Sometimes that can mean working until 3 A.M. In addition to all this, there is plenty of homework.

Despite the hard work and the unpredictable hours pages have to endure, Mr. Knautz says he would gladly do it all over again for the unique opportunity of seeing firsthand how government operates. And, he claims, there were certain advantages to the job. For instance, the Iran-contra scandal broke after he had been on the floor for a month, and he says that he and his colleagues had an inside line to the story. For instance, the young page says he could have told the rest of the country in February 1987 that Lt. Col. Oliver North was going to be a hero. Even that early on, one of the pages at the dorm had bumper stickers that read, "God bless this country and Oliver North."

Even when Mr. Knautz and his cohorts weren't on the floor, they often monitored the proceedings by watching C-SPAN in the dormitory lounge. "Pages are supposed to be neutral, and on the floor we were neutral," he says. "But when we went back to the dorm room, we were like anybody else— a lot of debate went on. The speed limit bill, the budget, the trade bill—a lot of that stuff was discussed at length." He says they also watched in the dorm to see when the sessions would end to find out when the rest of the pages would be coming off the floor.

When Mr. Knautz returned to Illinois, he maintained his friendships with other pages, and he kept up his C-SPAN viewing. But as summer gave way to the school year, he found he had less and less time to take in the congressional proceedings. Such activities as the church choir, school drama club, and sports left fewer hours for TV viewing. However, he still watches in the evenings. He finds it to be valuable for his American government and political science classes.

Keith Knautz recognizes that most teen-agers, given the choice, would probably opt for *Return of the Jedi* or *Rambo* over reruns of Congress. He understands that most high school students don't share his interest in politics, and it doesn't bring memories back for them as it does for him. Besides, he says, most high school students are too busy with athletics or extracurricular activities and homework to devote their time to something like C-SPAN programming. "I really don't think it's over their heads. It's just that most kids my age don't have the patience to sit down and watch a show that is that deep, that meaningful," muses Keith Knautz.

He believes that most high school students consider C-SPAN to be "adult" programming—something they're not concerned about yet. Perhaps, he says, "when they turn 21 or 22 their interest level will go up."   —R.C.

Keith Knautz reminisces about Congress by watching MetroVision of Glendale Heights.

"The Feminist"

Suzanne Lauer

Decatur, Georgia

At 36 years of age, Suzanne Lauer of Decatur, Georgia, still believes she can make the world a better, more decent place to live.

"I am of the generation that wanted to change the world. I am first a humanist, because I believe in individual freedom and dignity, as exercised by the responsible use of reasoned judgment and tolerance. I am a feminist because I believe women should participate equally in all expression and institutions of dignity and freedom."

Ms. Lauer's dreams for herself were fashioned in college, where she realized that her main aspiration was "to become an active citizen and to participate in the responsible development of freedom." For many years now her work and studies have been dedicated to promoting and protecting the rights of women and disabled people.

An active member of the DeKalb County Democratic Committee, Ms. Lauer also volunteers as legislative coordinator for the Atlanta chapter of the National Organization for Women. She chairs the Patient Advocacy and Government Relations Committee of the National Foundation for Ileitis and Colitis. For both of these groups she tracks federal and state legislation, organizes people to lobby for their rights, speaks on behalf of individuals who need help, and distributes information and position statements to the media and politicians. In essence, Suzanne Lauer is a lobbyist, and a very busy one at that.

But there's something else to know about Suzanne Lauer. She suffers from Crohn's disease, a chronic digestive ailment that sends its victims into periodic states of severe disability, and often leads to mandatory bed rest or even hospitalization. The disease "stops me in my tracks," she says, and even prevents this busy woman from holding down full-time employment.

In the summer of 1986, Ms. Lauer's condition flared up, forcing her to quit law school at Georgia State University. Confined to bed, she now says if it hadn't been for C-SPAN, her convalescence "would have been a complete waste of time." Instead, it was "one of the most instructive periods in my life." Fresh from classes in constitutional law, she was drawn in by the confirmation hearings of Chief Justice William Rehnquist and the ongoing series on the federal judiciary, "America and the Courts." "I felt enormous excitement at being able to see deeply into the confirmation process, understanding the issues involved, and then watching as many programs as I could on the judiciary," Ms. Lauer says.

As a feminist, one of Suzanne Lauer's special constitutional interests is the 14th Amendment's equal protection clause, which, she believes, must serve to protect women's rights in the absence of the Equal Rights Amendment. "The subtleties of the 14th Amendment contain the nuances of women's political, economic, and social equality before the law of the United States," she explains. Hence, when the Senate Judiciary Committee questioned Judge Robert Bork in 1987 on his interpretation of the equal protection clause, Suzanne Lauer was taking notes.

Congressional hearings, interviews with presidential candidates, and bills introduced on the House and Senate floors are all fertile ground for Ms. Lauer's grassroots activism. When a congressional hearing topic affects the groups she lobbies for, Ms. Lauer videotapes the hearing and passes the coverage along to other members. Hoping to inspire others to activism, she wrote an article in NOW's Atlanta chapter newsletter, advising members on how to use the network and commenting on the various programming that affects their work as feminists. "I've seen, to my surprise, that feminists have a lot of friends in Congress," she advised the NOW membership.

Suzanne Lauer's commitment to fighting sex discrimination began in 1976 when she experienced sexual harassment at her United Nations secretarial job in Vienna, Austria, and brought charges against her American male boss. Found guilty by an all-male panel, he subsequently lost his diplomatic immunity. Similarly, her work for the National Foundation for Ileitis and Colitis was inspired by her own disability and the myriad difficulties she sees that other sick people have. "I want to use my education and background to speak for individuals with all sorts of chronic illnesses, and to become an effective lobbyist for everyone who is sick."

Suzanne Lauer won't permit her debilitating disease to keep her from working to advance her causes. She has learned that even her "limited energies can make a difference. I've realized you don't need to be in the best of health to do the job of legislative coordinator. What you need is to be informed and to know who to contact, and how. As a result of C-SPAN I am becoming an effective lobbyist, something which I imagined would lay far in my future, not right at my doorstep in the present." —M.C.

Ms. Lauer is a Prime Cable subscriber.

"The Letter Writer"

Stephen J. Liesen
Wyandotte, Michigan

Stephen J. Liesen is an inveterate letter writer. From his home in Wyandotte, Michigan, he fires off at least one letter every day. "It costs like hell in stamps, paper, and typewriter ribbon," says Mr. Liesen, "but I've always thought a citizen's duty did not stop at the ballot box. We elect them and we have a duty to tell them what we think."

For Stephen J. Liesen, a letter a day is his way of being involved in the democratic process. "If everyone who can would only write once or twice a week and give those people the benefit of our thoughts, we would see a big change in the way Congress operates. I can see some small changes already," maintains Mr. Liesen. If he makes "one point out of a thousand," he feels that he's made a difference.

He has been writing letters for over 30 years, and he says the pace picked up dramatically in 1975 when he retired from his job as mechanical inspector for Detroit Edison. Like many people in his community, he came to Michigan in the late 1930s to find work in the auto industry; later he went to work for Detroit Edison. He's lived in Wyandotte, which he likes, since the early 1960s. He describes it as a working-class community that's down river from Detroit. The residents of his town work mostly in steel mills and chemical and auto assembly plants. It's a Democratic town; however, he says "I fly no party flag."

Mr. Liesen gets more pleasure out of writing letters than just about anything else—it's his "main hobby." His interest in woodworking, knitting, and sewing takes second seats. For him letter writing is a form of self-entertainment. "I'm one of those guys who never got hooked up to anybody," reflects 75-year-old Mr. Liesen. "I live by myself, always have, always will."

He admits that his letters can be very critical. Sometimes he gets so enthusiastic about some of his letters that he tears them up because "they're a little too rough" on the addressee. "The first thing I do when I look at someone is to see their faults," he states. His pessimism and his opinions stem from his "study of the human species. I get puzzled as to why people do things. Then I read through history at how our species evolved. When I do that, I get very depressed. I'm cynical about the human race. Man has a lot of nerve saying he was created in God's image. I think that's an insult to God." He doesn't think there is anybody living whom he admires unconditionally. He says he used to think John Wayne was the greatest until correspondence with "the Duke" revealed some glaring faults.

C-SPAN has received scores of letters from Mr. Liesen, which he has addressed to just about every department at the network. Many of his missives have been reprinted in the network's weekly newspaper. Practically every morning he takes in a C-SPAN call-in with his breakfast—a habit he says that has become too costly because "I wind up writing a letter to someone on something that I agree or disagree with." Sometimes he writes to make comments about the call-in guests; other times he's just concerned with the issue or wants to make a comment about C-SPAN programming. But around the C-SPAN offices, Mr. Liesen is most famous for his "blooper-by-blooper accounts" of mistakes he notices on his screen:

> If you're doing something that is perfectly innocent, but might look bad to the viewers, for crying out loud, get on the boob tube and tell us what's going on. Don't just assume we have X-ray vision that can see into your mind. In short, communicate!

He is also not shy about expressing his opinions of C-SPAN's programming choices:

While I have the paper in the machine, I would like to comment on the caucuses you have been broadcasting. While they may be interesting to someone involved in that part of the race, I find them to be boring as hell. In fact, they brought back memories of a time in my youth when I got involved in that kind of thing in Kansas City, Missouri, back when Pendergast was running that town. It was boring as hell then, and I see it hasn't changed a wit since. Guess that's why I never got into politics.

There was excitement in politics if you knew where to look. The strong-arm boys hauled their tommy guns right on the back seats of the cars for any one to see who cared to look. There were parts of that town where you voted the way the machine wanted or you had better stay home. But the caucus rooms were still dullsville, nonetheless.

For years, Mr. Liesen has been writing his own congressman, Energy Committee Chairman John Dingell (D-Michigan), whom he says is "as good as they have down there." And Rep. Dingell usually responds to his letters. His efforts often take the form of suggestions for running Congress more efficiently, and thereby saving the taxpayers money. In one such letter he wrote to Rep. Dingell:

If all the time both the House and the Senate waste on such games and useless oratory just stalling around were added up, it could very well put the waste bill at the Pentagon in the shade.

Put a scorekeeper in each chamber to record all the time wasted by any member. Then take the cost of running by the hour, multiply that waste by that cost. Then take 10 percent of that off the pensions of all the members in direct relation to the time they have wasted. If such a rule were adopted, we would see a lot faster Congress or a lot smaller pensions for some. It would be like using a cattle prod on them. Really spark them up!

However, as you might have guessed, even Congressman Dingell is a "long way from perfect," according to Stephen J. Liesen, who "votes the person, not the party." The self-described maverick says party affiliation "just clogs your brain." He characterizes his politics as "free swinging. I reserve the right to take a swing at anyone I want to."   —*J.D.*

Mr. Liesen writes letters while watching C-SPAN on a system run by Wyandotte Municipal Services.

Nackey Loeb

Manchester, New Hampshire

The motto of the 125-year-old Manchester *Union Leader* is drawn from Daniel Webster: "There is nothing so powerful as the truth." With longtime publisher William Loeb at the helm, this small New Hampshire daily was very often the subject of national attention. Editorials referring to President Gerald Ford as "Jerry the Jerk" and to President Johnson as "Snake Oil Lyndon" caused quite a stir. And on the eve of the 1984 New Hampshire Democratic primary, one of the paper's attention-getting front-page editorials urged Democratic voters to write Ronald Reagan's name in on their ballots.

The *Union Leader*'s president and publisher, Nackey Loeb, maintains that the paper is performing an important function: "We try to get people involved, whether they agree with us or not."

Ms. Loeb took over the paper after the death of her husband William in 1981. By big city standards, its 70,000 plus circulation is relatively low. But that doesn't accurately reflect its reach. The *Union Leader* is the only statewide newspaper in the home of the first-in-the-nation presidential primary. In the words of the *Wall Street Journal*, "William Loeb took great joy in editorially pummeling presidential aspirants every four years." Politicians feared the paper's influence over other media and the voters. Today, although its tone has softened,

William Loeb's legacy lives on. "I may not be as hard-hitting as my late husband," Nackey Loeb speculates, "but we have the same principles."

C-SPAN cameras recorded the *Union Leader*'s operations during the 1984 and 1988 New Hampshire primaries. These visits to the paper's headquarters in Manchester featured interviews with Ms. Loeb and the staff, viewer call-in segments, and live coverage of editorial meetings. Ms. Loeb says she "loved it." An enthusiastic C-SPAN viewer herself, she encourages *Union Leader* writers to watch the public affairs programming in order to keep up with developments in Washington.

Nackey Loeb writes most editorials and reviews from her Manchester home, generally going to the paper's downtown office about once a week. After becoming partially paralyzed in a 1977 automobile accident she's now wheelchair-bound and spends "quite a lot of time generally getting set up for the day. Fortunately, the sometimes dull but necessary routines can be completed in front of the television."

Watching C-SPAN call-in programs has become part of her routine. "I get a perspective on what's going on around the country with other people in the newspaper business and the people who read the paper. I like to hear how other journalists are making news decisions. The calls coming in also give me an overview of the things people are concerned about. That's so interesting. Very often, 'the story' at one end of the country is much less important at the other end. The callers tell me what the big stories are and how they are relating to them."

Occasionally, Ms. Loeb learns something from watching C-SPAN that she'd rather forget. She heard, for example, that Steve McAuliffe, the husband of the late Christa McAuliffe (*Challenger* astronaut and New Hampshirite) had supported a presidential candidate whom he'd first seen speak on C-SPAN. But that candidate also happened to be one of Ms. Loeb's Democratic "targets." "That's the first time I've ever been unhappy with C-SPAN," she quips.

For Ms. Loeb, the combative newspaper presents a powerful truth. "We are not dull, to put it bluntly," she says of the *Union Leader*. "We come out very strongly. We say what we think. We put editorials on the front page. This practice in newspapers is disappearing, which is unfortunate." She hopes the paper will have a role in "continually getting people emotionally and intellectually involved with the government. Papers aren't doing it, for the most part. We do."

Ms. Loeb adds that "citizens cannot form an opinion if they aren't presented with the facts and with other people's assessment of those facts. I firmly believe that the public can do a darn good job, but only if they know what's going on."   —*M.H.*

Nackey Loeb receives C-SPAN from United Cable Co. of New Hampshire.

"The Leaguer"

Katherine Loew

Honolulu, Hawaii

Katherine Loew moved to Hawaii in 1972. "The thought of doing dolphin research at the University of Hawaii appealed to me tremendously," she says. After completing a doctorate in social psychology, she moved back to the mainland (the dolphin research "was fun," but she only did it for a year). She soon found she missed this charming cluster of islands in the Pacific Rim, more than 5,000 miles from the mainland.

Today she lives with her husband and three-year-old daughter in the predominantly Japanese Kaimuki section of Honolulu. The Japanese are one of the largest immigrant groups in Hawaii, second only to the "haoles"—or white mainlanders. Ms. Loew is a haole who now calls Hawaii home, and she's become quite involved in the state's issues and politics.

For the past five years Ms. Loew has been an active member of the League of Women Voters of Honolulu—one of more than 1,250 local chapters of that organization nationwide. Although she's not a television producer by trade, for the past several years she's been producing the league's monthly program, "The League of Women Voters Presents." It can be seen four times each month on the local cable access channel. "We've had some great shows," she says. "We did one on housing development in central Oahu—the cane lands, another on mass transit, and another on Japanese investment in Hawaii. That was one of my favorites. Basically," she adds, "we cover current issues and events."

When Ms. Loew first moved to Hawaii, keeping up with current events was difficult. Back then, news from the mainland was anything but timely. Limited by expensive technology and great distance, "today's" news in Hawaii was "yesterday's" news on the mainland. Now that satellite technology and cable have become as common as coconuts, Hawaii is as close to Washington, D.C., as Virginia is, at least in terms of having instantaneous access to information.

Today in Hawaii, for example, the Loew household is one of more than 211,500 homes wired to receive C-SPAN. Ms. Loew first tuned in to the network four years ago because she "wanted to know what was going on in Washington." Today she watches regularly because it helps her with her work for the league. Even though most of her shows focus on local issues, she finds that watching Congress and call-in programs often sparks her imagination. "The Japanese investment show came out of some remark someone made on C-SPAN," she recalls. "Someone was talking about trade issues and I thought that sounded directly relevant, and possibly of concern to a lot of people here."

Hawaii, with its seven main islands and dozens of smaller ones, joined the union as the 50th state in August 1959. Despite tremendous growth, the state's population only numbers one million people today. Main industries are tourism, the military, and sugar, but none is particularly secure. Ms. Loew feels that the most pressing state issues are "housing, education, and concern about the impact of Japanese investment in the local economy."

Ms. Loew is one of 250 members in the league's Honolulu chapter. The league describes itself as a nonpartisan, multi-issue, activist organization whose mandate is "to make democracy work better." It's organized like the federal government with local, state, and national levels. Since Ms. Loew's is a local chapter, it only deals with local issues and, when it comes to elections and debates, local candidates.

Politics in Hawaii are different from politics on the mainland, Ms. Loew says, for several reasons. "This is a small place. And this is a one-party state. Sometime in the '60s the

Democrats took over, and they've been controlling things ever since." Ms. Loew is a Democrat, and considers herself a liberal, but she says, "I think that the Democrats have been entrenched for so long that people who really might fit in better with the Republican Party are Democrats here because that is their only choice."

Although she had taken a few television and film courses in college, Katherine Loew was not a television producer before volunteering for this program. "It's so much work," she says. "It's just amazing how much time it takes and how tedious and wearing it is." She relies on volunteer crews and unpaid guests and, when not dealing with a crisis or an emergency, she spends most of her time on the telephone. But as she works, she also listens to Congress in Washington. "I keep the TV on and watch it between phone calls," she explains. "And if something interesting happens, then I stop making phone calls and start watching more."

While her interest in producing television is new-found, her interest in current affairs is long-standing. When Katherine Loew was growing up in Michigan, the family dinner conversations always revolved around current events. "In order to participate in the conversation, you had to pay attention to what was in the newspaper or what was on TV," she recalls. "Otherwise you got left out." Her parents were both "very civic-minded and very active in community affairs." Her mother, in fact, earned her living as an activist. "My mother was a civil rights worker when I was a kid. She was a social worker. It's true—she was always running around doing good."

Her upbringing had a lasting impact on Ms. Loew, who is "around 40." The fact that she's thousands of miles from her birthplace, yet still in her own country, makes public issues all the more interesting, she says.   —M.C.

Ms. Loew's Oahu home is served by Oceanic Cablevision.

"The Communications Professor"

Manny Lucoff

Tampa, Florida

Even in the midst of the communications revolution, students who study the growth, change, and regulation of the broadcasting industry often have to rely on textbooks that are printed months or years after the events they record have been swept away in a tide of more developments. But in Prof. Manny Lucoff's classes at Tampa's University of South Florida, federal action on the telecommunications industry is accessible as it happens.

That's because Prof. Lucoff, 55, brings principals into his classroom with television coverage of congressional debates and hearings on telecommunications issues that he says couldn't be there any other way: for instance, Sen. Tim Wirth (D-Colorado), who chaired the House Telecommunications subcommittee during his years in the U.S. House. "Here was a rare opportunity to see the people about whom I had taught in class, people who were making decisions in Congress. My students could actually see the debates I've been describing."

"C-SPAN is a resource that can't be duplicated," declares the professor. He has an extensive library of videotapes he's made of congressional debates and hearings for use in his courses on programming, introduction to broadcasting, and telecommunications law. No longer does he have to send his students to the reserve reading shelf at the library. "I'm always excited to be able to show my students testimony from commercial broadcasters, network presidents, NAB (National Association of Broadcasters) lobbyists, and industry experts." Now, he says, his "students can match faces and personalities and content."

Manny Lucoff, who heads the broadcasting department at the University of South Florida, has been teaching there since 1963. His forays into the fifth estate began after high school when he realized that his desire to be an athlete, as he remembers, "exceeded my talent, so I decided to get a degree in broadcasting and do sports programming. I went to work in television as a producer, writer, director, announcer, and cameraman—I did all those things while I was getting a college degree."

While Prof. Lucoff was working as a sports announcer for the Tampa ABC affiliate, a local football coach told him that he was good teacher material. The advice appealed to him; with his days free, he decided to teach American history and civics in the Orange County public school system. "The more I taught," says Prof. Lucoff, "the more I enjoyed it." He decided to return to the University of Florida "to get a master's degree so that I would qualify for better opportunities." After working for a while as a producer/director for public broadcasting, he started his ongoing stint with the University of South Florida by agreeing to take responsibility for putting the university's television station on the air. Later on he completed a doctorate in communications, taught classes, and eventually became the department chairman.

Although a 30-year veteran of the television industry, Prof. Lucoff claims disenchantment with a communications medium that he felt had such great potential. "To me commercial television is the movies on television, it is the radio on television. TV took forms that were in other media and grafted itself onto them—just modifying them for TV. We had sports, soaps, and news and drama before there was television. But what we never had before was an opportunity to see democracy in action." And for Prof. Lucoff, "what C-SPAN is doing is really what television is most fitted to do."

That's why Manny Lucoff was incensed when his local cable television system announced it was going to remove C-SPAN from its offerings. "I hit the ceiling," he says. "I couldn't believe that I would lose this teaching resource shortly after I had gotten it." So Prof. Lucoff told the cable system he was going to use the public access channel as a base to criticize them for taking C-SPAN off the air. "He videotaped a speech at the local access station and invited the local CBS affiliate and the press to come out and cover it. "I was claiming that the local cable company was denying the citizens of Temple Terrace an opportunity to see the American government in action," he recalls.

Shortly after Prof. Lucoff had taped his address, and informed the cable company that the issue was going to be covered on the 6:00 news, management offered a deal: They would put C-SPAN back on the system if the professor promised to stop talking about it. Even though Prof. Lucoff's tape never ran, the local press ran an above-the-fold story on the controversy, saying that the cable system had changed its mind about C-SPAN.

After his showdown with the local cable system, Lucoff was able to rest easy. He could continue building and updating his tape library on telecommunications. "I wouldn't know where else to get this information," says the professor. "C-SPAN brings a degree of life and enthusiasm" into his class. And besides, notes Manny Lucoff, it gives the students a break—they "get tired of seeing the same face lecturing day after day."   —K.M.

Prof. Lucoff creates C-SPAN videotapes from Jones Intercable.

"The Anchorman"

Patrick Lynn
Bismarck, North Dakota

"Even if I weren't a newsman I would still be watching C-SPAN, because contemporary government in action is a beautiful thing to watch."

Not many people ascribe aesthetic values to gavel-to-gavel coverage of government affairs, but for Patrick Lynn, 51-year-old television news anchor at KXMB-TV in Bismarck, North Dakota, uncut public affairs programming gives him a watch on Washington that would otherwise be difficult to come by in his small-sized midwestern capital city. "I go to the office, and, very frankly, as a result of watching C-SPAN and being an avid reader, I find myself much further advanced in terms of contemporary knowledge than my colleagues in the newsroom," says Mr. Lynn. "You don't have to worry about quotes and misquotes, or whatever. You can make your own decisions and base your own judgments on the full record."

Mr. Lynn is something of an expert when it comes to bringing national news to small-city viewers. Although he's had job offers in bigger markets. Mr. Lynn prefers not to live "armpit to armpit." The 30-year veteran of print and broadcast journalism has chosen to work in small cities or towns in California, Florida, Mississippi, and other states. Big cities are "too inconvenient, too busy, and they smell," he says. "I like my space." Attracted to "places that are remote," Patrick Lynn even spent a few years at the CBS affiliate in Anchorage, Alaska.

As producer and anchorman for the 6:00 P.M. and 10:00 P.M. news at KXMB, it's Mr. Lynn's job to select the stories and format the news show, help other reporters with their stories, and, of course, produce and anchor the live newscast. He also does the "afternoon cut-ins," which consist of 90-second headline updates on the air. The station's 10:00 news show is reserved for major national news stories, which are interspersed with the "more important local stories," says Mr. Lynn. As a CBS affiliate, KXMB has access to the CBS video feed, the network's library, and certain stories from "CBS Evening News." The station also relies on several wire services and has an in-house library with over 400 hours of one-of-a-kind videotape. To prepare himself, Mr. Lynn takes in daily extracurricular information; he reads several newspapers and watches various public affairs programs. He works from 2:00 P.M. until 10:30 P.M., so "my work habits dictate my viewing habits."

KXMB has developed a reputation for delivering hard news to its statewide audience. "We have an excellent news director here in Bismarck who does not care for any frivolous, lighthearted news. We delve very hard into social issues, such as poverty in the prairie and government on all levels. We don't go for happy talk and flowery features and sentimental, piglets-born-to-a-sow stories," insists Patrick Lynn. As a state capital, Bismarck is a political town. Many state employees live in the area, and they want to know what's going on in government, especially at the state and local levels.

Mr. Lynn made the transition from print to broadcast news in the 1960s, when the owner of the newspaper for which he was reporting "was having problems with his broadcast property." Patrick Lynn was recruited to "straighten out the problems in the newsroom of the TV station." He was reluctant to make the transition to television but admits that, after he got into it, "I sort of enjoyed it and I stayed."

All of his assignments have been at CBS affiliates. "It's just a superior system. It has higher standards of journalism. I would not work for either an ABC or NBC affiliate."

In light of what he calls the "tremendous advances that TV news has made within the last 20 years," he finds public criticism of television "fascinating." He cites the varied news programming available to viewers—Cable News Network, C-SPAN's public affairs programming, and network news specials—as proof that the industry has "more depth and more heavyweights." And "the news is virtually instant worldwide. We used to move film around in canisters by airplane, then it was by microwave, and now it's by satellite," he explains.

All this technology means that even local news isn't just local anymore. He also points out that while network news shows are confined to 30 minutes a day, affiliate news programs are stretching to 90 minutes in some major markets. So, for TV newsman Patrick Lynn local stations will remain "the place to be."   —P.K.

Patrick Lynn follows the government process on Bismarck Mandan Cable TV.

Tony Maidenburg

Marion, Indiana

Tony Maidenburg was born in Marion, Indiana, in 1947 and practices law there today. As a junior high school student in 1961, when his classmates were still young enough to want to grow up to become president, the 14-year-old tagged along with his father to speeches before City Council meetings and presentations to planning commission hearings, and dreamt the more down home fantasy of serving as Marion's mayor. He didn't know then that in 18 years, at about the time his school chums were settling down with their families and their first homes, he would already be Marion's former mayor, and would find himself eschewing the political scene for time with his wife Jennie and his three children.

Yet old habits die hard. Today, Molly is 10; her brother Micah is seven; their sister Nancy is three; and Dad, now 40, has decided to run in 1988 for a state Senate seat. In the meantime, he is actively encouraging, among the youth of Marion, his friends, and his fellows at the Jewish Sinai Temple, the same sense of direct involvement in public affairs that his father gave him.

The former mayor (he served from 1976 to 1979) starts with an assumption about democracy that is universal in American political culture: "If we want to preserve it, we sure as heck better participate in it." That elusive goal is easy to reach, he believes, simply because once someone sees the democratic process at work, he'll be hooked.

The hooks are close at hand: The City Council is just downtown; the legislature is a little further away in Indianapolis; and Washington is on C-SPAN in the living room.

"I still occasionally get invitations to speak to classes in the Marion community school system. The teachers remember my willingness to visit classes from my years as mayor," he says. "I usually start by talking about getting involved in the political system, not just by being good students in the classroom but by participating as active citizens even though they may not be old enough to vote yet.

"I end up by quoting one of the founding fathers about the need for an informed electorate, and I'll encourage them to visit City Council meetings on the local level or the state legislature. For an in-depth look at our federal system, I urge them to tune in to C-SPAN, because whatever people are concerned about is eventually going to show up somewhere on C-SPAN."

Teens, for example, might be interested in knowing that the music they dance to was the subject of a news-making committee hearing in the Senate. "However much one wants to watch the nightly news or read a newspaper, there's nothing like having the chance to really hear an advocate for one position or another give a full speech, and that's what I try to outline to the students. It may not be practical to attend a committee hearing, but if you can tune in to one when they are discussing Tipper Gore's work to get rock music labeling—that's something that has a direct effect on high school kids. That's something they've only really heard about on a very superficial basis, but if they have the chance to tune in a hearing where they have Tipper Gore on one side and somebody from a rock band on the other, you can really make the whole process come alive."

Mr. Maidenburg always attends the annual Jewish Federation Dinner at his temple, where he served three one-year terms as president. Among the many pictures hanging there is an old photo of the men and women of the congregation standing outside the temple, behind a jeep. In 1947, Marion's small Jewish community raised enough money to purchase the vehicle; one of them drove it to New York, where it was shipped to Israel. The photograph is the congregation's favorite, perhaps because it symbolizes the fruit of its members' efforts to assist other Jews in America, in Israel, and around the world.

"These are people who are for the most part politically interested and astute," Mr. Maidenburg says. Even his fellow members at the temple, however, were once admonished against the specter of complacency. This was after he had watched, on C-SPAN, a panel composed of former congressmen espousing views on aid to Israel that were at odds with the efforts of the congregation. "I remember talking from the pulpit and with others from the congregation about how we sometimes get in a rut of going through these local fund-raising campaigns year in and year out, but we ought to keep in mind what some folks are saying about the kinds of efforts we're doing—the kinds of things we're comfortable with that others are very upset about."

He taped the program, and made it available to his fellow members at the temple. "It was a rather startling reminder that there is another point of view, and that we simply ought not to go through the motions of having an outside speaker come in and having a deli dinner once a year and writing a check and forgetting about it."

At one time, Mr. Maidenburg thought he might want to run for Congress, but when he saw the schedule that his own congressman has to keep he realized "that life is just a series of choices, and I don't want to put myself in a position of having to choose between being the kind of father I'm enjoying being and being an officeholder as well." But the proximity of the state capital—Indianapolis is just 90 minutes from Marion—makes it possible, he says, "to have my cake and eat it, too.

"State capitals are a growing source of power," he observes, "and I'd like to be involved in efforts to help mold these public policies on education or farmers' problems." In his current campaign, he'll have an asset that he didn't have as mayor in the late '70s. "I've been paying attention to some of the governors and state legislature conferences on C-SPAN. Those forums have demonstrated potential for airing state-related issues. Those of us who are either in or aspire to be in the state legislature can learn what other states are facing."

"I certainly would have enjoyed having C-SPAN when I was mayor of Marion," he says. "Occasionally I would have a chance to attend a National League of Cities convention or a U.S. Conference of Mayors meeting or an Urban League convention, but no mayor can go to all these things. Anyone who's involved in running a city, no matter how large or small, is going to find coverage of these things fascinating."

Today, as he attempts a trek to the state capital, Tony Maidenburg is, in a sense, still tagging along with his father, whether those footsteps lead to Indianapolis, to a temple meeting, or to the living room where a committee hearing is playing on TV. "Dad was an interested citizen and always expressing his concern, or urging a council or commission to do this or that. I would go with him because sometimes that's what fathers and sons do with each other. The more I did that sort of thing, the more interested I got in what was going on locally, and it helped me develop the conclusion, at an early age, that the right people in the right places in Marion could really get a lot of things done.

"I guess C-SPAN has shown that the bottom line, whether you are talking about the Marion City Council or the Senate Judiciary Committee, is by and large men and women who are trying to do a good job, who have perhaps different levels of education and involvement, but who are all good citizens trying to do their best to make the process work."   —*P.K.*

Mr. Maidenburg watches C-SPAN on Marion Cable TV.

Aimee Maxfield

Marietta, Georgia

What was your most treasured extracurricular activity during high school? Were you an exercise nut—trying out for first string everything? Or perhaps you were more into, as Miss Piggy the Muppet says, "snacksercise," scarfing down the very best all-purpose, vitamin-free junk food you could find. Some kids diligently hone their acrobatic skills on state-of-the-art skateboards. But not Aimee Maxfield.

At age 16, Aimee Maxfield of Marietta, Georgia, has something else on her mind: politics—and major league politics, at that. In a letter to C-SPAN, in the summer of 1987, she wrote:

> Though I am only 15 years old, I already have big plans for a career in politics. C-SPAN, with its speeches, briefings, conventions, and daily coverage of the proceedings of the House of Representatives, has helped me learn a great deal about the federal government. I especially enjoyed your nighttime rebroadcast of the Iran-contra hearings. I work and go to school during the day, and it was wonderful to know that I wouldn't have to mess with the VCR and that I wouldn't have to worry about missing anything.

Today, 75 percent of her television viewing is devoted to C-SPAN. Add to that her extracurricular work on the school newspaper and the dance committee, and special after-school history classes, and her plans to run for class office in her senior year, and longer term plans to intern for the summer in Washington, and even further-off visions to attend college in the nation's capital, someday go to law school, and then work on Capitol Hill—and it's clear that this high school sophomore is not sophomoric.

Nor is she without political opinions. Ms. Maxfield is a self-described "die-hard conservative." She's against abortion and tax increases, and in favor of a strong defense. She believes there should be more conservatives on the Supreme Court; Robert Bork appealed to her. She considers herself something of a feminist; that is, she'll "raise a fuss" if she thinks she's not getting a fair shake. But she doesn't align herself with the National Organization for Women. "They portray women as screaming and nasty . . . and they're not," says Aimee Maxfield. She admires former Transportation Secretary Elizabeth Dole because "she has a good grip on things. I consider her a role model."

And she doesn't like people telling her how to think. "I am firm in my convictions, but I am aware that how the material is presented affects what I think. One of my favorite things about C-SPAN is that it allows people to think for themselves. The network cultivates your intelligence instead of insulting it."

Her political philosophy is something she has picked up from her family. "My parents are both conservatives, and in the last couple of years I think I've become even more extreme than they are," muses the honor student. But even so, her feelings about those on the opposite side of the political aisle have softened. "Growing up I heard my parents complaining about the awful Democrats, and I think for a long time I was sort of under the impression that Democrats had three eyes and horns. After watching some of the Democrats on C-SPAN, I've come to the conclusion that they are not as big idiots as I thought they were." Today one of Aimee Maxfield's favorite politicians is Sen. Sam Nunn (D-Georgia): "He's moderate and respected, and has wide appeal. I think he's good for Georgia's image, which people think of as a 'hick state.'" She has already written Sen. Nunn to inquire about internships in his Washington office.

Activism, in many forms, seems to come naturally to Aimee Maxfield. Her letter-writing efforts compete with her other activities. She says she has written to "absolutely everybody" and that includes members of Congress, President Reagan, the first lady, the vice president, and several people she had seen testify during the Iran-contra hearings. She got a personal reply from Nancy Reagan, "which was kind of neat," and mailings from the White House and the Bush campaign.

"Though I am currently torn between Vice President Bush and Sen. Dole," Ms. Maxfield wrote to C-SPAN in November 1987, "I am interested in all of the platforms of all the candidates. I have written to each and every candidate, requesting information on their ideas."

As a young Republican, Ms. Maxfield claims to meet plenty of opposition at what she sees as her liberal-leaning high school. She's been trying to organize a teen-age Republicans group, but so far response has been poor—she knows of only four possible student recruits. Her school, Galloway High School, "has something of a political past," she explains. "Martin Luther King Jr.'s children went to Galloway, and the headmaster, Elliot Galloway, was a friend of King's."

Being a conservative in a school of liberal thinkers doesn't bother Aimee Maxfield too much. In fact, she seems to thrive on it. She says she often talks politics with her more liberal classmates. Their differing views don't cause friction: "Everybody just laughs about it," says Ms. Maxfield. Her best friend is a liberal, and they disagree constantly. "We like to argue about things, and, in a way, it has brought us closer," she says. "You know, opposites attract."   —S.S.

Aimee Maxfield's family subscribes to Wometco Cable TV of Cobb County.

Bob McBarton

Redondo Beach, California

At the age of 25, Bob McBarton of Redondo Beach, California, has started compiling an impressive résumé. The ambitious young man is a law student, full-time dictaphone salesman, member of the California Democratic Party's Central Committee, and until its unusual end, a volunteer staff member of Sen. Joseph Biden's (D-Delaware) presidential campaign.

In the fall of 1987, soon after his candidate withdrew, he added another line to his list of credentials: a "My Turn" column in *Newsweek* magazine. "I am a political junkie," he wrote. "I get my fix nightly from Ted Koppel or, on demand, from C-SPAN."

His obsession with politics thus framed in the metaphor of his TV viewing habits, the former campaign staffer went on to give his rendering of the full picture to future presidential candidates. He wrote: "Grassroots activists like me bind ourselves to the fate of our candidate, giving money and time because we believe in his vision of the future. It's a leap of faith, but this year there was a disillusioning crash. . . . Maybe it has something to do with a yuppie ethic of cutting your losses, but candidates today are quitting at the first whiff of crisis, before a single vote has been cast. More important, they're leaving their supporters stranded—and less eager to volunteer in the next race."

Mr. McBarton grew up in Rochester, New York, with a

Republican father and a mother whom he calls a "sometime Democrat." He has been volunteering for presidential campaigns since he was 12 years old. An eighth grade teacher got him interested in Rep. Mo Udall's (D-Arizona) 1976 contest. In 1984, he worked as a student organizer for Sen. John Glenn's (D-Ohio) presidential campaign. And, for the 1988 race, he signed on with the Biden campaign. At his age, he's a fairly experienced campaign volunteer, and he takes it very seriously. He expects the same seriousness from his candidates: "Democrat or Republican, liberal or independent, consider this fair warning. If you want to become president, you must run in good times and bad, in hell or high water. Those of us who volunteer in your campaigns also put our lives and our careers on hold. If you want my help, I want a commitment from you. If you can't give that commitment, don't run."

Someday, perhaps, Bob McBarton will run for public office himself. He says he wouldn't mind being a state legislator, but recognizes that "it's very difficult to break in." He notes that "if a state assembly person from my district dropped out, there would probably be 10 to 15 people in front of me who could express more electable liberal credentials than I could." It's also very expensive to run. He estimates that a race for "the average assembly seat in California costs anywhere between half a million to $750,000. That's every two years."

Mr. McBarton has already had at least a taste of running for office. He ran for a delegate seat to the Democratic National Convention in 1984, and although he was beaten by Hart and Mondale supporters, he did manage to chalk up 5,000 votes. Before the collapse of the Biden campaign, he had hoped to win a delegate seat to the 1988 convention. Now that those dreams have been dashed, he won't be going as a delegate. But he's still hoping to go as an observer.

After working 40 hours each week selling dictaphones, and going to evening classes at least 20 hours each week at Loyola University's School of Law, Mr. McBarton divides what's left of his time among studying, taking part in political activities, and keeping abreast of political news. He watches C-SPAN about 10 hours a week, and more when something big happens like the Iran-contra investigation or the Robert Bork confirmation hearings. One of his favorite programs, not surprisingly, is the '88 campaign series, "Road to the White

House." "In the past, we'd only find out about a candidate who was hot stuff after he did well in the Iowa caucuses or a New Hampshire primary situation. We didn't know that much about them beforehand. Any time there's been an election, there have been good candidates who, for one reason or another, didn't get decent exposure. Maybe they didn't have a lot of money and therefore couldn't attract a lot of money. Maybe the message was garbled. 'Road to the White House' allows candidates who might normally be forgotten in the process to have a chance to have their views heard," he says.

He loves hearing their views. And he loves being able to see politicians in action. Bob McBarton feels that there's no shame in quitting if candidates run out of money or support by the time of the Iowa caucuses or the New Hampshire primary. Then, at least, they've given it their best shot. But, as he explained in his *Newsweek* article, "They can't talk about idealism and self-sacrifice and then walk away at the first sign of trouble. I expect politicians to try and turn a crisis around; after all, the *are* politicians. There is something to be said for someone who will stand up and fight. A little guts can't hurt a campaign for leader of the free world."

Mr. McBarton has been watching C-SPAN since 1984. He believes "it's a really good way to find out how democracy works." While watching, you'll often find him reading law briefs. After he finishes law school, he hopes to join a firm with connections to the political process. He has one Los Angeles firm in mind "where a lot of former Democratic candidates and officeholders have ended up. It also has a lot of up-and-coming people."

Whatever his future, it's a safe bet that Bob McBarton will always have a hand in politics. "I want to get involved with a campaign or person who can change things so that things can be better—a candidate that I can be proud of. A grassroots activist gets involved early on," he says. "There are a lot of people who are hooked on the romance of politics, only to be burned by the reality. I want to be involved. I hold no illusions of what I intend to be. I don't have a secret cache of 'McBarton For President' bumper stickers. What do I want to be? I don't know. At my age, what was Ronald Reagan doing?"   —*P.K.*
Bob McBarton watches C-SPAN on Century Cable of Southern California.

"The Area Man"

Michael McGough
Pittsburgh, Pennsylvania

For many Americans who watched the hearings, the nomination of Robert Bork to the Supreme Court in 1987 was a watershed event in U.S. judicial history. But did it play any differently for the folks in the judge's hometown of Pittsburgh, Pennsylvania?

When a local boy makes it to the major leagues, national news takes on a provincial meaning for the people who knew him when. But Michael McGough, editorial-page editor of one of the judge's hometown papers, the *Pittsburgh Post-Gazette,* disagrees. He's turned on his TV and seen a new age, where so-called hayseeds are glued to televised Senate Judiciary Committee hearings and following the scholarly ins and outs of jurisprudence. He sees a new trend towards a national community emerging "in the age of C-SPAN."

Mr. McGough's special beat is constitutional law and the courts. So when Robert Bork—the former U.S. solicitor general from Steel Town—defended his judicial philosophies to the Senate Judiciary Committee, Mr. McGough watched the televised hearings "almost nonstop," and wrote regular editorials as the nomination progressed. Yet as he worked, he knew that these hearings appealed to his readers not because their subject was a so-called "area man." Rather (as he was to write in a 1987

New Republic piece), he saw that "inside the Global Beltway, everyone's an Area Man."

Michael McGough, 36, a graduate of Allegheny College, has lived in Pittsburgh his entire life. A career in the fourth estate was almost a given for this self-described "lifetime news junkie," who was editorial-page editor of his high school newspaper and afternoon copy boy at the *Post-Gazette*. "We used to talk politics in the hall at school. Now when we do it, at least we get paid for it," he jests.

Mr. McGough's newspaper, in various incarnations, has been serving the people of Pittsburgh for 200 years. Its current daily circulation is 173,000. Mr. McGough says of his newspaper's editorial philosophy: "We're probably liberal on social issues, less so on economic issues, strong on civil rights and women's issues, and we support arms control negotiations." Although the paper endorsed President Carter and presidential candidate Walter Mondale, it has also endorsed President Nixon and past Republican governors of Pennsylvania.

C-SPAN's public affairs programming is common knowledge among the editors at the *Post-Gazette*. "We have a meeting every day with the executive editor and the other three editorial writers, and I would say a couple of times a week someone will make reference to something on C-SPAN," he notes.

In a format somewhat similar to C-SPAN's televised forays into the print world, the *Post-Gazette* has an unusual marriage with the local PBS affiliate station. Each evening they co-produce a broadcast from the paper's newsroom that features interviews with the writers talking about the lead editorial of the next day. "It's been an interesting experiment. I'm not sure how many people watch, but I think it would probably appeal to the same sort of people who are C-SPAN watchers," says Mr. McGough.

As a print journalist who covers politics, Michael McGough understands that the ever-increasing number of electronic eyes on the political scene "is a major part of the political process. It's really part of the story." And he believes that the press has been slow to get comfortable with this invincible union. "Not too long ago newspaper people were paranoid about television. There was a real reluctance to write about television in newspapers, especially television news. TV columnists wouldn't even write about anchor people." But he believes a good newspaper will treat television the way it does any other subject. "Just because somebody watches the Robert Bork hearings on C-SPAN, it doesn't mean they're not going to buy a newspaper. My guess is that you are really talking about the same people. That is, the person who is fixated enough on politics to actually sit and watch roll call votes and all sorts of procedural things is probably the same person who can't get enough of the subject generically."

The *Pittsburgh Post-Gazette* has a strong editorial page tradition that Michael McGough inherited when he took the post. "We have a very enlightened publisher who keeps a large, healthy, well-traveled editorial page staff," says Mr. McGough. Each day the editorial page carries four unsigned pieces, with at least one on national politics. With the exception of the paper's Washington correspondents, the editorial writers are usually the only staffers who speak to national issues. "For the record, most of us will insist that our real satisfaction comes from those hard-hitting local editorials that effect real changes in a benighted city government and have the additional advantage of guaranteed feedback. Deep down, however, we also treasure the opportunity to hold forth on more cosmic matters," wrote Mr. McGough in the *New Republic*.

But sometimes he questions whether the effort spent by "non-Washington, non-New York editors" covering national issues is worth it. "You know the drill," wrote Mr. McGough. "'In Pittsburgh, they're more concerned about the Steelers than they are about the Iran-contra affair.' At the risk of seeming defensive," he concludes, "there is something atavistic about this attitude in the age of C-SPAN. Today's precocious Pittsburgh kids can gather at a drugstore and watch Bob Bork's confirmation hearings on the tube, and then come up with their own instant analysis." —*K.M.*

Michael McGough receives C-SPAN on Tele-Communications Inc.

Bob Michel

Peoria, Illinois

In October 1977 the House of Representatives passed H. Res. 866, which established procedures for the televised coverage that would begin 17 months later. The profile of the House leadership was slightly different then: Now-retired Speaker Tip O'Neill (D-Massachusetts) had been at his post only nine months; Rep. Bob Michel (R-Illinois), the current minority leader, was Republican whip; and current whip Trent Lott (R-Mississippi) was a member of the House Rules Committee, which had reported the television resolution. All three had supported it.

Toward the end of that month, Reps. Michel and Lott were on the House floor to debate Section 4(b)(2) of the television resolution, which stated: "No coverage made available under this resolution nor any recording thereof shall be used for any political purpose."

"There are all kinds of ramifications to this issue, and there can be members who, frankly, may be hurt," minority whip Michel asserted. Noted for his attentiveness to the political needs of the minority, Rep. Michel was referring to less senior members of the House who might not get much air time and, thus, no political benefit. "Mr. Speaker, I think the committee would be well served to really look at all of the alternatives very carefully, lest any one of the members of this House be hurt in some fashion by whatever 'broadcast time' he does or does not get."

"I appreciate the gentleman's making these points," Rep. Lott responded, "because I am sure he is one of the members who is going to benefit from this live broadcast coverage."

Seven years later, Speaker O'Neill would look back on the history of House television and proclaim, "Television is here to stay now," implying perhaps that there were once some doubts about its prospects. And indeed there were. In 1982, some deemed House television "in jeopardy" in the aftermath of an internal controversy involving the political use of House footage. The target had been Rep. Michel himself.

The son of a French immigrant, Bob Michel, 65, represents the city where he was born—Peoria, Illinois. A combat infantryman in World War II, he was wounded in the Battle of the Bulge and awarded the Purple Heart, two bronze stars, and four battle stars. After graduating from Peoria's Bradley University with a degree in business administration in 1948, he came to Washington, D.C., to work as administrative assistant to Rep. Harold Velde, the congressman whom he succeeded in 1956. In 1972 he began to move up through the Republican leadership ranks. Fellow House Republicans elected him their leader in 1980.

That year was the beginning of a watershed era in the modern history of House Republicans. The party had not ruled the House since 1954, but with the working majorities behind President Reagan's budget and tax plans, the minority leader became, in the eyes of some political observers, a de facto majority leader.

Two years into the Reagan administration, however, the economy in Mr. Michel's hometown was hurting. A decline in the construction industry and in agriculture diminished demand for products of the city's leading employer, Caterpillar; the administration's decision to prohibit American participation in construction of the Soviet natural gas pipeline further cut Caterpillar's sales.

In his bid for re-election that year, Rep. Michel was challenged by a 31-year-old Democratic attorney named G. Douglas Stephens, who was making his first foray into national politics. Mr. Stephens' campaign tried to make the point that the incumbent was insensitive to the economic troubles of his constituents. To buttress that claim, Mr. Stephens aired a 30-second ad on Peoria television stations that featured Rep. Michel. The campaign commercial included a short clip taken from actual House floor footage in which the minority leader said that some Social Security recipients were "fairly well-heeled."

In November 1982, Rep. Michel won the race, but it was an unexpectedly close finish for the longtime House member, 52 percent to 48 percent.

Mr. Stephens' unprecedented use of House floor footage pointed up a significant irony: The fraternity of the House could enforce Section 4(b)(2)'s restriction against political use of footage only among its own. To attempt to enlarge that jurisdiction to nonmembers risked violating the First Amendment right to free speech. In the halls of Congress, members worried that their attempt to open up government to the people had a major flaw; the price of opening up the gavel-to-gavel proceedings of government to television could be the members' willingness to speak candidly on issues. In a video game version of mutual assured destruction, both parties began assembling an arsenal of potentially damaging House television footage to be used if the other side struck first.

The arsenal was never needed. House commitment to television enabled its members to reach a solution that left the cameras, and their comity, intact. Although the members could not stop challengers from using floor footage for political purposes (and Rep. Michel himself was firm in making that point) they did reaffirm the need to refrain from using House tapes themselves—a general understanding that extends to the parties' congressional campaign committees as well. So far the intent of Section 4(b)(2) to keep congressional telecasts out of the realm of partisan politics remains effective. Minority leader Michel is still the only congressman ever to be challenged with House footage.

Shortly after Rep. Michel's successful re-election he appeared on a C-SPAN call-in program. The topic was not his recent election, but rather his observations about the network's February 3, 1984, airing of the "Day in the Life of Congressman Bob Michel." In an unprecedented day-long program, C-SPAN had committed all of its cameras and technicians to give viewers a behind-the-scenes look at congressional life.

The minority leader was trailed by C-SPAN cameras from his home, to fund raisers, and to his office.

To a viewer who had watched the program and called to comment on Rep. Michel's rapport with his colleagues, the minority leader responded, "There's that one word: Trust. Confidence in one another. . . . It does go across party lines. After 28 years in Congress in the minority, I never get anything unless I'm able to get something from the other side. To have had to scratch and work for it has made me a better congressman."   —M.M.

At home in Peoria, Congressman Michel watches C-SPAN on UA Cable Systems of Illinois.

"The Bureau Chief"

Jack Nelson

Bethesda, Maryland

Jack Nelson, Washington, D.C., bureau chief of the *Los Angeles Times,* has never been shy about his goals. He wants his newspaper to be recognized as one of the very best in the country. "We are to the West Coast what the *New York Times* is to the East Coast," he says. "We have the second-largest bureau in Washington with 50 people, plus 25 foreign bureaus, and 13 domestic bureaus." Yet, in 1979, when his newspaper ran an article about a not-yet-operating cable service called C-SPAN, he was not yet satisfied that the *Times* was getting the national recognition it deserved.

Shortly after C-SPAN began operating, and perhaps with his newspaper's reputation in the back of his mind, Nelson visited the network's start-up facility. Today he says he can remember when C-SPAN was "a two-person operation in one room in Arlington, Virginia." He also recalls appearing as one of the network's first guests on the call-in program from that same little room and realizing that no one in Washington, D.C., could see him. Cable had not yet come to the nation's capital, but it had come, Mr. Nelson realized, to his home base of California and to the rest of the country. Thus, through the foresight and media savvy of Jack Nelson were sown the seeds of a long-standing professional relationship between the established and influential *Los Angeles Times* and the fledgling C-SPAN.

Why cooperate with C-SPAN? "The editors in Los Angeles," he says, "have always seen [exposure on C-SPAN] as an opportunity to get the *Los Angeles Times* known in other parts of the country and as a way of broadening communication."

The Southern California-based *Los Angeles Times* is the flagship of the Times Mirror Corporation, a communications company with media properties, including other newspapers and cable television systems, across the country. Its editors were sensitive to the possibility that their "flagship" paper could remain essentially regional in appeal and recognition. They, too, had an interest in having their daily work recognized beyond the more than one million Southern California homes that receive the paper every day.

The *Times* is often referred to as "the writer's paper" because it features long, in-depth stories. Says Mr. Nelson, "I recognized that we are complementary [to television]; our participation just might whet people's appetite for reading a longer piece." C-SPAN's format also presents an opportunity to be on television long enough to have a lasting impact. "People remember you," says Mr. Nelson. "Many of our reporters have appeared over the years. That's a kind of national exposure that gives us more clout in Washington. People begin to know that we're a big bureau. That helps our reporters get their telephone calls returned. It's also made our people more comfortable with television. Now they take it as a matter of course."

One reason the *Los Angeles Times* people take television "as a matter of course" is because under Mr. Nelson's supervision the paper has been associated with several C-SPAN firsts:

- The first "Day in the Life" program, in February 1981 (only one month after C-SPAN aired its first gavel-to-gavel congressional hearing), focused on the *Times'* Washington bureau. The network covered editorial meetings, interviewed *Times* correspondents, and took a video tour of the bureau. C-SPAN would use this format in at least 30 visits to other papers such as the *Des Moines Register* and *USA Today*.

- The first journalist to appear on C-SPAN's new regular morning call-in was *Los Angeles Times* Washington correspondent Paul Houston, in November 1982. More than 750 print reporters have followed him on that program.

- The first publication to allow C-SPAN to record one of its meetings of reporters and editors with high-level sources was the *Times,* in January 1983. The paper's "newsmaker breakfasts" are an occasional part of C-SPAN's fare. As Mr. Nelson says, the breakfasts have proven to "make good television and good news."

- The first major daily to carry C-SPAN's program listings was the *Los Angeles Times,* in May 1984. The move paved the way for other papers to list the network's often complicated schedule.

Mr. Nelson joined the *Times* in 1965, when he was hired to open an Atlanta bureau. An Alabama native, he began his journalism career in 1947 with the Biloxi, Mississippi, *Daily Herald.* He joined the *Atlanta Constitution* in 1952, and in 1960 won a Pulitzer Prize for a series that exposed conditions at Milledgeville (Georgia), the world's largest mental institution. At the *Times'* Atlanta bureau he covered the civil rights movement throughout the '60's. He moved to the Washington bureau in 1970, when the newspaper was making a deliberate effort to expand its Washington presence. Today he supervises the bureau's reporters and editors while continuing to cover politics and the White House.

As for using television to push the print medium, he notes, "Newspapers promote television and TV news when we report about them." Turnabout, then, is only natural. To support his equation he could point to the fact that the *Times* reported about C-SPAN from the beginning, or more accurately, from before its beginning: The first article to appear about C-SPAN in a major daily paper was in the *Los Angeles Times* in February 1979, one month before the network went on the air.

Mr. Nelson has talked with C-SPAN viewers a number of times via the call-ins. On one occasion in 1986, he brought his co-panelists from public television's "Washington Week in

Review" to C-SPAN. The group discussed its book, *Beyond Reagan: The Politics of Upheaval,* which Mr. Nelson had co-authored with program regulars Haynes Johnson of the *Washington Post,* Hedrick Smith of the *New York Times,* Charles McDowell of the *Richmond Times-Dispatch,* Charles Corddrey of the *Baltimore Sun,* and "Washington Week" moderator Paul Duke.

In April 1987, the bureau chief appeared again on C-SPAN during "Covering the South," a reunion at the University of Mississippi of journalists who had covered the civil rights struggle. Mr. Nelson, one of four organizers of the conference, had alerted C-SPAN about it two years ahead of time. Based on viewer response, it may have been one of the more provocative programs in the network's history.

When Mr. Nelson first sat down on C-SPAN's makeshift call-in set back in 1980, he recalls that he liked the idea of a network "that would bring in differing opinions and let viewers decide." Although his own organization dwarfed the small network, Mr. Nelson treated C-SPAN as an equal. From his paper, the network received news coverage, access to public affairs events, and a reliable supply of call-in guests.   —*P.P.*

The Los Angeles Times Washington Bureau receives C-SPAN through The Capitol Connection; at home, Jack Nelson subscribes to Cable TV Montgomery.

Marian Norby

Arlington, Virginia

In 1941, Marian Norby went to Washington, D.C., for a two-week vacation and never left. Since then, she's been around government enough to have seen just about everything. She started her career with the War Economic Administration and retired as the Air Force project director for President Jimmy Carter's Plain English Project. In between, she worked at the White House as a secretary during the Truman administration and rode "Give 'em Hell, Harry"'s famous whistle-stop train through the American heartland. She was the only secretary on the train, so she did all the dictation for President Truman's speeches and all the typing. "Whenever the train went around a curve, the typewriter would fly off the table," she says. She lost 20 pounds on that hectic trip.

It was a long journey for a girl from Kansas who grew up on a farm, 17 miles from the nearest village, in a house her father ordered from a Sears catalog and built himself. She can recall life in the dust bowl, when people would hang wet sheets over the windows during the day to keep the dust out. "The sheets would be mud by the afternoon."

When her family's farm was close to financial ruin, the policies of the Roosevelt administration, she says, helped save Ms. Norby, her younger sister, and her parents from destitution.

That's why she's a Democrat. "Only the Democrats cared about saving people," she claims.

Marian Norby's extensive past contact with the inner workings of the White House and Washington and present activities in political groups have led her to appreciate unedited coverage of Congress and political events. "What C-SPAN does is destroy the stereotypes," she says. "The press tends to create stereotypes. For instance, when I first went to work in the White House, I thought Congress was a bunch of lazy louts. That was the perception that existed and was backed up by columnists and commentators. The longer we worked with them, the more we found out that many of them worked very hard. Today, you can see what these congressmen are doing, and you can see the difference between the good ones and the bad ones."

Ms. Norby's perspective on the press developed while she was working on the Truman campaign. "There was a perception that Truman would not win, so the press merely backed up that perception by downplaying Truman's appeal out in the country," she says. At one point on the whistle-stop tour, she recalls stepping off the train into a crowd of journalists: "I was looking over the shoulder of one reporter, and I could see that he had written: 'Mr. Truman spoke here today to a crowd of about . . .' and he turned around to a policeman and asked, 'How many people are there here?' And the policeman said, '2,000.' And so the reporter continued, '. . . to a crowd of about 1,000.' So that's how the newspapers were distorting things." The result: that famous *Chicago Tribune* headline declaring a Thomas A. Dewey victory when, in fact, Truman had won.

One of the most striking things Marian Norby has seen on C-SPAN, she says, was the insider's look at the Iowa caucuses. (In 1984 and 1988, television viewers across the country could watch actual caucuses in progress.) "I got insight into how these people thought," she says. "It was unbelievable that I could sit here and hear the conversation in that Iowa farmer's living room."

And she also likes hearing the opinions of other viewers. "You can take the temperature of the country from the calls on the call-in show," she says. "Not long ago the attitude of most callers was: 'How dare you speak about my president that way!' These days, the callers are more skeptical: 'Why is the president sending those troops to the Persian Gulf?' And the callers are more likely to point out the contradictions in the president's policies."

But most important for Ms. Norby, complete coverage of hearings often yields information that members of the press omit in their haste to get the story out. The Senate confirmation hearing for Supreme Court Justice Antonin Scalia, she says, is a case in point. Long after the press had left, a woman lawyer from New York who had spent years studying Judge Scalia's record testified. Ms. Norby thought her testimony was "deadly." "The only thing left was the C-SPAN camera, and it alone caught the testimony," she recalls.

The next day she got a transcript of the remarks and gave it to a *Washington Post* columnist, who used it in a story that week. That, she says, was the only mention she saw in the press of that witness' revelations.

Indeed, Ms. Norby says she's become a "self-appointed monitor" for the many organizations she belongs to, including the National Organization for Women, the Women's Equity Action League, and the Woman's National Democratic Club. "When I watch TV or hear news that might be pertinent to something that they're working on, I alert my organization. I found out while working in the White House that people responsible for getting things done never have a chance to read the papers, so I try to help out by sending articles in the mail."

There is, of course, another reason Marian Norby likes in-depth politics on television: "It gives you something to tune to on Sundays besides football," she says.   —*P.W.*

Marian Norby watches C-SPAN on Cable TV Arlington.

"The County Administrator"

Robert O'Brien

Dover, Delaware

"We were kind of a little puffed up here in Delaware," recalls Robert O'Brien, a Dover Democrat who volunteered for the presidential campaign of Delaware Sen. Joseph Biden. "We had two people who were presidential candidates this year. I guess the world knows that now."

The world may know, but not long remember, that Delaware produced two major candidates in the 1988 presidential campaign—Sen. Biden, the first Delaware Democrat in a century to be a serious candidate for president, and former Gov. Pete DuPont (R). But the political world will not soon forget the unusual role that television played in the campaign of Delaware's junior senator. The *Almanac of American Politics* had written of him: "In an era dominated by the cool political medium of television, he is a hot politician." And it was television's unblinking eye that set in motion a chain of events that led to the candidate's withdrawal, a tremendous let-down for the would-be president and supporters like Robert O'Brien.

Mr. O'Brien, 53, is the county administrator for Delaware's mostly rural Kent County (population 105,000). He is responsible for formulating policy alternatives for elected officials and then implementing the decisions. He came to Kent County from New Castle County in 1968 as its first planning director; 15 years later the County Council appointed him to his current post. His wife Judith works to promote the local arts.

When Joe Biden was a New Castle County councilman, Robert O'Brien knew him well. And when, at age 29, Joe Biden ran for the U.S. Senate, Robert O'Brien supported him wholeheartedly. By the 1984 Senate campaign Judith O'Brien had joined the effort, too, organizing coffees and speaking events in the county. "When you get to know him as well as we do," Mr. O'Brien says, "it is impossible not to like him."

In the television age, getting to know the candidates "up close and personal" is a challenging proposition. C-SPAN's "Road to the White House" went on the campaign trail in January 1987, a year and a month before the Iowans cast the first votes of campaign '88. In the beginning, the program wound mostly through Iowa and New Hampshire, where candidates were testing their mettle in the "retail" politics of the early contests. The series' goal was to let voters across the country share the experience of voters in the early states. Viewers got to know not just the image the candidate attempts to portray in his commercials, but also the person himself; and to witness that presidential campaigns are often more grueling than glamorous, more monotonous than momentous.

Perhaps no one followed the series more closely than the campaign staffs themselves. Robert and Judith O'Brien were ad hoc Biden campaign operatives. They would get a call from the senator's Wilmington headquarters with news that the candidate would appear on C-SPAN at a certain time. The O'Briens would tape the program, and "we'd get it into the hands of his staff people. They'd view it, analyze it," Mr. O'Brien says.

In April 1987, in a "Road to the White House" episode, viewers saw the Delaware senator addressing a small gathering of voters in a Claremont, New Hampshire, kitchen. When a member of the group, 44-year-old teacher Frank Fahey, asked Sen. Biden what law school he attended and how well he did, the candidate shot back testily, "I think I have a much higher IQ than you do," and ran down a list of academic credentials—a full academic scholarship to law school, a finish in the top third of the class, three degrees from college, and an award for outstanding student in the political science department in college. Upon closer scrutiny, his credentials turned out to be exaggerated.

That scrutiny did not occur for another five months, however. When the program initially aired, the tone of the remarks, and not their content, drew some attention in the *Manchester Union Leader's* weekly "Granite Status" column, below a note about a judicial appointment. But in the Biden campaign offices and in the living rooms of people like Robert and Judith O'Brien, there was some immediate concern, Mr. O'Brien says, "about his rapport with some of his audiences."

In September, a rival campaign supplied the news media with what has been called an attack video demonstrating that Sen. Biden had lifted other politicians' passages for his own speeches. To compound the senator's problems, evidence surfaced that he had plagiarized sections of a law school paper. Eleanor Clift, a *Newsweek* reporter, was tipped off by an unnamed source about the earlier Claremont, New Hampshire, exchange. She telephoned C-SPAN and asked to look at the network's archival copy of the coffee klatsch video. Ms. Clift's subsequent story told of the New Hampshire incident and laid out Sen. Biden's true academic record in graphic detail. TV news programs requested copies of the C-SPAN tape, and the exchange was aired over and over. Delaware's hopeful called a press conference and withdrew on September 23, 1987.

That week, *Newsweek* wrote: "So far the question has been whodunit to Joe Biden. . . . It's an accepted game to spread negative research about one's opponent, as long as it's accurate. Beltway regulars . . . know which reporters to leak to. . . . But the more intriguing question may be whatdunit. It's the weapon that provides the surprise twist, and testifies to the new techno-political age. Biden was strangled with C-SPAN."

Half a year later, the Biden volunteer O'Briens would say, "It hurts because you believe in the guy and you support him, but you've got to know that it hurts him, too, and it hurts his family as well."

Yet the O'Briens don't blame the messenger. "Media coverage is a vital part of our lives, and it proves that the system works." —*P.K.*

The O'Briens subscribe to General Television Inc.

"The Caregiver"

Raymond O'Dette

Foster, Rhode Island

Raymond O'Dette, 70, keeps a leather-bound commonplace book. For many years, he has been writing down his impressions of his daily routine and recording the important events of his life. The marriage of a child or a grandchild's first tooth go into the book for preservation and rereading.

The book also bears entries offering insights into a larger world, a world that has become part of Raymond O'Dette's own existence. Mr. O'Dette watches government go through its own daily routine on television and jots down what he sees in his commonplace book. An entry about a visit to the doctor or a phone call from a friend sits side by side with a passage recounting what happened during a televised hearing of the House Special Committee on Aging. "The government is part of my life now," says Mr. O'Dette. He has discovered a whole new sphere watching Congress, opened himself up to it, and made it important. His unusual chronicle of government running through the life of an ordinary citizen would make an archive entry worthy of examination for future historians.

With his wife, Mr. O'Dette owns and runs a nursing home in rural Foster, Rhode Island. He gets up at 5:00 in the morning to help make breakfast for his residents, watching C-SPAN as he prepares their food. Each day he makes his rounds of the building and checks on everyone's well-being. Part of every day is spent watching C-SPAN or writing.

Despite his schedule, Mr. O'Dette claims that he is "fully retired" from the nursing home he and his wife have operated for more than 27 years. "We had a dream," he explains, "and we put it all together," starting with one bed, then six beds, then eight. Today, the Nancy Ann Convalescent Home has 17 workers and is home to 18 residents who range in age from 76 to 98 years.

Their philosophy at the home has been "to restore the dignity of these elderly people who so rightly deserve it. Someday I'm going to be old," Mr. O'Dette says, "and, besides, that's what life is about, the giving of oneself."

A few years ago, at the urging of a friend who is a C-SPAN fan, he installed a satellite dish on the nursing home grounds. Despite the many television offerings, the House of Representatives continually captures Mr. O'Dette's interest and attention. He observes members of Congress closely for signs of compassion. He keeps an eye out for what he detects as strength of character and dignity in public persons. He says that the House proceedings on television give him "a chance to get to know what they stand for."

Watching Congress has allowed Mr. O'Dette to watch the political process unfold in its own time according to its own rules. To better understand the legislative procedures, Mr. O'Dette consults *Gavel to Gavel,* a key to watching Congress, to guide him through the process of passing laws and reconciling budgets. By now Mr. O'Dette knows the way so well that he likes to think that if he were a younger man he would run for office himself: "I'd know the rules of the game."

He's proud of this new-found education, claiming "I've just missed so much in life. At this stage of my life I have all my marbles and I'm able to sit back and listen to this stuff, and comprehend it. I didn't get it in school."

Raymond O'Dette grew up in Providence, graduating from high school "back around the crash, when jobs were hard to come by." Unable to go to college, he instead found work doing "a little bit of everything."

He has not always held public officials in high regard. He says, "I had a sour impression of government, based on what I was reading in the newspapers." After exposure to the big picture that government presents on television, "I feel we have some brilliant men and women in Congress."

Writing about what he sees has helped him put it all in order and mull over ideas. When the telecasts are over, he can look back at the observations he has saved in his book. Like the House of Representatives itself, the book is a continuous, ongoing tableau of events, changes, and the daily compromises of life.

Although Mr. O'Dette is moved by politics, he says he's slowing down a bit these days, spending frequent afternoons relaxing in front of the television set: "I watch the leaves fall and watch C-SPAN." But he continues to make a special point of being available to others: "What I've been trying to accomplish in life," he says, "is being an understanding guy who lives on the block, who, if you need a helping hand, you could give him a ring." —S.S.

Raymond O'Dette watches C-SPAN on a satellite dish he installed on the grounds of his nursing home.

Thomas P. "Tip" O'Neill

Harwichport, Massachusetts

On many a pleasant Thursday night, his former aides say, House Speaker Thomas P. "Tip" O'Neill would slip away to his beloved Cape Cod for a weekend of golf. After all, even if the Congress were holding a Friday session, the speaker could tune in to C-SPAN to keep an eye on the floor, and he could phone instructions to his staff on Capitol Hill if he saw something he didn't like.

Years later, former House Speaker Tip O'Neill would call televising the House of Representatives "one of the best decisions I ever made." In 1977, his first year as speaker, the Massachusetts Democrat agreed to put House television on his agenda; by March 1979, the first live, gavel-to-gavel telecast of the House went out by satellite to 3.5 million cable homes. "Thanks to television, the House of Representatives is now recognized as the dominant branch of Congress," wrote Speaker O'Neill in his 1987 autobiography, *Man of the House.*

However, wary of its impact on the legislative process, Tip O'Neill had not always supported House television. "We were disgusted with how the major networks covered the Republican and Democratic conventions," he wrote. "If a delegate was picking his nose, that's what you'd see. . . . . No wonder so many of us were skittish."

But after six years of debate on the issue, the new speaker saw it was time to move ahead. So, with the help of Democratic Party leaders, a proposal was crafted that gave the office of the speaker control of the television cameras. "That," he says, "struck me as a reasonable compromise." On October 22, 1977, the House passed a measure permitting full coverage of its sessions—on its own terms and with tight controls—by a vote of 342–44.

After the measure passed, a telecommunications task force headed by Rep. Charlie Rose (D-North Carolina) helped Speaker O'Neill lay down the rules for the telecasts. A $1.6 million system was installed. Cameras would be trained on the speakers at the podium, and would not be allowed to pan the chamber. During 15-minute votes, an electronic vote tally would cover the screen. Proceedings of the legislative body would be covered live, uninterrupted, and "gavel-to-gavel" and would be offered to all accredited news organizations. Only C-SPAN, however, committed itself to telecasting the House of Representatives whenever it was in session.

The speaker recalls that some members of the House continued to grumble about the television measure after it passed. "Many of the members, of course, were skeptical. . . . Today, of course, it's hard to imagine Congress without it, and the results of our broadcasting experience have exceeded my wildest hopes," he says.

It may have taken a few years, but House TV gained a loyal following among those members who saw the potential of the unblinking television eye. "I see a young fellow come on the floor with a blue suit and a red necktie, hair groomed back, and an envelope under his arm," the speaker explained, "and I know that he's going to make a speech and that speech is for home consumption. His office has already notified the local media that he's going to be on and he's going to give a talk."

The audience for congressional telecasts grew as well. Just five years into its run, the speaker was calling the audience for Congress "unbelievable." One avid viewer was the speaker himself, who said, "I really enjoy it when I come in at night and put it on and see a committee hearing."

During his eight years of congressional TV coverage, the speaker became a familiar figure to many Americans. People began to recognize the speaker when they saw him in airports or on the street. Appearing in a televised interview with C-SPAN to mark House TV's fifth anniversary in early 1984, Speaker O'Neill said, "Television is here to stay now. . . . Everywhere I go, people say, 'Well, I saw so-and-so on the show,' or 'I listened to this bill,' or 'What are your views on that?'" He said he believed that coverage of the House had "whetted the curiosity of America as far as the running of the government is concerned," calling it "very informative for the American people."

Within months, though, a controversy would follow the speaker's rosy assessment. In May 1984, Speaker O'Neill asserted his control over the House cameras, provoking cries of protest from House Republicans and leading to a disruption on the House floor. In the process, the way that television covers the House underwent permanent change.

On May 10, 1984, the speaker ordered House cameras to break with precedent and provide a full view of the empty House chamber during Special Orders speeches. With Rep. Robert Walker (R-Pennsylvania) on the floor, the cameras for the first time showed a representative gesturing and talking to a chamber of empty seats.

Minority whip Trent Lott (R-Mississippi), watching in his office, dropped what he was doing and raced to the floor to denounce the surprise camera angle as "an underhanded, sneaky, politically motivated change." The press picked up on the story immediately and gave it the name of "Camscam"; *Washington Post* TV critic Tom Shales called it a "knockabout slugfest" and wrote that "the brouhaha over control of the cameras has ignited the House and in the process served to dramatize again the huge presence television has in the political process."

"Camscam" came to a head on May 15, when harsh words flew on the House floor between Rep. Newt Gingrich (R-Georgia) and Speaker O'Neill. Mr. O'Neill called a Gingrich speech "the lowest thing I have ever seen in my 32 years in Congress"—a remark that the House parliamentarian ruled out of order. The speaker's words were taken down and the phrase was struck from the official congressional record, the first such rebuke to a House speaker in this century.

In time, "Camscam" died down, but today the cameras continue to show the whole chamber during Special Orders, giving audiences a fuller view of the post-legislative business proceedings. Later, in response to an initiative by the Republican leadership, cameras also started showing varied shots of the House members during votes. Slowly, the early restrictions on what the viewing audience could see through television were easing.

Speaker O'Neill, 75, likes to say that his social policies brought many poor people into "the great American tent of opportunity." During his years as speaker, many Americans were brought into the halls of Congress via television. His decision to support televised coverage of the House of Representatives ushered in a new era of government accessibility. House TV went through its growing pains, but its success eventually influenced the Senate to follow suit, voting to let itself be televised in 1986. When future generations remember Tip O'Neill—the man who served the longest consecutive term as speaker—they may well remember him as the man who let Americans see their government at work.   —C.E.

Former House Speaker Tip O'Neill keeps his eye on Congress through Cape Cod Cablevision.

"The Cartoonist"

Mike Peters

Beavercreek, Ohio

Editorial cartoonist Mike Peters likes to use his cartoons to educate people, to focus their attention on things he thinks are "weird," and even to rile them up. "My cartoons kind of point out something; they say 'Here's something that I think is really stupid' or something that I would sure like to have changed. I always try to have a little twist in there to entertain people so they'll keep coming back to me. But there's no future, if you're an editorial cartoonist, in doing something just to have people enjoy it. You want to be affecting them somehow."

Mr. Peters has a wide audience for his brand of humor. His political cartoons are syndicated in 280 newspapers. In addition, 300 papers carry "Mother Goose and Grimm," his comic strip chronicling the trials of a collection of confused animals. His work has been printed in countless magazines and earned him numerous awards, including a 1981 Pulitzer Prize. Cartooning has been a lifetime vocation for Mr. Peters from his boyhood years in Ohio: "Ever since I was four, or something like that, I was always doing my little drawings." Forty years later, the youthful Mr. Peters works at home and delivers cartoons every day to his home paper, the *Dayton Daily News.*

Political cartoonists rely on political scandals, gaffes, and turmoil for inspiration. While Mr. Peters' political humor has a lighter cast than that wielded by his more vituperative colleagues in the business, his zany drawings often feature politicians with distended limbs, buggy eyes, and open mouths, and sometimes the politicians get mad: "We always get in trouble from whatever faction we're drawing. Somehow I'm always doing something terrible to them."

In order to ply his trade, Mr. Peters has to be aware of what politicians are doing. He also has to have an accurate idea of what they look like so that his pen can transform them into the wild creatures of his imagination. To fill these requirements, Mr. Peters often turns to C-SPAN for its continuous, uncut coverage of sessions of the House of Representatives and Senate.

"The main reason I watch is to stay abreast of what's happening in Congress. I turn it on for education," he says. "I turn it on because I'm fascinated by the process. I'm fascinated by being there and hearing the arguments and hearing who believes in what. I switch back to the news stations to see what's going on, but I have C-SPAN on all the time. It's like audible wallpaper. It's like sitting right next to an AP wire machine."

Mr. Peters finds that his intensive viewing of government on TV has increased his political awareness to the point that his cartoons sometimes jump the gun on the average citizen's knowledge of public events. They even occasionally jump the gun on his employers: "When I bring cartoons to the newspaper, the editor will not understand why I have drawn about certain topics, because all he's getting is the news off the wires or the stuff that he reads in our paper. That's how C-SPAN has changed my cartoons directly—I'm much more up-to-date. I'm much more timely."

Political cartoonists can be too timely, however. "You've got to guard yourself from being too current. Most people will know what's going on in two or three days from reading and from Dan Rather, but they won't have seen it that day on C-SPAN. Most people just don't have the time to watch. They're too busy making ball bearings and stuff."

Watching government officials gesticulate and cogitate on television also helps sharpen Mr. Peters' eye for the visual eccentricities of his targets. "That's one small thing that C-SPAN has given me. When you do a caricature from a picture, it's nothing like doing it from life, and C-SPAN is the next best thing. You can get a feel for the face, a feel for how the person's skull is actually formed, large forehead and small nose and stuff like that—things that you can't necessarily get from a photograph, but you can get from TV."

Mr. Peters says he looks at every person from two perspectives: as a citizen and as a cartoonist. "The editorial cartoonist in me loves Vice President George Bush and Sen. Paul Simon [D-Illinois] and people who make real good caricatures. I love Simon, not because I necessarily think he'd make a good president, but I love the way he looks. I would want this man to be my dogcatcher just so that I could draw him." Another Peters favorite is Sen. Jesse Helms (D-North Carolina): "He's really wild-eyed. His eyes are like a Picasso painting—they're on different planes going all different directions."

As a citizen, Mr. Peters says his opinion of Congress has changed for the better now that he has seen the legislature carry out its duties. "It turned my beliefs around about our elected officials being sleepy façades standing up there with their aides feeding them things. I found that our congressmen are literate, educated debaters, people who think on their feet, people who have convictions and strength and courage."

One politician in particular won over both the citizen and the cartoonist in Mr. Peters. During the 1988 presidential election, Mr. Peters watched C-SPAN's "Road to the White House" series, which introduced him to Sen. Joseph Biden (D-Delaware), then active on the stump as a candidate. "I thought, 'Man, that's the guy.' I woke my wife up the first time I saw him making a speech." Cartoonist Peters also took a liking to Sen. Biden's smile. Before Sen. Biden left the race, Mr. Peters' cartoons were "kind of nice toward Biden."

When not ticked off by Mr. Peters' depictions of their antics, politicians are often tickled. Some even ask him for original editions of his work. Those requests can rub Mr. Peters the wrong way: "It's kind of a put-down because you're usually trying to hurt these people. You're usually trying to say, 'Hey, you turkey!'" So, from time to time, Mr. Peters will send the cartoons and use the opportunity to write little notes at the bottom. "How many times can you write a politician and know *for sure* the guy is going to read it?"

The demands of Mr. Peters' career keep him tied to his

information sources. His free time is scarce, and he rarely goes away with his wife and three daughters. It's a pitfall of the trade, he laments. "Cartoonists never go on vacation. We always go wonderful places, but it's never a vacation. We're always working. I can't go somewhere unless it has C-SPAN and CNN and Federal Express so I can send the stuff back."

Mr. Peters works in a medium defined by the quick glance and the laugh on the run. ("The average amount of time that someone reads a cartoon is about three-and-a-half seconds," he says.) So it's ironic that he should use an ongoing, unhurried service to inform and shape his work. "C-SPAN is all depth. It's all deep background. That's the beauty. It's the 'network of record,' and I think that's one of those extremely appealing things for me."

In 1983, the network devoted a full week of call-in programs to editorial cartoonists. Mr. Peters appeared on one of the programs. He wore a colorful striped sweater and carried a big drawing pad and a thick black magic marker. As he took viewers' questions, the cartoonist drew big, loopy renditions of President Reagan. As he responded to the questions, he waved his arms around, pointed, smiled, laughed, looking for all the world like a man who enjoys his job very, very much.   —*N.G.*

Mike Peters is a subscriber of Continental Cablevision.

"The Golden Fleecer"

William Proxmire
Madison, Wisconsin

Not everyone is enthusiastic about gavel-to-gavel coverage of the Senate. Today, more than two years after Senate television's inaugural, Sen. William Proxmire (D-Wisconsin) has a plan for televised Senate proceedings: "Turn off the lights, sell the cameras, close down televising of Senate proceedings, and send the proceeds to the treasury to help reduce the deficit."

One of 21 senators who voted against televising the Senate, the soon-to-retire William Proxmire remains the most outspoken of the lot. The 30-year veteran of the Senate didn't like the idea of televising Congress when it was in the conceptual stage, and, true to his convictions, he continues to oppose the idea. On the first anniversary of Senate TV, he took to the floor to proclaim: "Nobody, I mean nobody, is watching."

About 15 million homes currently receive Senate telecasts carried live on the C-SPAN II network. But the skeptical senator estimates a zero audience share for Senate television, based on the "up to 1,000 letters" he receives each day and his personal conversations with constituents when he goes back home: "I have people tell me or write me that they have read my speeches in the *Congressional Record,* or they tell me they have sat in the Senate gallery and heard my speeches. But response from a TV audience? Never." And, notes the senator, "I speak daily on the floor on controversial issues."

On June 29, 1986, the day the Senate debated and approved permanent television coverage, Sen. Proxmire argued that cameras would capture members in undignified moments and that regulations banning candidates from using congressional debate in campaign ads could not be enforced. He envisioned "bloopers programs" based on Senate television, adding, "Who doesn't make 25 seconds of blunders over five years? I hope we have not blindly opened a Pandora's box, and I am afraid we have done that."

Sen. Proxmire warned his colleagues that "television will make it easier for demagogues to win election to the Senate." He calls television the "the Che Guevara of modern society . . . a revolutionary tool of such power that even the firebrands of the American Revolution—Patrick Henry or Sam Adams—would think twice before approving it." He believes television makes it more difficult than ever to make progress. "Instead of an institution where sharp differences are ground down and compromised, this floor will become a place where they are sharpened."

But beyond the "demagogues" pandering to the public eye, Sen. Proxmire is convinced that there's really not much of a show to be seen in the well of the Senate. Back-to-back quorum calls, he claims, can take the zip out of any issue of great moment. Instead of locking horns on the Senate floor, the senators are off privately negotiating their differences. Viewers look for an exciting debate, and what they get is "boring, boring, boring," insists Sen. Proxmire. How boring? He says it "may drive Sominex off the market."

Sen. Proxmire's opposition to cameras is consistent with his no-frills approach to Congress. During his many years in the Senate, he's gained fame for his opposition to what he considers wasteful government spending. He consistently annoys his colleagues on both sides of the aisle by refusing to support congressional salary increases and by opposing the development of a deluxe gym in the Hart Senate Office Building.

Through the years, the senator has earned national recognition for the monthly award he bestows on government institutions that he thinks spend foolishly. His "Golden Fleece" has been awarded to such questionable government projects as a $6,000, 17-page Army report on "How to Buy a Bottle of Worcestershire Sauce," and a National Institutes of Health

$103,000 project to study the effects of tequila and gin on the behavior of fighting fish. The award is also given to pioneers of prudence in spending, like Max Cleland, a paraplegic and former veterans administrator, who declined the use of a chauffeur-driven limousine, and instead drove himself to work.

Senate television, however, has not yet been honored with the "Golden Fleece." Despite the myriad faults he claims to find with it, Sen. Proxmire is promoting one application for TV in Congress in keeping with his fiscal philosophy. He told colleagues he'd like to flash Senate campaign contributions across the screen as the lawmakers vote on legislation that would affect the donating special interest groups. So far, fellow lawmakers have failed to enact his proposal.

Despite his protestations, the man who predicted TV would turn the Senate into a "vaudeville act" came prepared on the first day of Senate TV with show-and-tell tools to enhance his daily speech. Decrying the cost of President Reagan's Strategic Defense Initiative, he displayed a red and blue, hand-lettered chart. He also exercised an extra bit of sartorial flair for the occasion: His blue tie was emblazoned with the words: "Wisconsin is Great."   —J.E.

Sen. Proxmire's Capitol Hill office receives C-SPAN and C-SPAN II through an internal congressional cable system.

"The Priest"

John Putka

Cincinnati, Ohio

When you say the words "Special Orders" to hungry adolescents, they most likely think of cheese and lettuce, and "special orders don't upset us!" But Father John Putka of Cincinnati's Moeller High School says that the young men in his political theory class seem to have an appetite for another version of Special Orders—those offered up at the end of each day in the U.S. House of Representatives. In fact, the students were so taken with the legislative procedure, which they watch on C-SPAN's cablecasts of House floor sessions, that they introduced the concept into their student government meetings. Now, at the end of their sessions, anyone can be recognized to speak on any topic.

We learned about Father John Putka in 1985, when he wrote an enthusiastic letter to C-SPAN about his students' interest in Congress:

> Several of my students have become "C-SPAN junkies," and thrive on the telecasts of the House in session. Many of them have become fascinated by the use of Special Orders to call attention to significant issues. Congressmen Newt Gingrich, Vin Weber, Bob Walker, and others are well-known to the students, and in discussions they refer to what "Newt"

or "Bob" or "Vin" had to say on the House floor with so casual a reference that you would think that they were referring to mutual friends or someone in school.

Father Putka, who reads the *Congressional Record* every day, has always been interested in politics and government, and has passed on his enthusiasm to his students at Moeller High. He takes about 40 students to Washington, D.C., each year for a school trip, and, by using C-SPAN in the classroom, has familiarized his classes with the workings of government. In years past, the itinerary for the Washington trip included lengthy visits to the House and Senate galleries. But that has changed, because Father Putka believes that one can actually learn more by watching the floor proceedings on television. He says his students agree.

"I think C-SPAN is much better than actually watching Congress in session," says Father Putka. "When you're sitting in the gallery at a distance, unless you're really on the ball, you have no idea what the procedures are, what they're talking about. You know that if you go in when they're voting, it's just absolute chaos. It looks like a zoo; you don't know what's happening. With C-SPAN, however, you do know. You've got the name of the member up there, where he's from, what his party is, and every now and then they run across the screen what's being debated, or what the pending business is. And during the votes they tell you what's going on, and you can see the running tabulations. It's much better."

Father Putka, a 49-year-old Marianist priest, lives in a religious community in Cincinnati, Ohio. He holds a doctorate from the University of Cincinnati, where he did his dissertation on the Supreme Court and judicial activism. While doing theological graduate work at Georgetown University in Washington, D.C., Father Putka worked as an intern in the office of former Sen. Barry Goldwater (R-Arizona).

For some, telling students to watch television as a study tool may seem like telling them to use Cliff Notes instead of reading the novel. Father Putka admits that using television in the classroom can make teaching easier "because students respond well to video." But he always links the TV assignment with some written work and some specific class discussion:

In other words, there will be a test. "It's so easy to watch something," he says, "and because you watch it, sometimes you give way to a fallacy, 'Well, I saw it, I watched it, therefore I understand it.' But that's not true. Just because you witness something doesn't mean you understand it or you realize what's going on."

Father John Putka subscribes to Tip O'Neill's famous observation that "all politics is local," but he applies the rule not to issues but to people. "If voters like their local congressman, they're going to vote for him over and over again, and most of them don't even realize how he votes on most major issues." Thus, when his students look at politics, particularly election campaigns, he admonishes them "to look at the personalities involved and to see the extent to which the personalities affect the outcome of the campaign and the eventual outcome of the election. They are very naive in terms of democracy: They actually think people are very conscious of the issues and they know how people stand and all that."

Joe Burbee, a 20-year-old junior at Miami University in Oxford, Ohio, and former Moeller High student, remembers Father Putka as the teacher whom everyone admired. "His lectures were scintillating, packed with information," he recalls. "He was always adding little asides to political theory." Joe says that even though Father Putka was his only teacher who used C-SPAN in the classroom, he was the teacher who least needed visual aids to enhance his lectures. Father John's classes were never monotonous, insists Joe, and televised portions of House debate in the class usually added valuable insight to the lectures.

Joe, who has been interested in politics since the eighth grade because he "was bored with everything else," says that he was sometimes amazed at the number of classmates who acquired the C-SPAN habit. "They would come up to me and talk to me about it in school. They'd say, 'Joe, I saw this debate on C-SPAN last night,' and it would shock me that they were often football players, and people you would never think would be watching C-SPAN."

Father Putka's annual trip to Washington, D.C., made a lasting impression on Joe Burbee. Father Putka thinks that Joe has a future in politics, and if Joe's assessment of his former teacher is true, then Father Putka is probably correct. "Father

John knows everything about Washington," Joe says. "The neat thing that Father John does is, he knows a lot of these people who work in the Capitol. So we're following him around, and all these signs say 'Senators Only,' and we're walking right past them and going up these stairs. We went into Tip O'Neill's office. And we were on the steps of the Capitol and Ted Kennedy walked out and Father John ran over and told him he had a group of students visiting from Ohio. He asked, 'Won't you come over and tell us something about what you do?' And he came over."

Joe says "I think Ted Kennedy is probably the most impressive person I've ever met," which is generous, bipartisan acclaim from the student who calls Republican Newt Gingrich "my hero." Yet Joe saves his highest praise for the man who taught him to pay attention to people instead of labels. "I try to pattern my life after him. He's always on top of everything, very organized, very intelligent, very articulate, and those are the things I'm trying to work up to. And I guess Father John would be the ultimate kind of person I'd like to be." —*M.C.*

Father Putka and his students watch Congress on Warner Cable Communications.

"The President"

Ronald Reagan
Washington, D.C.

In the days of Abraham Lincoln, presidents could check on Congress with little ado. If Mr. Lincoln happened to be curious about what congressmen were discussing on the floor, he'd simply put on his stovepipe hat and ride down Pennsylvania Avenue to the Capitol. If it were a nice day, he might even walk.

Today, of course, no president could ever simply stroll out into the streets or sit in the Capitol. A swarm of schedulers, aides, and Secret Service agents surround the president at all times. Any place he is going to be has to be checked, wired, and patrolled. Security considerations have made a congressional gallery seat off limits to the president. And, until recently, modern presidents couldn't have instantaneous knowledge of pending legislation. They had to rely on the telephone calls of aides to fill them in on what was going on.

Such was the case until President Ronald Reagan was connected to C-SPAN's live, unedited telecasts of Congress in 1982. President Reagan now watches Congress regularly from a television set in a small study adjoining the Oval Office. He has other C-SPAN hookups in his private residence at the White House.

When the first telecast of the House took place in 1979, Washington was not wired for cable. Government buildings and homes could not receive the service. That included the residence at 1600 Pennsylvania Avenue. Duluth housewives and Hawaiian retirees could watch Congress deliberate national issues, but not the president of the United States.

In late 1981, George Mason University Prof. Mike Kelley started The Capitol Connection, a microwave transmission service that made C-SPAN and other educational programs available to Washington, D.C., businesses. The White House signed up for the service in early 1982. Ever-present security regulations prevented The Capitol Connection's technicians from entering the White House, so the antenna was passed through the White House gate. President Reagan was ready to watch Congress make decisions on contra aid, the budget, and the war on drugs.

Soon afterwards, White House insiders began to tell tales about the president's Congress-watching. President Reagan's television set, they said, was often tuned to channel 10, which picked up C-SPAN. On December 23, 1982, The *New York Times'* "Washington Talk" column reported: "Mr. Reagan has C-SPAN, the cable-satellite network that televises House sessions, in both his living and working quarters. He was riveted to his set during the recent House debate on the MX missile, even as he shaved. Presumably the president uses an electric razor; how else to explain the lack of nicks on his chin after that particular debate, which ended with the House killing the missile project?"

House members would report that they occasionally received telephone calls in the House cloakrooms directly from President Reagan after they had made speeches on the floor. He would call to set them straight on their facts, or try to change their minds about issues. Rep. Robert Walker (R-Pennsylvania) says the president is "an avid viewer. . . . A lot of times he's said to me, 'Bob, I saw your speech on C-SPAN.'"

President Reagan's habit of picking up the phone to make surprise calls to people he'd seen on C-SPAN suggested that he was watching more than just Congress. In five exclusive appearances arranged in conjunction with the Close Up Foundation, President Reagan met with high school students at the Old Executive Office Building to answer their questions face to face. C-SPAN televised the half-hour student question-and-answer sessions. At the end of two of those sessions in

1983, the students returned to C-SPAN's Capitol Hill studio to review their encounter with the chief executive on live television. As they spoke, a phone call came into the studio—it was the president, who had been watching the students on his White House television. President Reagan phoned to give the students a chance to ask a few more questions.

On another occasion, the president placed a call to a reporter to protest a statement she had made about him on C-SPAN. On a June 1984 morning call-in program, *Los Angeles Times* reporter Betty Cuniberti said that presidential aides often "roped off" the president from reporters who covered White House social functions, fearing that President Reagan might make a gaffe. The president happened to be watching a replay of that program. The next day, Ms. Cuniberti received a call from President Reagan.

"I was watching you on television last night, and something you said touched a nerve," the president told Ms. Cuniberti. "This is not a complaint, and this is not your fault, but I am frustrated by the continuing belief that I have to be protected from reporters because I say so many wrong things." Gently but firmly, the president challenged reporters to send him a list of his supposed mistakes. "Every time they've said I was wrong, I checked it out and found that I was right and they were wrong."

President Reagan has confronted others he has seen on C-SPAN with what he feels are misrepresentations of his record. Once, during a National Governors' Association meeting, President Reagan confronted then-Gov. Anthony Earl (D-Wisconsin) as the governors made their way through a receiving line at a White House function. "I was watching television," the president said, "and I heard some criticisms that were unfair, that we have benefited the rich at the expense of those who aren't rich." As it does each year, C-SPAN had covered that day's entire National Governors' Association session, during which the governors had proposed military spending cuts and tax increases.

Even as recently as Harry Truman's administration, presidents could stroll out to Pennsylvania Avenue, enter a nearby card shop, and chat with ordinary citizens to find out what was on their minds. Today, such casual, easy presidential contact with the public is obviously impossible. A president can rarely get a sense of public opinion except through the hard numbers of polls and surveys.

President Reagan, though, has found a way to listen to the concerns of the man on the street. "I'm a fan of C-SPAN's national call-in shows," he told executives of the cable television industry. "People across the country phone questions and comments on the issues of the day. I am continually struck by the sophistication and intelligence of the questions that are asked. And I think it shows once again that the old Washington opinion that the people in this town are way ahead of the people 'out there' is all wrong. In fact, more often than not, the people out there are way ahead of us."   —M.C.

The White House is served by The Capitol Connection.

"The Camscammer"

T.R. Reid

Denver, Colorado

It was the end of the day and official legislative business on the floor of the House of Representatives had ended when someone handed Rep. Robert S. Walker (R-Pennsylvania) a note that enraged him. Unbeknownst to Rep. Walker, who was making an after-hours speech, the House TV cameras weren't focused just on him. Instead, they were showing the nationwide TV audience a full, wide shot of the lawmaker talking to an empty chamber. It was the first time in five years of televised gavel-to-gavel proceedings that the House cameras had deviated from the policy of focusing only on the person speaking.

"A cheap political trick," said Rep. Walker of the sudden decision by then-House Speaker Thomas P. (Tip) O'Neill, Jr. (D-Massachusetts) to order the TV cameras to show the nearly vacant House chamber. Over at the *Washington Post,* reporter T.R. ("Tom") Reid, who covered the May 1984 story, described it to his readers as "Capitol Hill's newest situation comedy." He even coined a new term for the political brouhaha: "Move over, Abscam! Step aside, Debategate! Make room for official Washington's latest political scandal: Camscam."

As editor of the *Post*'s "Federal Page," a daily section on the activities of the federal government, Tom Reid was familiar with Congressman Walker. A couple of months earlier, his editors, "who know something about the world, were really stunned that a guy like Bob Walker, who is pretty much a nonentity in official Washington, had a national following," Mr. Reid said. They asked him to write a background piece about the House on television.

Long fascinated by technology (he pens a regular column on computers and is the author of a book on the same subject), Tom Reid decided that one way to learn about C-SPAN was to experience it for himself. He spent an hour on a live call-in program so he could talk directly with viewers about their Congress-watching, encouraging those who couldn't get through to send their comments to him at the newspaper. His article, "The Best Little Soap Opera on Cable," appeared in the *Post* in April 1984, one month before the turmoil erupted in the House.

Aspects of "Camscam" resulted in nearly 10 articles bearing T.R. Reid's byline. Now Denver bureau chief for the *Post,* Mr. Reid recalls that at the time the affair occurred, he and his colleagues thought the debate reflected fundamental tensions in the institution and the battle over Special Orders rather than concern about TV coverage. "Now I think that's wrong," he says. "I've changed my mind. I think C-SPAN is a fundamentally important part of modern democracy."

Tom Reid, a Baltimore native, graduated from Princeton and has a law degree from George Washington University. He joined the *Post*'s national news staff in 1977, specializing in congressional and political affairs. He was named editor of the *Washington Post*'s "Federal Page" in 1981.

Readers of the *Post* will always see Tom Reid's articles bearing the byline "T.R. Reid." He explains why:

"My father is Thomas R. Reid, same name. Years ago I was freelance writing in Japan. I was writing for a magazine I had never seen in Japan called *Oui*—it's a dirtier *Playboy*. I didn't know it at the time, but I was writing stuff, which they would edit to make much more racy. I couldn't see this magazine. I didn't know. And my dad writes me a letter saying, 'Stop putting my name in that filthy magazine!' I changed my byline."

Shortly after the Camscam articles, he moved to Denver for personal reasons—so his wife could be near her family— but says he does not feel out of touch with Capitol Hill. "I discovered when I moved out of Washington that I didn't lose my love for, and fascination with, Congress—and never will."

Like others across the country, Tom Reid is watching Congress on television. "The real use for C-SPAN," he says, "is further out of Washington." Mr. Reid believes that the public's initial response to viewing lawmakers on television is often surprise at seeing how human they are. "Many of them are not articulate people," he says. "The guy on your town school board could be in Congress and do just as well," he says. "Once you internalize that realization, then you watch a little longer, and you sense that, while they are human, they are incredibly concerned and hard-working and energetic about serving the country."

"I think in the end it enhances people's feelings for Congress. And it certainly gets them involved. They know more and they know the people. I think it's sort of turned Congress into a town meeting," says Mr. Reid, "and it encourages people to walk up to congressmen they recognize on the street and start talking to them."

In fact, Mr. Reid believes that public recognition of House members was a key reason the Senate decided to televise its proceedings: "People knew their congressmen better than they knew their senators."

In a way Tom Reid considers himself to be even closer to Congress now that he lives in Colorado: "One of the things I noticed was that the debates are a lot more interesting when you're looking at the person talking. I've spent my life listening to congressional debates from the press gallery. I was always looking at the backs of their heads."

Ironically, Tom Reid can't watch the network at home right now. Because his children were watching "too many music videos," the Reids had their cable disconnected. Now, Tom Reid only sees C-SPAN while on the road.

However, the Reid children may yet succeed in capitalizing on one of the more inventive uses of C-SPAN mentioned in these chapters: "There's a major war on among all of my children to get cable back," he says. "And one of the arguments is that they'll let me watch C-SPAN more if I bring back the cable." —N.G.

Once the family cable conflict is resolved, Tom Reid will be able to watch C-SPAN on Mile Hi Cablevision.

"The Role Model"

Barbara Reynolds

Washington, D.C.

Barbara Reynolds, editor of *USA Today*'s "Inquiry" page, has a vision in mind. "I want to bring more black role models into the paper and help to correct the wrongs that have existed and endured. . . . My mission, if you want to use that word, is broad. Excellence will come about when there is no color, no gender." One way that Ms. Reynolds hopes to uphold positive images of blacks is with the publication of her book, *And Still We Rise: Interviews with 50 Black Role Models*. Ms. Reynolds' work is among the first published by *USA Today* Books.

And Still We Rise, a collection of interviews from the "Inquiry" page, is a labor of love for Ms. Reynolds. The book includes interviews with athletes, activists, and educators. Entertainers such as Bill Cosby and Oprah Winfrey, journalists Tony Brown and Carl Rowan, and black politicians like Reps. Mervyn Dymally (D-California) and Cardiss Collins (D-Illinois) are profiled in character sketches and asked their views on work and life.

Ms. Reynolds is a familiar figure to viewers who have watched C-SPAN's annual telecasts of "A Day in the Life of *USA Today*." Each anniversary date since the paper's first in 1983, C-SPAN has featured an 11-hour live telecast of *USA Today*'s operations. The program covers editor John Quinn and his staff, from the morning meetings when they plan the paper until the evening when they "put it to bed." With a daily circulation of 1.5 million, and an estimated readership of 5.5 million, *USA Today* is readily available to C-SPAN viewers nationwide. And, through call-ins with the *USA Today* staff and coverage of editorial board meetings, viewers can watch the step-by-step process of assembling a daily paper.

Ms. Reynolds says that those telecasts catch the true spirit of *USA Today*'s operations. But, she adds, when the staff hears C-SPAN is coming "the ties go on and I try to remember to put my make up on." She also takes time to call her family in Ohio so they can "let me know how I look."

Barbara Reynolds says that "Day in the Life" telecasts help viewers understand newspaper operations, and also give *USA Today* staffers "a tool to evaluate ourselves, and the process." C-SPAN cameras have captured entire editorial board meetings, watching as the group selects a topic to be covered on the opinion and editorial pages and develops the editorial position the paper will take.

During one of those televised editorial meetings Ms. Reynolds characteristically stuck her neck out. "We had a debate on creationism, and I was the only one who didn't agree. I believe that creationism should be taught in the schools, maybe next to evolution, but certainly taught. I stood firm. . . . After the meeting, I was a little down. I said, 'Dag, nobody agrees with me.'" Then, during the viewer call-in portion, calls came in "11 to one on my side. Everybody said, 'Barbara, we support your position,' and took the rest of the board to task. That convinced me that in my position as a Christian on that board I was going to stand even firmer. . . . No more backing down."

One issue that the editorial board took a strong stand on was Senate television. Before the Senate voted to allow cameras into its chamber, the *USA Today* editorial board encouraged the move with unanimous approval. "We do everything to try to protect First Amendment rights. And television in the Senate, I feel, enhances our understanding of the process," she says. Today, Barbara Reynolds and other members of the editorial board tune in to Senate debates and other C-SPAN telecasts for background on issues they cover.

Ms. Reynolds also says that one of her C-SPAN appearances may have inspired her next book. "When I was on a call-in show, people calling in had so many weird ideas about the role of black mayors. I said that black mayors were the crown jewels of America. It made somebody mad, but I could prove it. That may be the genesis of a book, something that came right across on C-SPAN."

An instinctive inclination drew Ms. Reynolds to writing as a teen-ager in Columbus, Ohio, in the 1960s. "It was a natural. All I could ever do was write. When I was 14 or 15 I was writing short stories. People in town would say, 'Barbara, she's the writer.'" After graduating from Ohio State in 1967, she joined the staff of the *Cleveland Call & Post,* covering the black community. "The metropolitan newspapers didn't hire blacks. It was the only training ground blacks could get." Stints at the *Cleveland Press* and *Ebony* magazine followed. Ms. Reynolds became an urban affairs reporter for the *Chicago Tribune* in 1972, in the meantime writing freelance articles, teaching, and founding *Dollars and Sense* magazine, a periodical for black professionals. In 1981, "disillusioned" with the *Chicago Tribune,* Ms. Reynolds established her own news service.

She joined the staff of *USA Today* in 1983, a career move she likens to "a religious experience. . . . It's a multimedia operation here. A creative mind can find many areas to explore without going outside of Gannett. . . . It's hard to believe that you could wind up like this after you'd always been told that you couldn't write, or couldn't make it, or that you didn't even belong in journalism. One day, you look up, and you're respected, and people want to know your views."

Gannett's production of Ms. Reynolds' book gives her hope for the kind of society she envisions. "Black people usually come last, but this is one of the first books Gannett is going to publish." She points out that a black artist designed the cover and that her senior editor is a black woman from the staff of *USA Today.* "When you lay the burden of race down and stop fussing about it, there are so many things we share in common," she says. "We can just be creative and we don't have to argue—it's amazing what you can do."   —*M.C.*

The USA Today *offices receive C-SPAN programming via Cable TV Arlington.*

"The Crusader"

Brent Riley

Logan, Utah

If you spend enough time on Capitol Hill, you're bound to run into a few people like Brent Riley, people so committed to particular issues that they travel to Washington, D.C., at their own expense to patrol the hallways of Congress. Their hope is to garner that seemingly elusive Washington commodity—the personal, if fleeting, attention of lawmakers.

For Brent Riley, a 43-year-old youth counselor from Utah, the issue is the Middle East. His latent passion for Arab-Israeli affairs surfaced about 10 years ago when he engaged in long conversations with a close friend and his new Palestinian wife. "Meeting her just sparked an interest that was already there," he explains.

Their friendly discussions began to call into question all Mr. Riley's previously held ideas on the Middle East. Intrigued, he sought more and more information on the region and on U.S. policies toward it, finding that the more he learned, the more upset he became. He came to believe that "the prevailing views do not convey the reality of the area," and is convinced that the U.S. government "is not keeping its obligation to help the Israelis and the Palestinians reach a solution."

Being an activist by nature, Brent Riley decided to do what he could to advance the issue, embarking on a campaign to inform politicians and journalists. At one point, deciding that the "average senator doesn't know very much about the Middle East and doesn't get very good information," Mr. Riley found a good price on blank videotapes and set about making copies of two televised documentaries on the Middle East that he believed would accelerate his information campaign. In all, he thinks he gave copies of these tapes to 50 senators—"either personally, or to someone on their staffs." He would show up where he expected them to be, stopping individual senators for hallway briefings.

Earlier lobbying experiences had taught him "not to be too overbearing or pushy" when meeting members of Congress. Although one senator who chairs a key subcommittee spurned Brent Riley's attempts at dialogue, he reports that most of his self-styled lobbying experiences "have been pretty good."

The Middle East isn't the only cause that motivates Brent Riley. Nuclear waste disposal and other ecological issues are also subjects that keep him percolating.

Love of the environment can come easily to a person living in Logan, Utah, a city of some 27,000 people that's surrounded by imposing mountains and national forests. Brent Riley's not native to the area; he grew up in Virginia and was raised as a Mormon. His first years in Utah were spent at Brigham Young University, where he fell in love with the scenic beauty of the West. He has lived in Southern California, Arizona, Washington state, and other parts of Utah.

The city of Logan is home to Utah State University, where Mr. Riley is currently working on a master's degree in journalism. He was attending Utah State University full-time until his father, still living in Virginia, became ill. Frequent trips back East forced Mr. Riley to cut back on his studies, although it allowed him more time to visit Capitol Hill.

For Mr. Riley, studying journalism is not necessarily a means to the obvious—a media career. In fact, one may never see a Brent Riley byline, since it's his firmly held conviction that journalists shouldn't be political activists. Journalism is a way for him to see what he considers "the larger picture." He says it should supply a context for events. "Personally, I get fired up or driven when the collective viewpoint is off track and you get leaders talking in a way that shows they are not incorporating the larger picture. Then I'm in a state of discontent and agitation."

Whatever the burning issue, he'll likely go it alone in his lobbying efforts, enjoying "the freedom of not being restricted to having to speak for an organization."

Back in Utah, Mr. Riley stays in touch with Congress the way other self-styled activists often do—by tuning in to C-SPAN on his local cable system, with his audio recorder on standby to record notable remarks. Frequently, he'll fire off letters to members of Congress or journalists after hearing them speak about the Middle East.

"I've always been one who's stood up for the underdog," he explains. "I don't like unfairness, so if something comes along, I just have to pipe up about it."   —K.B.

Mr. Riley watches C-SPAN on The Cable Company of Logan.

"The Rancher"

Joyce Robinson
Great Falls, Montana

Rancher and farmer Joyce Kropp Robinson sticks to a few sound principles to keep things running on her land: "Hard work, an informed mind, and a willingness to never count the hours or the days, but to just go forward." The native Montanan's skill at growing wheat and barley and raising cattle has won her the respect of her neighbors. When Ms. Robinson has trained her vision and tenacity away from the day-to-day labor and hard numbers of running a ranch, she has lobbied for farmers in Washington, D.C., testifying before congressional committees on agribusiness and throwing herself into the fight to get the farmer a fair deal. In the thick of country life, Ms. Robinson uses C-SPAN to help stay informed: "Out here in the rural USA, you could get very narrow. We're working so doggone hard to make a dollar in agriculture, we can become very confined. These politicians could come through here and tell us anything. Oh, boy, they'll have to tell us the truth now," she laughs, "because we can see it on C-SPAN."

Ms. Robinson, part of a third generation of family ranchers (the Kropp family has been known among sheep producers since 1880) was born and raised in Montana. The state, she says "is the grandest of all the 50." She's a graduate of Northern Montana College and is now president and chairman of the

Joyce K. Robinson Ranch Corporation, a family-run business. Her main ranch lies near Choteau, a town of 2,000 in Teton County. With her children, Ms. Robinson owns another spread in Idaho, a shopping center, and a Safeway store. A special method of animal husbandry yields prize calves on the ranch; the family no longer raises sheep.

From her years on the ranch, Ms. Robinson developed an understanding of agriculture issues early. After serving as Teton County deputy treasurer, she helped organize the state chapter of a group called WIFE (Women Involved in Farm Economics) in the 1970s. A few years later, this self-described "Lincolnian Republican" began to travel to Washington, D.C., mostly as a delegate of the American Agricultural Movement. Ms. Robinson has fond memories of the friends she made in the nation's capital.

Her first trip to Washington was in 1976, to represent the American Meat Producers. The group wanted to tell Congress that imports were damaging their business. Ms. Robinson's testimony on the issue before the International Trade Commission had won her a standing ovation from an audience of cattlemen in Rapid City, South Dakota, earlier that year, so the association chose to send Ms. Robinson to make its case. When the time came for her to present the meat producers' argument before the ITC in Washington, D.C., Ms. Robinson had to improvise: "I had to sit and listen to everybody and then attempt to rebut their points—everything they said about our position."

The opposition's lawyers told the neophyte lobbyist she had made quite a hit. "'Darling, we are giving you a one-way ticket home!'" Ms. Robinson says. "After it was over, we all went out to dinner. They kept insisting I was an attorney and I said I absolutely was not. I just have an analytical mind."

Ms. Robinson put that analytical mind to work along with a natural affection for people and a zest for her profession. On behalf of WIFE and AAM, she enjoyed "pounding the congressional offices, calling on congressmen and senators and presenting the best case you possibly can." People in power, she says, "always liked me whether I voted or not. They're human, too, and if you present your testimony in an attractive way, start with a little humor before you get too deadly serious and pound them over the head, and use a gentle but firm approach, you'll usually get what you want."

Perhaps the apex of Ms. Robinson's lobbying career came when she testified before President Carter as the only woman in a group representing varied agricultural organizations. After complimenting her on her "stimulating" testimony, the president made a remark: "There will be a rosy future for those who can survive." Ms. Robinson wrote the statement down on White House stationery, feeling that it set a tone for what the farm community was experiencing and what the future might hold. "I happen to be one of those who survived," she says.

Now 66, Ms. Robinson doesn't lobby in the federal capital anymore. She gets involved in Montana and local politics, which she says are more genial. "We take our politics quite seriously, but we don't have any knock-down, drag-out fights, because we are all friends." She stays abreast of events in the national and global farm system by reading newspapers and watching C-SPAN, as well as staying in touch with her congressman, Rep. Ron Marlenee (R). (A staffer in Rep. Marlenee's office told C-SPAN that the office gets calls from Ms. Robinson whenever a televised debate on agriculture takes place in the House.) She frequently watches the House of Representatives in action and asks wryly, "What are they sneaking by us; what raise are they going to give themselves today?" Ms. Robinson also hopes to share her interest in C-SPAN: She recently wrote a check to buy the Choteau high school 35 copies of the viewers' guide to Congress, *Gavel to Gavel*.

Joyce Robinson expresses fears that the economy is "too uneven" and weighted toward defense at the expense of vital areas of production. "I see a terrible approaching danger, because any time your producers—agriculture, mining, lumbering, fishing—are not making a profit, eventually you're going to destroy the rest of the economy." At the same time, Ms. Robinson retains a light touch. "I'm just an ordinary ranch girl from Montana, but I enjoy life. It's a good time to be alive." —P.K.

Great Falls, Montana is served by Tele-Communications Inc.

"The Doctor"

Tom Rose

Stillwater, Minnesota

Often, the people profiled in this book have described themselves as being "addicted" to public affairs television. Tom
Rose, a Minnesota physician, says he's proof that there can
indeed be a cure for this television addiction: the printed word.

Dr. Rose, 49, immersed himself in C-SPAN-watching for
several years. He's now convinced, however, that he "learned
all I was going to learn about the process of how the government operates." Today, he satisfies his thirst for understanding
with books. Last year, for example, he estimates he read 35 on
Central America alone.

Tom Rose is an internist/endocrinologist in the St. Paul
suburb of Stillwater, Minnesota. For most of his life, he has
"maintained a deep interest in politics." This Twin Cities native
likes to tell people about his years as an undergraduate at the
University of Notre Dame (class of 1960). Former Democratic
presidential hopeful Bruce Babbitt was Tom Rose's next-door
neighbor during their senior year; President Reagan's 1980
campaign advisor, John Sears, was a classmate; and syndicated
columnist Mark Shields, "a political junkie even then," was in
the class ahead.

Tom Rose describes himself as "moderately, but staunchly,
liberal." His "original political idol" was Adlai Stevenson; the

two-time Democratic presidential candidate attracted the admiration of then 13-year-old Tom Rose in 1952.

Throughout his adult years, Tom Rose has maintained his intense interest in politics, but "more so with content than the process." The only exceptions were the nominating conventions. Every four years since his teens, Tom Rose has "stayed up all night" to watch his party select its nominee.

So it was probably no surprise that Tom Rose eventually found his way to C-SPAN. "I was talked into buying a satellite dish by my brother-in-law," who in 1980 was "one of the first people interested in satellite technology." Soon after he discovered that his dish gave him access to uncut congressional hearings and House floor debates, he was watching two to three hours a night. "There were many evenings when I watched right up until midnight, or one, two, or three o'clock. Past 10:00 P.M., I usually watched alone."

Back then, not many of his colleagues at the University of Minnesota Medical School, where Dr. Rose has taught medical residents for 16 years, had access to cable television. They became quite interested in what Tom Rose was picking up from all his hours in front of the television set. "I worked with a group of people who were politically aware," he explains, "and often they would ask me, 'So, what did you see last night?' I was sort of their source of information."

Tom Rose's high-intensity viewing lasted for several years. He became so interested that in 1986 he penned a lengthy letter to the network suggesting changes he would like to see in the call-ins, congressional telecasts, and other programs. He agreed to allow his suggestion-filled letter to be reprinted in the *C-SPAN Update,* the network's weekly newspaper, so other viewers could react to his comments.

But eventually for information-hungry Tom Rose, even C-SPAN was simply not enough. "I just got dissatisfied with the depth you would go into any particular issue," he explains. He realized that "I just wanted to spend more time on specific issues in a little more depth." So instead of watching television, Tom Rose found himself doing "more reading and talking to my friends."

Tom Rose says he's "pretty discouraged by the general level of political dialogue" in the nation. He claims he had "higher hopes that more people would become involved" in the political process by watching C-SPAN. Dr. Rose doesn't think that's happening. "I don't think it's activated a lot of people," he says. "The people who watch it are the people who are already interested."

Two people already interested in the political process are Tom Rose and his wife Karen. They still tune in C-SPAN. But instead of spending several hours each evening, they tune in for specific events, like the Robert Bork Supreme Court nomination hearings.

"There are certain things that are happening live that are fairly dramatic," he concedes. But Dr. Rose, who yearns for in-depth "political dialogue," now thinks that television alone can't satisfy his needs. "Television tends to produce political rhetoric rather than true political dialogue," says Dr. Rose. "C-SPAN's consistent message should be that what you see is merely the tip of the iceberg." The doctor is so convinced of the salutary effects of his reading regimen that he prescribes it for other viewers as well: "For some call-ins you should announce required reading two weeks in advance and restrict calls to those who have done their homework."   —M.C.

Dr. Rose still occasionally watches C-SPAN via his own satellite dish.

"The Risk-Takers"

Bob Rosencrans
Ken Gunter

Greenwich, Connecticut
San Angelo, Texas

Robert Rosencrans, the son of Austrian and Russian Jews, grew up in New York during the New Deal and World War II in what he calls "a very democratic environment—with a big and small 'd.' We were a very idealistic family." Ken Gunter was raised in San Angelo, Texas, in a family of "austere business-men"—Methodists whose ancestors had fought for the Confederacy during the Civil War. "My staunch Southern background is really the root of my redneck, right-wing politics," he says.

In spite of their glaring differences, these two men are very close friends. Their unlikely friendship has endured and flourished over the years. And something they and other cable executives helped build—C-SPAN—has likewise lasted and grown against the odds.

Mr. Rosencrans, 61, and Mr. Gunter, 54, were a pair of pied pipers who encouraged the cable industry to support the network. In 1977, Mr. Rosencrans was president of a large cable company, UA-Columbia; Mr. Gunter oversaw the company's Texas-based operations as executive vice president. Mr. Gunter, usually the pair's doubting Thomas, persuaded Mr. Rosencrans to take a risk and donate desperately needed seed money to C-SPAN when the network was just starting out. Their gift inspired other cable companies to give money as well, establishing the network as cable television's contribution to civic awareness.

Mr. Gunter and Mr. Rosencrans took divergent routes to the growing cable business. Mr. Rosencrans' father was an importer of millinery supplies, his mother a dress designer for a New York couturier. "We were a very idealistic family," recalls Mr. Rosencrans. "The whole essence of democracy was developed through my home and my educational environment. Politics were always on the table as I grew up."

Young Bob grew up during World War II, and those years left him with an awareness of politics and world events. "Everything that happened during those years was so pervasive, so overwhelming. . . . Everybody who grew up in those times became very involved with history and those issues— they became paramount." The war also left Mr. Rosencrans with lingering scars; his older brother Herbert died in combat. "The most significant thing in my life was the death of my brother," he says. "It still is. But I think I remain idealistic in spite of it. I look for the better side of people."

After graduating from Columbia College in 1949, Mr. Rosencrans tried different professions for awhile before embarking on a career in television production, producing shows that demonstrated television's capabilities in movie theaters. (He remembers producing a TV short introducing "the beautiful Edsel car.") One of the companies he joined, TelePrompTer, got into the cable television field. Through TelePrompTer, Mr. Rosencrans became aware of the opportunity to buy a small cable company in Washington state. He assembled investors to purchase the company, and by 1968 the company, United Artists-Columbia, went public. That was the year he met Ken Gunter.

Mr. Gunter was born "from truculent stock" and raised in San Angelo. His father was an electronics salesman who built a cable system there in the late 1950s, by Mr. Gunter's account, "so he could sell more TV sets." Heated political arguments were also common fare at the Gunter dinner table, and Mr. Gunter grew up with "Southern ethics, a sense of right and wrong." Although he missed the war years, he says, "I'd like nothing better than to have been in a war. I fancy that I would have done pretty well as a military leader, while that would be the last thing Bob Rosencrans would want to do. Bob is simply a peaceful man who hates violence or altercations of any kind."

Mr. Gunter went to Rice University, where he joined the Young Republicans. "There was a pronounced liberal trend that we thought was going to be damaging to American values," he remembers. He had intended to go to medical school, "but I'd always been involved in science and electronic things, and medicine was beginning to look like a bore. I don't like whiney people, and I can't stand hypochondriacs, so I went into business with Dad." Mr. Gunter learned the cable business in International Cablevision, his father's company.

The two met when Bob Rosencrans' company was trying to buy the San Angelo-based International Cablevision. "There we were from different parts of the universe," remembers Mr. Rosencrans, "but we got along beautifully from day one." Before long, Mr. Gunter was running divisions for Mr. Rosencrans.

Twenty years down the line, the contrasts between the two men may have blurred somewhat. But the contrasts are still there, and they stand out immediately when Mr. Rosencrans and Mr. Gunter walk into a room. Years of rugged Texas individualism have straightened Ken Gunter's back and composed his face; he stands tall in perfectly pressed business clothes and talks at a smoothly modulated clip. The smaller, balding Rosencrans often breaks into a grin or widens his eyes to make a point, and his speech bears a staccato Eastern rasp. How can these two possibly see eye to eye?

"We like to do battle a little bit," admits Mr. Gunter. The two men argue over politics on occasion, but "never in a vitriolic way, just intellectual," says Mr. Rosencrans. "But it never entered our business view. I think we have the same ethical approach to treating people. Where we disagree on politics, we don't disagree on our system of government. We believe that everyone should have his day in court." This common tolerance overrode their differences; so did a strong mutual trust. Says Mr. Gunter, "If you learn to trust motives and simply trust the person, you can be in violent disagreement with philosophy and ideology and still love the person."

By the late 1970s, Mr. Rosencrans and Mr. Gunter had to unite their energies to meet a cable industry problem. Cable had grown as a business and an entertainment medium, but had come to a point where federal regulations prevented it from growing any further. This was partly because the regulators were unacquainted with cable and what it could offer. As Mr. Gunter puts it, the industry needed to prove to Capitol Hill that cable was more than a "smut peddler. We were getting our teeth kicked down our throats in Washington because politicians didn't understand our issues or know who we were."

In 1977, the idea of creating a public affairs network was proposed to a group of 40 cable executives. Specifically, the proposal called for the industry to finance a public affairs cable network that would televise Congress. By bringing government to the American people, such a network would heighten cable's civic profile and demonstrate to Congress the services cable could perform. UA-Columbia was asked to contribute $25,000 to the project; Mr. Rosencrans, it was hoped, would help raise money among his colleagues in the industry. Mr. Rosencrans, intrigued by the idea, brought it up with other cable operators. He was initially rebuffed. "The deal's off," he reported.

The decision roused Mr. Gunter's combative dander. As he saw it, "If nothing else, it would put us on the map in Washington. It would mean visibility for cable. I was tired of breaking down peoples' doors in Washington." He thought that C-SPAN would more than pay for itself by making Congress aware of cable's potential and good intentions. He argued that objective, gavel-to-gavel coverage of Congress "would give us congressional visibility that we couldn't buy with 10 times that much money."

Messrs. Rosencrans and Gunter decided to move ahead on the idea anyway. The company donated $25,000 in seed money toward the C-SPAN concept, setting an example for the industry at large. And, once Mr. Rosencrans had made the initial donation, he followed up on his effort. He prevailed upon more skeptical industry figures to make similar donations. This time "it was not difficult to persuade the heads of Warner, ATC, or TelePrompTer to donate money. I think we all saw the value of it. We saw it as another total piece of service that cable ought to provide." He used C-SPAN's apolitical perspective as a selling point: "The only way you were going to get the support of the industry was to have it completely nonpartisan—without any commentary, without any slant." He urged them to get involved "because we couldn't do it ourselves." Together, industry leaders pooled $425,000, and the network got its start.

Mr. Rosencrans agreed to serve as C-SPAN's first board chairman. He raised money, continued to bring in other cable operators, and helped the network along in its early days. Eventually more than 35 cable companies joined the network's board, making C-SPAN a true "cable cooperative." Mr. Gunter stayed behind the scenes, satisfied that he had helped influence the process.

Of course, C-SPAN is just one of many links between the mild-mannered Eastern liberal and the skeptical Texas conservative. "We come from entirely different backgrounds," explains Mr. Rosencrans, "but we just had a gift for communicating with one another." Together, the two men's gift for overcoming differences to reach and convey the essence of things helped persuade the cable industry to bring Congress to the nation via television.   —C.E.

Bob Rosencrans can watch C-SPAN on Cablevision of Connecticut; Mr. Gunter can tune in to Scott Cable Communications.

"The Mountain Belle"

Shirley Rossi

Pueblo, Colorado

When Shirley Rossi wants to get in touch with somebody, she usually picks up the phone and makes a call. Writing is fine, but calling is quicker.

For her, C-SPAN forms one link to government; the telephone forms another. As a retired telephone employee, Ms. Rossi has a monthly long-distance allowance at her disposal. When she has a question, remark, or objection for a government official, she dials away to say what's on her mind.

In 1982, Ms. Rossi's hometown of Pueblo, Colorado, was feeling the effects of a nationwide recession. The local steelworks had closed, and the town's unemployment rate soared to 20 percent. "The whole town shut down," Ms. Rossi recalls.

One morning, Ms. Rossi read a story in the local paper, the *Pueblo Chieftain,* about a group of Pueblans who were banding together to try and save their homes from mortgage foreclosures. The same morning, Ms. Rossi saw Rep. Henry Gonzalez (D-Texas) on C-SPAN making a speech about massive U.S. home foreclosures. Ms. Rossi called the *Chieftain* to ask the reporter how to contact the local homeowners' group. She then phoned their organizer to inform them of Rep. Gonzalez' sympathy to their issue and to explain how they could contact the congressman in Washington. A few days later, the congressman appeared on the House floor waving a piece of paper—a petition for federal assistance signed by the beleaguered Pueblo homeowners. Rep. Gonzalez further demonstrated his sympathy for the townspeople by talking about their problems for a week on the House floor and introducing an aid bill to ease some of their burdens. The bill took a year to pass, but Ms. Rossi believes it passed in time to help some of the people of Pueblo.

Ms. Rossi likes to tell this anecdote to show that ordinary citizens can reach government and that government can respond to citizens' needs.

Ms. Rossi is one of the network's longest and most loyal viewers; C-SPAN "met" her in 1979, when she began frequent calls to the network just one month after it had started sending out its signal. Her intensive daily C-SPAN watching prompted *USA Today* to write a story about her in 1982; the *Washington Post* wrote about her two years later. Even now, Ms. Rossi takes in 10 to 12 hours of C-SPAN a day, although she now holds off from calling the question-and-answer program "to give other people a chance."

While Ms. Rossi is an activist, stridency isn't her style. She likes to work on things slowly but surely. Ms. Rossi has been known to invite neighborhood children over for milk, cookies, and C-SPAN. "These kids come from homes where politics would never be discussed," she believes. One of the girls, a third-grader, had a severe speech impediment, and Ms. Rossi and her husband decided to take the time to work with the child. Mr. Rossi would play the piano and encourage her to sing along as a way of developing her vowel enunciation. The couple also made up a game called "playing C-SPAN," in which the child would imitate various members of the House of Representatives on the House floor (her favorite to imitate was then-House Speaker Tip O'Neill, the young girl said, because "he's in charge"). The Rossis' patient tutelage seemed to help the little girl overcome her linguistic obstacles. "Wouldn't you know, within a year she could really talk," says Ms. Rossi.

When an aide to Speaker O'Neill appeared on a call-in program, Ms. Rossi helped the nine-year-old place a call to the network. "She wanted to thank O'Neill for supporting aid to special education, which is important to her because of her speech impediment."

Ms. Rossi applies the same patience and steadiness to her gathering of political information and her work for causes. When a few cable operators across the country threatened to remove C-SPAN from their systems in 1982 and 1983, Ms. Rossi helped Bud Harris form "Friends of C-SPAN," an organization of loyal viewers who called and wrote to cable operators with appeals to carry the network.

More specifically, individual examples illustrate Ms. Rossi's telephone activism. She doesn't hesitate to call government officials when something she sees on C-SPAN captures her interest. During the 1984 election, Republican members of Congress were in the habit of using Special Orders—time after the close of official House business—to make strongly partisan speeches. "I have to turn the set down when those guys get up." said Ms. Rossi, a longtime Democrat. One night Ms. Rossi heard a member lambasting a Democratic senator and presidential candidate by name on the House floor. The speech pricked up her ears and prompted her to pick up the phone: "I was under the impression that members could not mention the names of senators and their voting records by name."

Ms. Rossi doggedly telephoned Capitol Hill until she reached the office of the House parliamentarian, who confirmed her reading of congressional rules: Members were not allowed to refer to other members by name when the House was in session, and, technically speaking, it was in session during Special Orders.

The following Monday, from her Colorado living room, Ms. Rossi had the satisfaction of seeing the speaker, on advice from the parliamentarian, cut off the offending representative when he began a personal attack. Told he could not mention the name of his political opponent, the member said, "Then, I guess I have nothing to say." Ms. Rossi believes it was her call that encouraged the enforcement of House rules: "I'd like to think I had something to do with it."

In addition, she has telephoned presidential campaign staffs to protest their television ad campaigns and has told syndicated columnists when she disagrees with their commentary. Ms. Rossi encourages others to be involved, too. Her other family members now all have cable in their homes and are watching Congress. And at her urging, a local political science professor is using C-SPAN to prepare his courses.

Still a hardy liberal Democrat, 62-year-old Ms. Rossi says her daily doses of C-SPAN have softened her views somewhat, and she acknowledges complexities in issues such as the death penalty. She has turned to other news sources for information: "I discovered *USA Today* through C-SPAN, and also three news magazines I didn't know about, like *The Nation*. C-SPAN is very important to me. It keeps me thinking and acting."

While Ms. Rossi rarely calls C-SPAN these days, she continues to take full advantage of her phone privileges with calls to members of Congress and public officials, demonstrating that satellite technology—telephone and television—makes it possible to be an armchair activist, thousands of miles from the nation's capital.   —*M.C.*

Shirley Rossi is a subscriber to Pueblo Cablevision.

"The Presidential Questioner"

Sally Salmon
Jackson, Mississippi

What high school student wouldn't jump at the chance to ask the president of the United States a question on any subject— on television, yet? Sally Salmon of Greenville, Mississippi, had that chance. In 1983, Ms. Salmon was chosen to participate in a special Close Up Foundation telecast, which allowed high school students from around the country to question President Reagan during a freewheeling half-hour session. "I was a nervous wreck," Ms. Salmon remembers.

Sally Salmon's high school teachers had encouraged political participation, and she volunteered in congressional campaigns by putting up signs, attending rallies, and canvassing door-to-door. She worked in student government and took part in a model United Nations. When one teacher recommended that she go to Washington, D.C., on the Close Up program, she leaped at the opportunity.

Founded in 1971, the Close Up Foundation brings more than 20,000 students to Washington every year for week-long personal introductions to the federal government. Some students are selected for Close Up by teachers; others simply apply on their own. Each week, a small group of Close Up students is chosen to participate in a televised meeting with top government officials. From 1983 to 1986, Close Up had the chance to add President Reagan to its list of participants. In all, President

Reagan faced the student questioners on five occasions, each televised exclusively by C-SPAN. Ms. Salmon arrived in Washington for her Close Up stint unaware that she might get a shot at asking the highest official in the land something that had been on her mind.

The Close Up students are taken on a tour through Washington that shows them the sights and steers them through the halls of power and into the offices of the powerful for lectures and discussions. For a student from a small town like Greenville, remembers Ms. Salmon, the experience was overwhelming. "You're in the center of power in the world and you sort of sense that." She became acquainted with students from all over the United States: "You couldn't find people more different than people from Massachusetts and people from Mississippi. They have different backgrounds and different views politically, and you're exposed to that through a program like Close Up."

"Just seeing the president was a highlight for me. I wanted to ask him a question so badly," she recalls. At first the opportunity passed her by: President Reagan did not call on Sally Salmon during the Close Up students' face-to-face "press conference" at the Old Executive Office Building.

However, Ms. Salmon got a second chance. After the press conference, the students returned to C-SPAN's studio to talk about their presidential experience in a session that was televised live. One of the viewers of that telecast was the president himself, who had gone back to his residential quarters and turned on his television to C-SPAN. There he found his young interrogators talking about him. He asked the White House operator to phone the program so he could get another crack at answering their questions.

The students were visibly delighted at having President Reagan on the line ready to take more questions. Sally gasped when Close Up President Steve Janger pointed to her.

Ms. Salmon wanted to ask about a pending jobs bill. "I felt that people were not giving him a fair shake on the issue, so I phrased the question so he could really come out and give his opinion and people could understand what he had been trying to get across." Her excitement got the better of her, though; all she can remember of the president's reply is his preface of "bless your heart." But Ms. Salmon does have the fleeting presidential encounter on videotape to refresh her memory.

A lot has happened since that 1983 Close Up experience. In college, she worked as an intern for former Rep. Webb Franklin (R-Mississippi), participated in a Washington semester program, and served an internship in the White House Office of Political Affairs. Now 23, Ms. Salmon holds the position of staff assistant to the Southern political director of the George Bush political campaign. She says she "thinks George Bush from 7:00 in the morning until 9:00 at night" while scheduling pro-Bush speakers for Republican events and maintaining ties between the Southern Republican leadership, the national campaign, and the Bush operation.

From working on the inside, Ms. Salmon has a perspective on the intricacies of politics: "In high school, you have an impression of how things are done in government. You never realize until you start to work that there are all the different factors that go into it—the personality factor, the real politics, the people factor, what's done behind the scenes. It's a lot more complicated than you'd think from reading a book."

The Close Up trip was Sally Salmon's first contact with C-SPAN. Her busy Bush campaign office keeps it on all day long, but Ms. Salmon says she's usually juggling too many balls to really concentrate on the programming. She's likely to be sending a member of the Bush team to a GOP luncheon or calling Republican officials to attend a fund-raiser. For Sally Salmon, her Close Up experience with the president is just one part of an ongoing life in politics.   —M.C.

Jackson, Mississippi, is served by Capitol Cablevision.

"The Conference Caller"

Ray Schwartz
Dover, New Jersey

Whenever there's an important political event brewing, everyone at New Jersey's Dover High School crowds into Room 108. That's where Ray Schwartz, who teaches social studies and government to the seniors, has set up a television for watching Congress and a telephone for making conference calls. It's an arrangement that brings history to life by linking students directly to what they're studying.

Mr. Schwartz has been teaching young people for nearly 20 years. "When I think of the history this room has seen through television," he says, he recalls events like the invasion of Grenada and the space shuttle disaster. "You name it, this is the room to be in when something happens. It's not unusual during major hearings to have three or four classes jammed in here to see it."

For Ray Schwartz, who has been known to watch C-SPAN on a small portable television while his family is watching entertainment programs in the same room on a different set, congressional and public affairs programming is not only a vital teaching aid, it helps him keep up with his longtime passion for politics. Besides being the kind of teacher whom his students say "gets us involved," the 40-year-old Schwartz has his fingers in several other pies. He works for the local teachers union and serves as the legislative chairman for the

Morris County Education Association. During the summers, he has also worked in Washington, D.C., as a congressional intern. Somewhere in between all these activities he finds time to put the finishing touches on his doctoral dissertation at Rutgers University. His topic is the political activities of the teachers union. His plans for the future are wide-ranging: "I'm investigating a whole bunch of things. I wouldn't mind working for a think tank or working with some group that has education as its primary concern—something that I believe in. I wouldn't mind getting the *Washington Post* every morning."

In the meantime, he obviously hasn't forsaken his teaching career: "I get paid for this; this is my hobby. I thoroughly enjoy it, and if you have to teach something, it might as well be about *now*."

His students watch everything from C-SPAN's call-ins to hearings and floor debate. "It's absolutely important," he says. "It's informative, up-to-date, and it's happening right before your eyes. You don't have to read about it—you can make your own judgment. And that, I think, is critical. Any time you put the glaring light of television on the people in government it will make a difference in getting information out to people. That is what makes social studies real and alive for everybody."

A permanent television in the classroom, as Ray Schwartz has, is a rarity. It's the envy of many teachers who are trying to cultivate their students' involvement in current events. But a television-telephone combination, which Mr. Schwartz has, is almost unheard of.

Through conference calling, the students have talked with historian Arthur Schlesinger, Sen. Bill Bradley (D-New Jersey), syndicated columnist Jack Anderson, former New York Congresswoman Bella Abzug (D), former presidential candidate Sen. George McGovern (D-South Dakota), and CBS anchor Dan Rather. The class has even made a conference call to the C-SPAN call-in program.

"The level of excitement in this class is pretty high," says Mary Beth Fritch, 17. "Sometimes it's a lecture, and sometimes we put the phone on. His excitement really travels through us. I would say everyone really likes this class."

One of the best exercises, students say, is holding mock hearings, which are recorded with the school's video camera and played back so that the students can size up their performances. Last year, for example, a state senator held a three-hour hearing on drug programs in the schools. Students spent two weeks preparing for the session. Some studied drug programs in other states while others looked at New Jersey programs. Then they wrote their own testimony, presented it, and had to respond to questions by the senator, just as they would if they were involved in a real hearing. Mr. Schwartz says that watching C-SPAN's congressional committee hearings is good preparation for the exercise. The students see the layout of the hearing rooms and take notes on how the politicians conduct themselves.

Being able to watch Congress on television has made learning about politics an immediate, and even emotional, experience for some students in Mr. Schwartz' class. "We always have great class discussions with Mr. Schwartz," says Jessica Sisto, 18. "And normally they're carried on outside the classroom because we always have strong opinions. A lot of our other teachers get mad because we're having discussions that don't pertain to their classes."

The nomination of Robert Bork to the Supreme Court was a major subject of debate for the students in the fall of 1987. "I noticed the Republicans, or the people who were supporting Bork, had a lot more facts and numbers, whereas the people who were against Bork had a lot of interpretations and opinions. That influenced me a lot," says Jason Sabozzi, 17. But for another student, Robert Bork was "too set in his ways, very hard-nosed."

The students also talked in-depth about whether President Reagan should have withdrawn the doomed appointment. "I tried to simulate that they were White House staffers. I wanted them to think about what it's like to take care of the president, and at the same time come up with something that is doable," Mr. Schwartz says.

This kind of exposure to politics has, in turn, influenced career choices. "I keep going back and forth on running for public office. C-SPAN helps me get a clear idea of what that's all about," says Jason Sabozzi. "It has influenced me toward going into politics and law, because I can see how everything is run. I can see how politicians have to be, what the possibilities are, and the pressures that they are under," says Joann Mazur, 17. She intends to go to college and law school, then run for Congress and possibly even run for president of the United States.

Already, two of Mr. Schwartz' former students have pursued careers in politics. One is a member of the City Council and one worked on Capitol Hill as a secretary for a congressman. For Ray Schwartz, the enthusiastic response by students to this unique approach to social studies is no small reward. "They now know what the *New York Times* looks like," he says. "They might ask: 'Did you see, Mr. Schwartz, where so-and-so said . . .' I mean, they actually know that the PLO is not some hamburger at McDonald's."   *—R.K.*

The students in Mr. Schwartz's class watch C-SPAN on Sammons Communications of New Jersey.

"The Legislative Addict"

Stan Singer

Harrisburg, Pennsylvania

"Politics, politics, that's all you ever think about," grumbled Phyllis Singer to her husband Stan. "I bet you don't even remember the date we were married."

"Sure I do, honey," he protested. "It was the day John Kennedy was nominated for president."

Stan Singer likes to tell this joke to illustrate his unromantic preoccupation with public affairs. Mr. Singer has been in and out of the doghouse for 28 years because his wife doesn't appreciate being widowed by his public affairs habit. But Mr. Singer can't help his addiction; his parents were political junkies, too. Truman's whistle-stop tour was as important as eating your vegetables in young Stan Singer's household, and no one got up from the dinner table without discussing the "candidate of the day." When the Singers got married in 1960, Phyllis Singer foresaw the day she would be yelling "Stann-*leeey*" in vain to her husband who remains periodically glued to TV election returns. On his wedding day, the 27-year-old Mr. Singer was hard-pressed to whisper sweet nothings in his new bride's ear when a radio broadcast of John F. Kennedy's nomination at the Democratic convention was begging for more volume.

Phyllis Singer first met Stan Singer when he was a promising young appliance store television salesman. Today, he's "gone from one side of the screen to the other," as executive director of the Pennsylvania Cable Television Association. Mr. Singer is responsible for keeping abreast of state and national issues that may affect the association's membership. He is pleased that he can combine television and politics, and "get a paycheck too!"

The PCTA represents the issues of cable operators to the Pennsylvania state legislature, local officials, and the press. It keeps its membership informed of legal and business developments in cable television. Consequently, Mr. Singer spends a lot of time in Pennsylvania's state capitol lobbying lawmakers.

In his rounds of the government offices, Mr. Singer has observed that public officials often harbor "great misconceptions" about cable, which for them conjures up visions of sexually explicit programming or third-rate reruns. Noticing that many of the lawmakers watched C-SPAN, Mr. Singer began to emphasize the network to public officials and cable operators alike. Offering C-SPAN he tells his members is a responsibility, a means of "paying civic rent," as he puts it.

Even if C-SPAN weren't a tool he uses to help "sell" cable to Pennsylvania politicians, Stan Singer, a man whose father made him subscribe to *Newsweek* at age 10, most likely would be a fan of the public affairs programming the network offers. In his monthly newsletter to PCTA members, he quipped that the installation of C-SPAN in his home made him feel as if he had entered "that great voting booth in the sky."

He's been a lobbyist for years now. He represented the Pennsylvania Pharmaceutical Association before joining the PCTA in 1981. Back in the '60s his colleagues in the appliance business drafted him to speak for their informal trade organization. "Since I was the guy who seemed to know the most about politics and knew the most state legislators, I got conscripted to represent the group. I soon realized that the legislative part was where my heart lay," recalls the veteran lobbyist. Mr. Singer says he is proud to be part of an industry he characterizes as "young and vital" in a state where the entrepreneurial spirit allows small cable companies to flourish. "Perhaps my greatest pleasure as association president is being able to help the smaller operators solve their problems," he says.

The good-natured association executive is quick to point out that Pennsylvania is the birthplace of cable television, claiming Mahanoy City as the home of the first cable system some 40 years ago. Pennsylvania also houses the national cable television museum, near the campus of Pennsylvania State University.

Stan Singer now brings his enthusiasm to a new project that's been a dream of many Pennsylvanians since 1982. Plans are coming together for the formation of a statewide network of public affairs programming. In late 1987, state representatives were about to vote on whether to set aside money to pay for a new lighting scheme in the statehouse chambers. He had planned to write to cable operators urging them to make room for a Pennsylvania public affairs channel.

Mr. Singer likes to watch C-SPAN for information, but also to pick up political nuances and to tickle his sense of humor. "Teddy Kennedy's going to run for something—he's losing weight." And in a letter to his association members, he joked that he sometimes likes to watch C-SPAN to tease his long-suffering wife: "I'm going to watch C-SPAN highlights from 1:00 to 4:00 in the morning—just kidding, Phyllis." —C.M.

Stan Singer watches C-SPAN and other cable programming on Sammons Communications of Pennsylvania.

"The Lone Star Reporter"

John Stolarek
McAllen, Texas

There are roughly 1,400 daily newspapers in the United States with a circulation of 50,000 or less. Day after day these papers supply their readers with local and state news. To a lesser degree, they also cover national and world events, getting their information from wire services, and, if they're fortunate, a news bureau in Washington, D.C. However, a growing number of small-town newspapers without a Washington staff are finding a way around that—their reporters use the televised coverage of Congress as a direct source of national news.

One local reporter who writes about national affairs regularly is John Stolarek, the political and education reporter for the *McAllen Monitor* in McAllen, Texas: "C-SPAN is how I track U.S. legislation. Sometimes I'll see a story on the wire about House floor debate or a committee hearing, and I'll come home at night and find that it's going to be on. Even if it's on at three or four in the morning, I'll make a point to watch the whole thing. That way I get a better view of what went on, because even in the *Washington Post* or the *New York Times* you know they only print about one-fiftieth of what actually happened."

Even though the *McAllen Monitor* is a small-city newspaper (daily circulation 35,000), it devotes a large portion of its reports to national and international news because it believes that action at the federal level will often directly affect its readers. Mr. Stolarek estimates that one-quarter of his writing is devoted to national politics, covering issues such as education, agriculture, and immigration.

McAllen (population 80,000) is one of a string of border towns; it's just 40 miles from Harlingen, the city that President Reagan described as a "two-day drive from Nicaragua." McAllen is more than 75 percent Hispanic, very Democratic, and not without problems: "They city itself is one of the nicest in the southern tip of Texas—very modern," says Mr. Stolarek. "But then you can go 10 miles from here and find what *Newsweek* called the 'new Appalachia,' an area with no running water and dirt roads, with a primarily Hispanic population." In fact, the entire 15th Congressional District of Texas is one of the poorest in the nation.

Hence, these national issues Mr. Stolarek covers with the help of television can be bread-and-butter concerns for the people of his small city. Agriculture is big business and a major source of employment in McAllen. So is Pan American University, a major state school just six miles down the road. And since McAllen is only eight miles from the Mexican border, inhabitants on either side of the Rio Grande constantly gauge the changing tides in Washington to decide if the river is fordable.

At first Mr. Stolarek watched C-SPAN simply for its congressional debate coverage, which his articles summarized for Texas readers. However, since he was responsible for interviewing the presidential hopefuls as they campaigned through southern Texas, he found C-SPAN's uncut coverage of candidates' cross-country stump speeches gave him the edge in interviews. "I've been able to refer to things they have said on C-SPAN and develop a more interesting dialogue, rather than ask the kind of pat questions they're used to getting from local reporters."

Although Mr. Stolarek has been writing about politics for more than 10 years, he's only been a reporter since 1984. What he refers to as a "kind of mid-career crisis" brought him from the ivory tower to the newsroom. He taught political science and American government at the University of South Carolina at Columbia for four years and at the Pan American University for another three years. During that time he wrote numerous articles for academic journals. Then, as he was interviewing several congressmen for his doctoral dissertation, he realized that digging for facts was the part of political science he liked most. Thus began his forays into journalism.

As a political reporter and former college professor, John Stolarek has been to Washington several times. While he has a good grip on the workings of Washington, he understands that for others the nation's capital can be a "very busy, complicated place. For a reporter there's an endless amount of information. C-SPAN helps give an accurate picture of what Washington is like." —E.Q.

John Stolarek monitors Washington through Heritage Cablevision of Texas.

John Sununu

Salem, New Hampshire

New Hampshire Gov. John Sununu (R) faces a perennial issue in his state: the construction of the Seabrook nuclear power plant. When he appears on C-SPAN call-ins, the issue becomes a national one as the governor fields calls from people around the country who want to know his stance on the plant. A July 1987 call-in was typical, as the engineer-turned-politician defended the plant's safety record to a California viewer: "There is no similarity between Chernobyl and U.S. plants, especially Seabrook. . . . We have done a good job in this country in terms of designing things to provide safety in the system."

Despite unavoidable hot issues, the governor enjoys call-in programs. "I have a ball," he says, and he occasionally does a New Hampshire version on public television. C-SPAN viewers generally get to talk with Gov. Sununu twice each year during telecasts of National Governors' Association meetings. As 1987–88 NGA chairman, he figured prominently in conference coverage. (His mother in Florida "was delighted.") Those telecasts also provide a way to communicate with the folks back home in the Granite State: "I probably get more feedback from New Hampshire people on those NGA appearances than just about anything else except local news programs," he says.

NGA chairpersons pick a theme for their term in office.

Gov. Sununu chose federalism for his. He hoped to focus fellow governors' attention on the balance of power between the state and the federal government. As governor of a state that upholds "Live Free or Die" as its motto and makes politicians take "the pledge" against sales or income taxes, Gov. Sununu is a firm believer in local autonomy. "I think most of the public is used to government at home being more logical and organized than the federal government," he says. Now that the public "has access to what's taking place on C-SPAN, a lot of people, I think, are going to question some of the strange antics that go on in Washington."

John Sununu was born in Cuba in 1939 and came to this country as a child. His father "has Lebanese roots," and Gov. Sununu considers himself an Arab-American. He earned a doctorate in engineering from the Massachusetts Institute of Technology in 1966. During the 1960's and '70s, he taught at Tufts University and worked as a business consultant and engineer, eventually founding his own engineering firm, Astro Dynamics. The Sununu family moved to New Hampshire from Massachusetts in 1969, feeling that the state offered potential for "improved family life," he says, for his wife Nancy and their eight children.

A two-year stint in the 424-member New Hampshire legislature, which pays its members $100 per year, introduced Mr. Sununu to state politics in 1973. In 1980, after serving as science and technology adviser to Gov. Meldrim Thomson (R), John Sununu ran for the U.S. Senate. Defeated in the GOP primary by Sen. Warren Rudman, he signed on as Mr. Rudman's campaign manager. In 1982, New Hampshire voters elected Mr. Sununu governor for a two-year term. He was re-elected in 1984 and 1986.

A typical work day for the governor begins at about 8:00 A.M.. At the capitol in Concord, he meets with agency or department representatives and state legislators to discuss bills in progress. Sometimes Gov. Sununu leaves the office for speaking engagements or campaign stops, but he rarely breaks for lunch—a cup of soup at his desk or a bag of microwave popcorn usually hits the spot. Office television sets are often tuned in to C-SPAN: "We watch some of the congressional debates on legislation that impacts the state," the governor says. He usually leaves the office between 7:00 and 9:00 P.M. for his house in

Salem, 40 miles away. The governor's mansion was too small to hold Gov. Sununu's big family.

At home, the governor will catch up on family matters, read his mail, and frequently watch news and public affairs on television until 2:00 or 3:00 in the morning. "It's like peanuts. Once you start watching it, you can't stop. I have been trying to figure out how I can watch both C-SPAN and C-SPAN II at the same time."

The 1988 presidential election disrupted Gov. Sununu's routine somewhat, for he served as chairman of Vice President George Bush's New Hampshire primary campaign. The governor maintains a matter-of-fact attitude toward the barrage of attention his state receives every four years as host of the nation's first primary. "We look forward to it. Contrary to everything everyone says, it is not important economically to the state. It is just something the citizens like doing. They feel a responsibility. No one's been elected president since 1948 without first winning the New Hampshire primary, and they take that very seriously. They want to do a good job."

Gov. Sununu feels that some candidates protest too much about the retail politics of the New Hampshire primary. "A lot of candidates are uncomfortable coming into New Hampshire because they have to answer questions directly without the installation of a pre-arranged message or media event as the mechanism. That's one of the advantages of New Hampshire—it does force candidates to come face to face with the public."

In the campaign off-season, the governor turns his attention to state matters and monitors his state's rapport with Washington. Unlike many states, New Hampshire doesn't have a Washington-based NGA office, preferring to "keep the power base at home," the governor says. To help stay on top of events in the nation's capital, Gov. Sununu and his staff watch C-SPAN. He keeps tabs on representatives from the region: "C-SPAN gives me a chance to see the degree of commitment of some of the New England delegation on issues like tax bills and so on. It gives me the chance to put some emphasis to my colleagues in the governors' chairs about getting some cooperation every once in a while. It's a good tool that way."

He adds, "I find it helpful in the sense that there's nothing you can put in a newspaper that conveys the flavor of the climate in which action is being taken. It gives me the feeling of what's happening in the Senate, what's happening in Congress, what's happening in hearings—and the hearings are as important as anything else."

His Congress-watching underscores Gov. Sununu's belief that local and state governments ultimately serve the people best. He feels that others will come around to his point of view if they watch the Congress: "You know that most of us back home think it's 'looney tunes' down there in Washington. I think you're confirming it for us."   —S.B.

Gov. Sununu's home and office are both served by Continental Cablevision of New Hampshire.

"The Independent Thinker"

Shani Taha
Seattle, Washington

Shani Taha bristles when people suggest that she doesn't fit their stereotypes: "We really are a nation that's so unwilling to accept diversity—race, sex, religion, political views. I think it's really easy these days, when you find a black female who's also a Republican, to wonder what's going on."

Shani Taha was born in Harlem and raised in Westchester County, New York. She was one of the few black students at Smith College in Northampton, Massachusetts, in the 1960s, where she observed the turbulence of that decade unfold. By 1969, she was working in New York City government, which she felt had become an unresponsive "mega-bureaucracy," insensitive to the needs of its neighborhoods and citizens. Over the years, her work took her from Europe to the South Bronx. Today, Ms. Taha lives in Seattle, Washington, where she is an executive with a large utility company. This product of the '60s is still an activist—as a Republican who has campaigned for the GOP presidential ticket.

Ms. Taha, traces her Republicanism to her experiences in city government and to her strong independent streak. She has a definite idea of what government should do: "Government can be so aggressive that it becomes intrusive and debilitating. There is certainly a role for government that I believe in very strongly. It should establish a tone and the ethics and the values of a nation. From my perspective, I believe in things like decentralization and local control." In Seattle she's found a "responsible, accessible government. The kinds of things I had worked for in New York, and found difficult to achieve, were all happening in Seattle. There's a kind of pioneering spirit here—very independent, and a real strong belief in the rights of the individual."

Ms. Taha was brought up with the belief that "as a woman, I could do anything I wanted to do. In our family we were raised to be very independent and very competitive and to get a good education." She became politically involved early. While still in high school, she was a member of the mayor's Task Force on Juvenile Affairs, and in 1963, she participated in Martin Luther King's March on Washington. In 1965, she decided to go to Smith College.

"There weren't many black students at Smith," says Ms. Taha. "That was a big difference, coming from a culturally diverse place like New York, but it didn't really upset me." The political upheavals of the time affected the all-women's college only subtly. "The 1960s on Smith's campus were very polite, but I could see differences that were going on in terms of political awareness and activism. There were revolutions on campus in different ways," she notes.

Ms. Taha graduated from college in 1969 and joined the staff of New York City mayor John Lindsay, a Republican. She threw herself into efforts to make city government meet people's needs, spending two years in the South Bronx with a juvenile justice program. "I would start with one citizen at a time. I would work with one family—one kid—and work to the extent that I could benefit one individual, whether it was getting a toilet fixed, keeping somebody out of jail, helping someone get a job."

In 1983, Ms. Taha had a chance to relive that spirit of activism when she watched a C-SPAN telecast of the 20th anniversary March on Washington. It brought together 300,000 people and speakers such as Jesse Jackson, Coretta Scott King, and NAACP head Benjamin Hooks. Ms. Taha watched the second march with her children, age 6 and 12, trying to convey to them "the size and scale of it all. I told them I had been there. I was a little nostalgic as one of those who went down there with a sense of responsibility."

Ms. Taha was disturbed at her son's lack of reaction to the ceremony. "Those were some of the finest speeches I had ever heard, but I don't think he got into them at all. It's like this whole world of history in the '60s is lost to another generation."

These days, Ms. Taha is a deputy superintendent at Seattle City Light, the nation's fifth-largest public utility company. She is responsible for a third of the company's service area. The utility, she says, encourages city residents to join in making service and environmental decisions. Ms. Taha feels that she is living out her combined beliefs in public service and local autonomy: "I may not be fighting service battles in the streets, but what I've enjoyed about my career is my ability to make life better for the people who are working for me."

In 1984, Ms. Taha expanded her work in state and local politics to serve as a Washington state co-chairperson for a group of GOP women supporting the Reagan-Bush ticket. One of the appearances she made on behalf of the campaign was on a C-SPAN call-in program. C-SPAN cameras were in Seattle as part of "Grassroots '84," a television journey to 14 cities around the country that aimed to gauge the electorate's mood. Ms. Taha represented the local Reagan-Bush organization on a call-in.

Initially she found the callers' comments "somewhat intrusive and personal," challenging her credibility as a black woman who supported the GOP ticket. But after a few prickly exchanges, the conversation expanded to take on a higher tone: "Callers ended up debating more about Democratic versus Republican philosophies of government. It was as if I were a catalyst or conduit for a national dialogue between callers. And that was just fine, because that's the dynamic of the whole medium of what you're doing."

After her appearance on the call-in program, Ms. Taha began to keep an eye out for the C-SPAN network. "You guys became people. You had a name." She now finds the network useful in preparing for her occasional visits to Washington, D.C., on behalf of Seattle City Light. "It's been my channel to keep up with the connections. A lot of what I've done in the past several years is influenced by federal action and what's going on at the national level."

Shani Taha is proud of her company's role in abetting citizen input in a town where "individualism adds up to collective action." And she is proud of herself: "The diversity of my experience has helped me develop really solid people skills and a leadership style that's unique. I do it well, and I like doing it." —S.S.

Shani Taha can watch C-SPAN on Tele-Communications Inc.

"The Runner Up"

Nelda Thompson
Applegate, Oregon

Nelda Thompson shares with her grandson Mike Kellington an "incurable obsession" with C-SPAN. In 1984, the former newspaper editor and the high school student teamed to write a 46-line poem about the network that won second prize in C-SPAN's national essay contest.

The poem playfully tweaked parliamentary manners, called on the Senate to open up its chambers to television coverage, and warned lawmakers that "the people are watching, so you'd better watch out." The pair was accustomed to spending hours watching C-SPAN and discussing what they saw, so they already had a natural rapport underway for their poetic collaboration.

Ms. Thompson had always been interested in public affairs. From her experience reporting political and society news for a California paper, she had developed an eye for issues and personalities. Mike was a high school debater who found that watching C-SPAN helped him polish his own forensic and rhetorical talents. Watching the channel gave the grandmother and her grandson something to share.

After a hectic but exciting career as a newspaperwoman, Nelda Thompson retired to rural Applegate, Oregon, to live near Mike's parents and "to get away from it all." She didn't realize just how far away she'd gotten. After a life full of news sources and publication deadlines, Applegate (population 800) soon left her feeling "isolated."

In 1980, while visiting her sister in Los Angeles, Ms. Thompson happened upon "that Congress station," as she calls it, and soon was hooked on the telecasts. "I told my sister I would kill to get it" in Applegate. Scraping together $3,000, Nelda Thompson installed a satellite dish in her back yard, and soon this woman who had never been to Washington, D.C., was spending hours watching the U.S. Congress from her rural Oregon vantage point.

Ms. Thompson said she and Mike "had a lot of fun" working together on their essay contest entry. They decided on the poetic approach early, thinking that it would be "different" enough to catch the judges' eyes. Together, they wrote:

> I suppose I should say that it "filleth"
>   my heart
> Makes me pure, patriotic, and born-
>   again smart . . .
> Expands my horizon and serves to erase
> My ignorant outlook, but that's
>   not the case.
> Call it vice. Call it virtue. Which one?
>   I'm not sure.
> I've just an obsession for which there's
>   no cure.
> When the gavel descends and that flag
>   is unfurled,
> The House is in session. All's right
>   with the world.
> No soap opera script, no HBO plot
> Compares with the action that C-SPAN
>   has got.
> No MTV rhythm could ever excel
> The decibel ratings that come from the
>   well.
> I view with alarm and loudly deride
> Walker and Gingrich and Weber and
>   Hyde
> But I glow with delight and applaud at
>   the sight

Of Schroeder, Gonzales, Ferraro, and
   Wright.
Biased I am, I cheer and I snarl
(But not Susan or Carrie or Brian or
   Carl)
Keeping cool while others are venting
   their spleens
(Whatever that hackneyed hyperbole
   means)
I've tried to entrap them, unravel the
   din. . . .
Which side are they *on* when the
   callers call in?
There are scholars and screwballs, elite
   Ph.D.
Mingled with nincompoops sounding
   like me.
I've a dialogue filled with drama and
   verve
That I sacrifice everything else to
   observe.
A thought sometimes haunts me,
   suppose I should learn
That the old founding fathers should
   somehow return
And be shocked from their shrouds and
   gaze at the scene
As their very own words are expressed
   on the screen . . .
"Freedom to say it, to comment, to quiz
By George, what an awesome
   contraption that is.
Though it took them many long years
   to invent,
They finally found out what it was that
   we meant . . .
But something's awry, they messed up
   the rules
The Senate is missing, go fetch it, you
   fools!"

Right on, founding fathers from
   whom we all sprang
Alexander and George and the rest of
   the gang
Their modern successors are left with
   no doubt . . .
The people are watching, you'd better
   watch out.
We see you, we hear you, the people
   report
But government's more than a
   spectator sport.
So I've sought to enumerate, tried to
   relate
How the founders and I have been
   brought up to date.
But I've dallied about, composing this
   rhyme
When I could have been C-SPANning
   all of this time!

Mike and Nelda learned they had won second prize in the contest on the night of Mike's high school graduation. "He came down the aisle with his diploma," Nelda remembers, "and the first thing he said was, 'Did we win, grandma?'"

The prize for their work was a trip to San Francisco, where they would meet the C-SPAN team and tour the network's on-site studios for the 1984 Democratic National Convention. They had a chance to watch as the Moscone Center readied itself for the arrival of thousands of political conventioneers. "It seemed almost chaotic to us," Mike recalled later. "Fifteen or 20 things were going on at once, and no one seemed to have overall responsibility." Mike even tested his skills as a television interviewer, asking questions of a Democratic consultant, later watching himself gleefully on videotape.

Back in Applegate, Ms. Thompson is still watching the House floor, often summoning up her writing skills to correspond with lawmakers. An ardent supporter of Rep. Pat Schroeder (D-Colorado), she relates how she once watched the congresswoman take criticism from male colleagues during a congressional telecast. She sent the legislator a telegram of encouragement, reading simply: "Give 'em hell, tiger!" "Thanks, I needed that," came the response. And, when Ms. Thompson's son-in-law recently ran for the State Assembly in California, she assisted in his campaign, at one point giving him tapes she'd made of C-SPAN's telecasts of campaign management seminars. He lost, but Ms. Thompson says she "loved working on the campaign."

Mike has gone to the University of Oregon, to study political science, an interest his grandmother feels was nurtured by their hours of C-SPAN watching. Although he's too busy to spend much time with television, Ms. Thompson occasionally videotapes programs for him. And you can be sure that whenever he's back home in Applegate the pair settles down to watch the network, and are soon embroiled in a hearty discussion of politics—just like old times.   —S.M.S.

In rural Applegate, Nelda Thompson has installed a satellite dish to receive C-SPAN.

"The First Caller"

Unknown Viewer
Yankton, South Dakota

A voice crackled over the telephone wires—the first viewer call was coming in. The caller, an older man, was ringing up from Yankton, South Dakota, 1,800 miles away from Washington, D.C. After a wail of feedback, his friendly voice said, "Thank you for C-SPAN."

Today, the voices of more than 13,000 C-SPAN viewers are heard every year during hundreds of call-in programs. But an unknown viewer from South Dakota started it all back on the 7th of October in 1980. The man was the first caller on the network's very first call-in program—and a pioneer in a format that was new to national television. C-SPAN, though, was not pausing to ponder the history-making implications of its foray into the opinions of America that day. The network's staff may have inwardly thanked the South Dakota caller for phoning in—but they were too preoccupied with the frantic business of keeping the set together, the phones working, and the power running.

Over the years, a few C-SPAN staffers have tried to find the unknown caller. Although they haven't yet tracked down the elusive Yanktonite, he occupies a special place in C-SPAN history and in the hearts of the people who pulled off the program in that harried hour. And for the people struggling to make C-SPAN grow, his call coming from Yankton—

population 12,000 and half a continent away—symbolized the fruits of C-SPAN's effort to establish a link between the nation's capital and the thousands of out-of-the-way communities across the United States.

C-SPAN rolled the dice when it opened up its phones that day. With a staff of less than 10, the network had only been in operation for a year and a half. And, although it reached about 5 million cable homes, it was unsure of the actual size of its audience. A modest budget forced the network to borrow a studio location and camera equipment. What couldn't be borrowed, 20-year-old chief engineer Richard Fleeson patched together. But C-SPAN's determination to host a dialogue between official Washington and the citizens of towns like Yankton compelled it to take the risk.

To transmit the call-in program signal, C-SPAN used a microwave transmitter lent by George Mason University's Michael Kelley. (Prof. Kelley supervises The Capitol Connection system that brings C-SPAN to Washington buildings not wired for cable.) Two RCA cameras provided by the Close Up Foundation as part of a long-standing agreement with C-SPAN supplied the video; the phones were on loan from the National Press Club. The young Mr. Fleeson hastily assembled a three-line telephone apparatus from a jumble of different parts.

The network set itself and its equipment up in the press club's east lounge, a small back room awaiting a well-deserved renovation. Creatively draped blue press club tablecloths formed a backdrop for the call-in set; 1980 campaign posters added a visual zing. Lack of space forced the program's producer, Gail Picker—a seasoned Capitol Hill hand with little television production experience—to place the phones a dangerously short distance from the call-in set.

Federal Communications Commission Chairman Charles Ferris was addressing press club members that day. The network covered his speech without a hitch. The sticky part came with the next steps of the plan. When he finished, C-SPAN's crew had to hustle the cameras over to the makeshift corner studio. Camera operators frantically untangled cables and switched electrical outlets as Mr. Ferris waited patiently for the interview to begin. Everything was finally in place, and the moderator was ready to ask the first question of the interview.

Someone turned on the television lights; all power promptly blew out.

The crew plugged and unplugged things, floundering desperately to find an electrical arrangement that would not overload the room's power supplies. They found it. Then they lost it and the lights went off again. When the interview with Mr. Ferris finally got underway, recalls C-SPAN employee Brian Lockman (now vice president for network operations), the atmosphere was one of apprehension. What could go wrong next? "It really only took 15 minutes or so, but it seemed like an eternity," he says.

Then it was time for the call-in program. Hoping to establish a profile in the communications industry, C-SPAN invited members of the communications trade press to analyze Mr. Ferris' speech and to discuss emerging issues in the industry in response to viewers' questions. Guests included Prof. Mike Kelley, then a member of the Corporation for Public Broadcasting; *Broadcasting* magazine managing editor Don West; Dawson "Tack" Nail, executive editor of *Television Digest;* and *Cablevision* magazine's Washington, D.C., bureau chief Pat Gushman. After a short interview, the panelists were ready to take the calls.

But was anyone listening? Was anyone watching? C-SPAN didn't really know. Not only had C-SPAN not promoted the program, but callers would have to pay for their own long-distance calls. There was a chance that this invitation to phone in might fall on the ears of a deaf, indifferent cable audience. That might mean an embarrassing silence.

To everyone's immense relief, the program's three phone lines lit up and stayed lit throughout the telecast. When the host picked up the first call, an ear-splitting screech of feedback blasted the guests and went over the network. Crew members scurried to repatch the phone system; producer Picker struggled to move the phone set-up a little further from the call-in table, although not far enough to keep the microphones from picking up her whispered off-camera questions.

After more tinkering with the phone system, a call finally came in that could be understood. The man from Yankton did not make the first C-SPAN call-in program call; he made the first intelligible call to a C-SPAN program. Other calls followed from people who were interested in earth stations, cable, and communications bills, but that first call made C-SPAN staffers take heart. It told the network that it was on to something.

Call-in programs have since become C-SPAN's hallmark. For more than 16 hours every week, the network's telephone lines are opened to allow viewers to talk directly to elected officials and journalists in a kind of no-holds-barred televised dialogue.

Yankton is a South Dakota plains town near an Indian reservation. It's tempting to ponder the identity of the enthusiastic Yankton caller. Was he a farmer? A small-business man? Or was he a salesman passing through who happened to turn on the cabled TV set at the Yankton Super Eight motel? Nearly eight years have passed since that first program. Does he remember making that maiden call? Does he still watch C-SPAN?

Many programs on cable television feature call-in segments now; thousands of calls to officials and political celebrities have faded into distant memory, part of America's ongoing national dialogue. C-SPAN has long since learned to run call-in programs smoothly. When that special call came through, it marked the beginning of both developments, a milestone in an oddly intimate and emotional moment.

Chances are, the unknown Yankton viewer has no idea that he was the first caller to break the ice on a C-SPAN call-in program. He probably doesn't know how his call eased the icy grip of terror on C-SPAN hearts. Nonetheless, it's certain that Yankton, South Dakota, will long hold a special place in C-SPAN's collective memory.   —*S.M.S.*

Yankton, South Dakota, is served by Yankton Cable TV.

"The Gambler"

Ken Uston

San Francisco, California

When something piques Ken Uston's interest, he usually learns the ins and outs of it and then writes a book. He's explained the skill and luck behind a winning game of blackjack and unraveled the intricacies of home computers. More recently, he wrote a "report card" that evaluates the television performances of U.S. senators, whom Mr. Uston calls "Clint Eastwoods" and "TV stars in their own right."

Ken Uston is not a political analyst, but his self-ascribed taste for "impulsive gadflying" and his analytical mind prompt him to "get to the bottom" of anything that intrigues him. In 1974, the Phi Beta Kappa Yale graduate and Harvard M.B.A. left a job as senior vice president of the Pacific Stock Exchange to devote his numerical abilities and intuition to blackjack. His skills won him millions. They also won him *persona non grata* status from Vegas to Bangkok; gambling houses in Europe, Asia, and the United States banned Mr. Uston because he was just too good. Mr. Uston later won a court case against an Atlantic City casino when the New Jersey Supreme Court ruled that the establishment could not banish him on the grounds of his talents.

Mr. Uston invites others to break the bank with his best-selling books, *Ken Uston's Blackjack and Poker,* and *Million Dollar Blackjack.* He is the author of 18 books in all, many of which are also instructional manuals such as *Puzzle Panic, Ken Uston's Guide to Home Computers,* and *Guide to Mastering Pac-Man.* Mr. Uston regularly contributes to computer digests and scientific and electronic magazines.

A chronic insomniac, Mr. Uston discovered C-SPAN's telecasts of congressional sessions at 3:00 or 4:00 one sleepless morning in 1986. He soon knew he had a new discipline to investigate. C-SPAN's gavel-to-gavel coverage of the Senate began on June 2; within a few weeks, Mr. Uston had decided to use his talents to develop a systematic evaluation of how senators presented themselves on television.

The blackjack specialist undertook the project from an apolitical point of view. "I pretended I was a professor evaluating the performance of 100 students. I also pretended I was sitting on the moon, avoiding the best I could any bias in any of the issues." He adds, "I couldn't have named 10 senators when I started this, but it's better that I did it than some political scientist with an ideological viewpoint."

He traveled to Washington, D.C., and watched 150 taped hours of Senate TV as a basis for his study. He looked at a 10-day period, during which the Senate passed the 1986 tax reform bill, mulled over a controversial judicial nomination that passed by one vote, and went over myriad other bills and amendments.

Mr. Uston entered each senator's remarks into a personal computer according to content, objectiveness, and effectiveness. He defined four criteria to rate the statements: (1) substance—was the senator's reasoning sound or constructive? Were his statistics accurate? (2) style—wordy, repetitive, or clumsy speeches earned lower grades; (3) emphasis of the national interest over regional (or personal) goals; and (4) individual traits, such as courtesy or leadership.

After collecting mammoth amounts of data, Mr. Uston made a ratings sheet for each lawmaker and awarded a final grade for overall effectiveness. For each he included "what I hoped were light and interesting vignettes" to illustrate how the senators had earned their ratings.

Mr. Uston's finished product weighed in at 411 pages and several pounds. It offered a remarkably detailed scheme of individual senators' performances on the floor, using graphs and a rating range from A+ to D+. It named senators' best and worst moments on television and even suggested ways that they could improve their television image. Mr. Uston put the report up for sale at $117, but sent each senator a copy of his own "report card" and another copy to the senator's party leader.

Then-majority leader Robert Dole (R-Kansas) pulled down an A+ for "invariably putting the nation's interests first" as he demonstrated "outstanding Senate leadership during the entire period." Democratic leader Robert Byrd (West Virginia) earned a solid B+ that took into account his "firm minority leadership" and "courteous graciousness." Sen. Bob Packwood (R-Oregon), who also received an A+, told a reporter he was "flattered" by the estimation.

Mr. Uston recommended that some senators shorten and sharpen their speeches, use more logical reasoning, and be sure to make proper contact with the microphones. He commented on senators' occasional floor faux pas. For instance, he revealed that he saw Sen. Albert Gore (D-Tennessee) chewing gum on the Senate floor. And finally, Mr. Uston believed that some lawmakers' TV images were simply beyond hope. He wrote of one senator: "His best TV moment is yet to come."

The writer/gambler was fascinated by Senate TV. "It's now possible to listen to debate over the issues—to hear senators disagree, debate, rebut, and sometimes get emotional, discourteous, or even angry." Senate TV, he felt, brings accountability to the political process. "The usage of television video equipment . . . now makes it possible to replay occurrences on the Senate floor—to get exact quotes, to more fully understand intentions, and to review behavior that occurred in the past." Mr. Uston believed that senators would deliver more messages of national scope as they grew accustomed to the scrutiny of TV.

Mr. Uston's blackjack winnings have made it possible for him "to do whatever I want to do." After completing his report Mr. Uston said he might even write a book about Senate TV. To date we've not seen one, but after all, he did admit, "I'm basically improvising as I go along." —B.L.

"The Neighborhood Organizer"

Jane White

Scottsdale, Arizona

At 45 years of age Jane White has forsaken housewifery—at least in part—to join the grassroots ranks of the politically active. She hasn't, however, entered politics as a novice. She has been studying the nuts and bolts of political organizing for over three years. Her curriculum and teachers are the American University Campaign Management seminars that she watches on C-SPAN and a constellation of House floor luminaries whom she looks to for elocutionary guidance.

Ms. White shared her story with C-SPAN—and its national audience—when she phoned a call-in program last year to apprise the audience of the skills and interests she had developed from the network's programming. "I learned how to map a political campaign" as a result of watching the campaign management seminars, asserts the former full-time housewife. Before this, "I had never given a public speech. I had never been interviewed. I had never talked to a mayor, or a state legislator, a governor, or anything like that."

But when a local controversy surfaced over whether the state would build a highway through her neighborhood, push came to shoving time for the Scottsdale resident, and she managed to do all of the above. Indeed, she did them with style, that is, the rhetorical style that she says she gleaned from watching "thousands of hours" of congressmen speechifying on the House floor.

Over two years ago the Arizona Department of Transportation decided to put a highway through her community. "That was okay," says Ms. White. The part she didn't like was the "on-again, off-again" tone of the deal. "We border an Indian reservation and they had negotiated a deal with the Indians where half of it would go in Scottsdale and the other half on Indian land." The only nice thing that developed from this "wretched situation," notes Jane White, is that she got to know her neighbors—the Salt River Pima Maricopa Indians, who have lived across the street from her for 17 years. She says they've joined forces to compare platforms on the "highway battle."

"As time went on the whole thing fell apart," she recalls. Then after a year the project was supposedly back on track, and she says, "The state started buying people's homes, and they approved ours, and said, 'We're going to get you out from under this mess.'" Then the state put a stop to everything once again in December 1986.

That's when Jane White and other community activists decided to form a homeowners' group to push the state to resolve the problem. "And what I found, much to my amazement," she says, "was that all those years of watching C-SPAN was like being in a classroom." Her campaign was launched with what she describes as "a real zinger of a speech" at a hearing before the transportation board with a crush of TV cameras on hand to tape the event. Soon after her speech, the local news programs wanted to interview her. The television appearances were "just terrifying," exclaims Ms. White.

The secret to her oratorical success, she claims, is a mix of the dramatic methods of her favorite congressional players. She takes notes on delivery and phraseology, and when she sees something that's effective or clever, "I steal it," she asserts. The lesson she's learned is: Be brief. "When I'm making a speech to the City Council, I don't want to drone on and on. I found out the best way was to make it snappy." Her congressional stars include Reps. Newt Gingrich (R-Georgia), Richard Armey (R-Texas), Steve Bartlett (R-Texas), Jim Courter (R-New Jersey), and Sen. Alan Simpson (R-Wyoming). And although she says she "hates" Massachusetts Democratic Congressman Barney Frank's politics, she admires his oratorical skill: "He can get a point across in one line. He can make a difference with one vicious thrust."

Watching Congress has demystified the political process and empowered Jane White to become a community activist. Not only is she involved in her neighborhood group on the highway issue, she follows local politics and City Council meetings on her cable system's local access channel. And her watch on Washington has helped to put Ms. White's political philosophy in perspective. "I've always been a pretty conservative Republican," she says. "Now I know why. Some of my conservative friends are angry with Reagan because he didn't completely change everything that started with Roosevelt. I understand why he didn't, because I understand the political process better now."

C-SPAN serves yet another purpose for Jane White. She says it makes her money. She has what she refers to as a "little piddling sewing business that I keep trying to quit. But I find that I may as well sew while I'm watching C-SPAN." Perhaps Ms. White is underselling the value of her business. With 60-plus hours a week of C-SPAN viewing maybe her sewing business is not so "piddling" after all.   —M.C.

Jane White tunes in C-SPAN on United Cable TV in Scottsdale.

"The Eternal Optimist"

Lawrence White

Culver, Indiana

This is the story of one man's personal crusade to give the people of his tiny Indiana town more access to their government in Washington. "It hasn't been easy," says Rev. Lawrence White, 77, of Culver, Indiana, who spent five years lobbying to get the town and First PIC Cable TV of Knox, Indiana, to agree to offer C-SPAN. But then Lawrence White—a retired Methodist minister, high school teacher, and video buff—is not the kind of person who gives up easily.

It all started in the summer of 1982 at a 4-H County Fair in Argos, Indiana, when Rev. White saw his first satellite dish. As a ham radio operator, he was interested in satellite communications technology. But something else caught his attention: C-SPAN was on during the demonstration, beaming the U.S. Congress right into the fairgrounds. "I thought, my land, that system gives us everything we want to know about government," recalls the retired Methodist minister. It was not long before he had bought and assembled the parts for his own satellite dish.

Sharing Congress and public affairs programming with the rest of Culver, which was something Rev. White felt was important to do, proved to be infinitely more difficult. In 1985, while attending a town council meeting, Rev. White made the first of many pleas for the system to add the network to the town's 35-channel system. But the cable company said its limited channel capacity and the cost of additional equipment for the small system precluded the possibility of carrying an additional programming service. Despite Rev. White's entreaties, First PIC said it could not add C-SPAN to its offerings. He wrote letters. He talked to the cable company's officials every time they were in town. He even tried to get elected officials interested in his crusade. (As the person in charge of the cable system's local access channel, Rev. White attended—and videotaped for community viewing—every meeting of the town board.) Nothing worked. Still, he refused to give up.

At the local access channel, Rev. White was basically a one-man band, serving as cameraman, editor, producer, and promoter for the community channel. One day he decided that if he couldn't bring C-SPAN directly to Culver citizens in its entirety, he could at least bring them part of the network's programming. He began to videotape C-SPAN programming off his satellite dish, and play the tapes on the local access channel.

Then, in the summer of 1987, Rev. White had a brainstorm. If the problem was that First PIC didn't have the equipment to put C-SPAN on its system, he'd lend them his own dish for a three-month trial, and run the service full-time on the system's local access channel. He hoped that others in his town would understand his zeal when they had the chance to see the public affairs programming for themselves. Rev. White even offered to pay C-SPAN's subscription fee himself—about $18 a month for the 600-subscriber system in Culver. On his pension, he says, "that wouldn't be just peanuts. But I was willing to do that as a service to get it on the air." The company agreed.

Rev. White mounted his stainless steel satellite dish on a small trailer; he was about to move it to the cable company when the telephone rang. He would not be permitted to take his satellite dish to the cable system, a member of the town board informed him, because of liability considerations. Board permission was necessary because First PIC's offices were on land leased from the city. As it turns out, liability may not have been the only problem. First PIC Cable and the town board had been involved in a running argument over the payment of cable franchise fees, and Rev. White felt he got caught between the two parties. "Well, I got pretty down-hearted, I'll tell you," he recalls.

By this time, however, others had become interested in his crusade. Joe Nixon, owner of a number of newspapers in Indiana and of a cable system in nearby Frankfort, was inspired by Rev. White's dedication and wrote a letter to the editor of the *Culver Citizen*. In the letter Mr. Nixon encouraged First PIC to carry C-SPAN, which he described as a top-priority channel on his system.

Why was Rev. White so set on bringing C-SPAN to Culver? One reason, he says, is that he hopes to "change the attitude of the public toward politicians. People are so hostile toward personalities like Richard Nixon, and Reagan." One way to clean up the image of politicians, Rev. White believes, is to change the government system by adding a direct vote on major issues. "I'd like to call the new system PDQ—Promote Democracy Quick. We could spend the price of one aircraft carrier to set up a system for a referendum or direct vote of the people. I've talked to a lot of people, and they have said that they'd be willing to go and vote once a month or so on some of the issues that are crucial." C-SPAN, Rev. White believes, could provide an important link in such a system.

Meanwhile, as Rev. White continued to videotape portions of C-SPAN programming and attend town meetings to carry on his campaign, the controversy was generating a fair amount of publicity. A cousin of Rev. White who works for the *South Bend Tribune* got a reporter to write a piece on the minister's struggles. His crusade was no longer a local one: The *Tribune,* with a daily circulation of 95,000, drew a lot of attention to the cause.

His dedication finally paid off. In the middle of August 1987, less than a month after the *Tribune* article appeared, the *Culver Citizen,* a local weekly newspaper, ran a front-page headline which read, "C-SPAN to Become a Permanent Part of Cable."

When asked if he could give a word of advice to others trying to bring congressional and public affairs programming to their community, he replied: "Persistence and education—that's essential. A public access channel like the one I've been using would be a good way of enlightening people and helping them to understand what C-SPAN is. And, of course, there's coverage. You must be in the press continually. You have to pound away at it. I put the pressure on them."

By September 1987, First PIC had ordered the equipment and was finalizing plans to put C-SPAN on Channel 32, right next to the Christian Broadcasting Network. But if there are ever any problems, Rev. White's stainless-steel satellite dish still sits on a trailer on his property, ready to go. —*M.H.*

The Citizens of Culver, Indiana, can now watch C-SPAN on First PIC Cable TV.

"The Localizer"

Kendall Wild
Rutland, Vermont

Rutland (Vermont) *Daily Herald* editor Kendall Wild knows from watching C-SPAN that his paper isn't the only one to hold "rather anarchic editorial meetings." He measures the *Herald*'s sessions against those he's seen on C-SPAN's "Day in the Life" telecasts, when the network spends time detailing the day-to-day ritual of running a daily newspaper.

With a circulation of about 25,000, the *Daily Herald* is smaller than most of the papers featured on that series. Nonetheless, it is one of Vermont's largest papers. It's also one of the nation's oldest, having started as a Federalist weekly in 1794. The *Herald* began daily publication during the Civil War—the local citizenry had a great demand for news of the war—and has continued to deliver its blend of state and national news every day since then. The *Herald* serves what has traditionally been an industrial region of Vermont, one that today is undergoing a "ski boom." Mr. Wild characterizes the paper's stand as "moderately liberal. We don't rattle the cage because it's fun to rattle the cage, but we don't mind taking unpleasant or unpopular stands if we think it's the thing to do."

The Wild family name has appeared on the *Rutland Daily Herald*'s masthead for many years. During World War II, Kendall Wild's father was hired as a fill-in reporter and ended up as editorial writer. Kendall Wild began his own career with the *Herald* as a teen-ager, rising early each morning to deliver papers to his Rutland neighbors. In 1952, one year after graduating from Harvard, Mr. Wild became a reporter there, covering the state legislature. Along the way he's occupied a number of positions, taking over as editor in 1976. His "great American novel" remains unwritten, but he still vows every year that he's going to complete it.

In addition to C-SPAN's newspaper programs, Mr. Wild watches House floor proceedings to keep a professional eye on Jim Jeffords (R), Vermont's representative-at-large in Congress. Rep. Jeffords' performance on the House floor and in committee hearings has impressed Mr. Wild, and the newspaperman has written editorials in praise of the congressman's "gumption" on controversial issues. Mr. Wild remembers a debate over dairy pricing, during which Congressman Jeffords "was getting absolutely squashed by the other side." That debate inspired an editorial, which read: "C-SPAN is a wonderful invention. There, right in your living room last week, you could have watched the House in raucous and sometimes rancorous debate over a dairy bill proposal." Mr. Wild told his readers that Rep. Jeffords remained as "gentlemanly and steady as a rock" in the midst of the controversy.

The editor often slips references like that into his editorials. In any given year, C-SPAN's news clipping service is certain to forward several mentions from the Rutland paper. Explains Mr. Wild, "It's such a good service that I try to spread the word around." Sometimes his references take the form of outright plugs, such as the one that suggested, "If people in this country could ever become intelligent enough to watch programs like [C-SPAN], turning from soap operas and money contests, this country would be in a considerably better position to cope with the realities of life in today's world." Members of the *Herald*'s editorial staff have been quick to follow the boss' advice, often huddling around the office television to watch congressional debates unfold and to discuss their implications.

Watching the House also appeals to Mr. Wild's sense of strategy and powers of political analysis. He even enjoys watching the 15-minute congressional votes: "It's like watching a ball game or the stock market," he says. "I can watch the tally change while the people are walking around in the background. It's very dramatic. After a while you can get a sense of the true personality of the place, the maneuvering that goes on. Suddenly, you'll get a block of votes for or against something."

Like many people, Mr. Wild is hard pressed to separate his vocation from his avocations, and after a long day on the job, one can often find him at home watching televised public affairs programs. And, for a while, C-SPAN watching even became a family affair. The 60-year-old Mr. Wild (who's not married— "not yet, anyway") would come home late afternoons to find his elderly mother, now deceased, engrossed in House floor debates. "She'd have been watching all day long," he remembers fondly. "She became an absolute addict, one of those 'junkies'" for congressional telecasts.

In 1986, he kept a close eye on C-SPAN when the network came to Vermont to cover the state's three-way gubernatorial race. It was a hot contest, which pitted incumbent Madeleine Kunin (D) against her Republican lieutenant governor and the socialist mayor of Burlington, the state's largest city. Mr. Wild worried that "coming into any state from outside, there are always little nuances you don't pick up on." In the end, he thought "C-SPAN did a pretty good job."

And for national issues, Kendall Wild will likely continue to watch the network to add to his perspective on news stories. Although he readily admits "I can read about a story on the wire," watching it for himself instills "more of a sense of participation. I just get more fired up."   —P.K.

Kendall Wild can watch C-SPAN at home or at the office on Rutland Cablevision.

Lee Wing

Durham, North Carolina

From the moment she first heard of it, Lee Wing was intrigued by the concept of simply showing, with the aid of television cameras, government at work. That fascination eventually led her to develop a statewide television series based on the C-SPAN theme. Today, her popular OPEN/net program provides North Carolinians with an inside look at their state capital.

In 1977, Lee Wing was a newly appointed policy adviser to then-governor James Hunt of North Carolina, and she was interested in the technological revolution then underway in the communications industry. After a few months on the job, she attended a telecommunications conference in Washington, D.C., at which the concept of "putting Congress on cable" was being considered.

The idea of government on TV struck Ms. Wing as something that could really take off in North Carolina, and she headed back to Durham and went to work. A state task force she helped establish resulted in the 1979 creation of the North Carolina Agency for Public Telecommunications, a centralized media production outlet for the state.

A few years later, Lee Wing helped organize another advisory group involving the cable, broadcast, and telecommunications industry professionals. The Electronic Town Hall Task

Force was charged with developing a strategy for improved communication between the citizens of North Carolina and their state government, and to increase the level of citizen participation. That group's recommendations led to a plan for a statewide television program distributed by satellite. By 1984, with the political support of Gov. Hunt and the financial support of several foundations, OPEN/net was on the air, with Lee Wing as its executive producer.

For the 60-year-old mother of two and grandmother of four, her job at OPEN/net is a dream come true. "It satisfies everything I've ever wanted to do in a surprising way." Growing up she learned "that it was very important to be a participating member in a democratic society, not only as a voter, but beyond that. I spent many years manning polls and being a poll watcher in New Orleans as well as here in Durham."

Lee Wing was born and raised in New Orleans and weaned on jazz, music, theater, and politics. As a student at Tulane University, she became involved in musical theater, often satisfying her penchant for politics by writing political satires, musical reviews, and songs. In addition to having a master's in psychology, she's a member of the American Society of Composers, Authors, and Publishers (ASCAP). Some of her jazz songs have been recorded by the likes of Pearl Bailey and Carol Sloane. North Carolinians have heard the theme song she wrote for one of the OPEN/net programs.

As executive producer of OPEN/net, Lee Wing says she has "a marvelous public service opportunity, with a very definite show business feel to it. For me it's the perfect combination." OPEN/net produces two hours of programming that air twice a week on cable systems, low-power television stations, and local public radio. Its scope encompasses "everything that goes on in the state capital," with an emphasis on the executive and legislative bodies. "We tend to cover committee action, not action on the floor of the House or Senate." Each week, one member of a rotating group of reporters acts as host, moderating a panel made up of elected state officials and appointees. The panel tackles a single topic each week, issues such as hazardous waste disposal, substance abuse, and teen pregnancy.

North Carolina viewers are encouraged to call in with questions and remarks. "Every call-in is more like live theater than television. People will tell you things on the phone that they will not tell you in person," notes Lee Wing. That's made for some interesting programs, as well as providing another avenue for North Carolinians to address state politicians or seek help. "We are trying to empower citizens to have the capacity to influence state officials. And we're trying to give state officials a chance to express their point of view on why they made their decision and to learn from citizens they might not otherwise have heard from," says Ms. Wing.

Initially, North Carolina legislators greeted the prospect of appearing on OPEN/net with a certain amount of skepticism. "They used to run the other way," Ms. Wing recalls. Now their attitudes have changed. "They love being on because they can explain things in their own words, whereas newspaper or television summaries may extract statements that don't represent their views quite as precisely."

"Getting OPEN/net started meant persuading a whole bunch of different entities to have the same vision of responsibility that C-SPAN's creators had," says Lee Wing. As a result, "we can have an ordinary citizen who is not a lobbyist and who has never put any money into a political campaign call a state official from the privacy of his or her own home and go directly on the air to talk with them." —C.D.

Lee Wing receives C-SPAN via Durham Cablevision.

"The Park Ranger"

Tom Winslow

Philadelphia, Pennsylvania

During 1987—the bicentennial year of the U.S. Constitution
—more than 7 million people toured the 23 national historic
sites that dot center city Philadelphia. At each stop, tourists
were greeted by U.S. Park Service rangers like Tom Winslow.

Each morning, Ranger Winslow, 33, dons the official
gray and green park ranger's uniform and places a "Smokey-
the-Bear" style hat on his head. He makes his way to one of
the centuries-old sites that make up Independence National
Historic Park, where he greets a continual stream of humanity.
Park rangers must be tour guides, guarantors of public safety,
and caretakers of priceless artifacts, all on the salary of GS5
(approximately $15,000 per year).

Tom Winslow works hard at interpreting monuments for
tourists. "We attempt to relate history in a way that's meaningful," he explains. "We try to take a very active role, not only
showing people the building, but trying to show how what happened there relates to their lives today."

History," he tells park visitors "is not a 'dead letter'—it's
very much alive and vital."

Each ranger is asked to develop an individual theme to
use on guided tours of the historic sites. Tom Winslow's
theme, as he puts it, is the Constitution as the final solution to
the "struggle between power and liberty." His love of the

Constitution made it especially interesting for him to work in Philadelphia during the Constitution's bicentennial year. He says he will always remember what it was like to give tours of Independence Hall on the 200th anniversary of the Constitution's signing, quoting Benjamin Franklin in the very room used by the founding fathers.

Ranger Winslow is very enthusiastic about his career, even though it wasn't one he had planned on. He earned a bachelor's degree in history from Missouri's Evangel College and spent several years as a substitute social studies teacher in northern New Jersey public schools. After a frustrating search for a full-time teaching position, someone told him about the Park Service, and he sent away to several national parks for information.

When an envelope arrived bearing the return address of Independence National Park, however, Mr. Winslow had misgivings. "I just threw the letter away," he recalls. Later he pulled it back out and thought, "Why the hell not?" Given his passion for American political history, the chance to work at Independence Hall made a move to Philadelphia seem worthwhile. After just one summer at Philadelphia's historic sites, Tom Winslow claimed he was "hooked on the Park Service forever."

"I was the kind of kid who wanted to go to Washington and Williamsburg instead of Disneyland," he explains. He says he use to convince his playmates to put on mock conventions "with self-made placards and the whole bit." As an adult he continues to make the three-hour trip to Washington, D.C., "pretty regularly."

More often, however, he checks in on Washington through cable television. Tom Winslow says he understood exactly what C-SPAN meant with its 1987 promotional line, "where the Constitution comes to life every day." For him, keeping up with the 20th century American legislature is one way to help people understand the activities that took place in historic Congress Hall.

"To see what's going on today gives you the confidence to talk with tourists about the past," he explains. "Here, we try to convey abstract terms like "balance of power," "consent of the governed," and the rights of the individual versus government authority. These ideals were put in place in this chamber, and when you turn on televised floor debates or hearings, you can see they are not just terms or concepts—they are still going on today.

During 1987, C-SPAN crews frequently ventured outside Washington to cover Constitution bicentennial events. Tom Winslow recalls one such commemoration that brought the network's cameras up to Philadelphia—the July 16 reenactment of the first meeting of Congress. Members of the House and Senate took part in ceremonies inside Congress Hall, where the U.S. Congress met from 1790 until 1800. "Those old rooms came alive again," he says. Seeing politicians mingle in the historic meeting rooms "really gave me the sense of what it must have been like 200 years ago."

Tom Winslow is a historian with an eye to future generations. Because of television, he says, our descendants will have a better understanding of the "spirit, the feelings, the atmosphere" of the 20th century Congress. "They will be able to see specifics about the Congress, the appearances of members, the rooms—all that ties together as part of the story. Just think what we could do if we had C-SPAN tapes of Congress Hall from the 1790s." —*P.K.*

Tom Winslow watches C-SPAN at his parents' New Jersey home via Suburban Cablevision.

David Yepsen

Des Moines, Iowa

The spectacle of the Iowa caucuses and early hoopla of the political campaign captures the attention of the nation for several weeks every four years. David Yepsen, chief political writer for the *Des Moines Register,* captures a fair share of attention, too. "The bottom line is, you don't let it go to your head," he says. "I'm under no illusions that this sort of attention comes my way because of something I've done. I like to think I've done a good job and I sure as hell work hard at it, but it's not a function of anything I've done. Somebody started these caucuses back in 1972 and they became a big deal and I happen to be the guy here."

As the chief political expert for Iowa's largest newspaper since 1983, Mr. Yepsen knows that, around Iowa caucus time, columnists and news organizations around the country watch his columns and choices carefully. During the months leading up to the caucuses, the 37-year-old journalist wields considerable influence. Despite the national attention he receives, he never forgets who he's working for. "I write for my readers," he says emphatically. "We have an audience to serve, and I know who these people are and I write about what they care about, what they're interested in."

Mr. Yepsen was born and raised in Iowa and, except for a brief stint in the Army, he has spent his entire professional life in his home state. He's been covering political campaigns for the *Register* since 1978. "We devote a high percentage of our news hole to political coverage, both presidential and local," he notes. "We've just always been a paper that likes to cover politics. And we've got a lot of readers who are interested in politics."

While he's inclined to downplay the national attention he receives, Mr. Yepsen takes his work very seriously. He reads five newspapers, follows political reports on three wire services, and regularly watches half a dozen television news programs. During the 1987–88 political season, another one of his staples was C-SPAN's "Road to the White House." "When I'm covering the campaign, a lot of it comes from outside of this state. So, just as I read the *New York Times* and the *Washington Post,* I watch the 'Road to the White House,'" he says. This presidential election series, which started a year before the 1988 Iowa caucuses, followed candidates on their campaign rounds, telecast stump speeches, and examined newspapers' election coverage— including the *Register's.* C-SPAN's on-location coverage of newspapers usually includes call-ins with writers and editors, newsroom action, and editorial meetings.

Increasingly, Mr. Yepsen has turned to television as a means of assessing the presidential contenders who canvass Iowa every four years. "I watch a lot more TV than I used to," he says. "I think you've got to look at the candidates on a TV screen to see who looks good and who looks bad. Those impressions count. Just ask Richard Nixon."

In Mr. Yepsen's eyes, the pervasiveness of television has changed the political process forever. Not only do candidates have to present a telegenic image; they also have to watch what they say. He cites Sen. Joseph Biden's (D-Delaware) sudden withdrawal from the 1988 presidential contest as a good example. Television, he believes, played an important role in the senator's decision to leave the race. "Having mobile video technology out there with these guys all the time," he says, "is really having an effect."

People will always speculate on the best way to run elections, maintains David Yepsen. "Whether it's getting rid of the Iowa caucuses or the New Hampshire primary or adding additional early states, or busting up Super Tuesday—everybody sort of complains about the process as it goes along.

That's just sort of the nature of politicians and political re-porters."

While he sees room for improvement in the election process, he remains optimistic. "I think we tend to dwell on the shortcomings of the campaign and coverage, as opposed to the strengths. There have been a lot of improvements up and down the line, not only in the process, but in the coverage of the campaigns. I think what C-SPAN is doing, for instance, is unprecedented. So, it's important to keep the crit-ics a bit in perspective."

When the Iowa caucuses are over, life gradually returns to normal for David Yepsen and his family. His wife, a medi-cal doctor, "is very good about helping me keep my ego in check," he says. Mr. Yepsen has no problems with plummeting moods once the camera crews and candidates have finally packed up and moved on. He just continues to cover national and state politics, albeit minus the fanfare he attracts every four years.

Iowans' interest in the campaign doesn't go away with the camera crews, either. "A caucus-goer is a highly motivated voter, an activist," he says. "We've got a lot of people here who are interested in politics." And Mr. Yepsen's readers hap-pen to be among the most politically interested citizens in the state. "We've got one of the highest rates of voter participa-tion in the country," he says. "Our readers are uniquely inter-ested in the race because they've seen these guys up close. And 230,000 of these people went to the caucuses. So, I figure there are 230,000 people who have a 'horse' they want to follow."   —E.Q.

The citizens of Des Moines receive C-SPAN through Heritage Cablevision.

"The Special Educator"

Joe Yerkes
Jacksonville, Florida

The Learning Center, a special high school in Green Cove Springs, Florida, exists to give students one more chance. It has one bottom-line requirement for its 40 pupils: They have to be expelled from other schools first. When regular schools dismiss them, students can avoid permanent expulsion by choosing to enter the Learning Center for an intensive 18-week period. Then they return to the regular school system for another try.

Most Learning Center students have run into problems with drugs, their families, or the law. Often withdrawn or indifferent, these teen-agers can be hard to teach. Someone has to reach them first. Enter Joe Yerkes.

Mr. Yerkes, who teaches history and politics at the Learning Center, has a special approach to his charges. "I'm kind of a laid back person, and these kids are kids who have been in trouble a lot. They are very trying. They will try your patience." He adds, "If you put a very strict, authoritarian, inflexible kind of person there, you can maintain control and you can keep them in a sort of prison environment, but you don't tend to reach them emotionally."

Mr. Yerkes, 30, tries to use a more relaxed nonauthoritarian style as a bridge to the adolescents. After 10 years of teaching and counseling in both special and mainstream schools, he says he feels motivated to make his students learn something any way he can. His goal may have been inspired by memories of his own dreary days in school:

"I remember sitting in school really liking politics and history and yet finding myself very bored in my history and political classes. I just began to feel that there were better ways to teach, better ways to get kids enjoying what they were learning. I figured I could do better. And that's what I try to do—be weird, be creative, be innovative, just anything to hook them, get them into what we are doing."

One hook that Mr. Yerkes uses to entice his students is C-SPAN. Green Cove Springs is part of the Jacksonville metropolitan area; most of its homes have cable television. Mr. Yerkes assigns C-SPAN viewing as part of the students' homework, sending C-SPAN air times and dates home with them from class. If he knows what is going to be on the air in advance, he writes down some general questions about the program for students to answer. Otherwise, he asks students to watch the network and write down their own questions to bring up in class.

Mr. Yerkes likes to suggest that his teen-agers watch with their families. He hopes that shared viewing will foster a sense of community: "Not only will it get the kids to look at the issues, it will get them talking to their families. These kids have very poor family relationships. But if I can get Mom, Dad, and the kids to actually watch something together and talk about it—well, there's a lot more going on there than just learning about the issues."

He says that his strategy has produced some hopeful signs. "I get notes that say, 'Mr. Yerkes, I cannot believe it. Stacey is reading the newspaper and watching things on TV and asking us questions about the Democrats and Republicans.' The kids have started talking about different things." So, he adds, have their parents. "If the kids are interested, then it piques their interest, too."

When Mr. Yerkes was interviewed, the 1988 presidential race was heating up. He had his classes use a wide variety of news sources to convey a sense of the race. "Where I'm at right now is just trying to get them to understand how this thing works. They have a hard time understanding why there are two separate races going on, a Democratic race and a Republican race, and they can't understand why people can't just vote for anybody. We've built the race up so that now it is a race. State by state, the kids are watching and waiting to see who's going to win."

Special bulletin boards in the classroom heightened the sense of excitement. "They've been watching those candidates," says Mr. Yerkes. "We've got a loser's bulletin board for each one who drops out. We have pictures of each of the candidates and one of their bumper stickers." Watching television has sharpened the students' perceptions of the candidates. "On the debate the other night, the kids were fascinated with Senator Albert Gore [D-Tennessee]. They were saying, 'Why isn't Reagan that macho?'"

After one student looked into Sen. Gore's 1988 campaign, the candidate's staff looked into him: "One of my kids got a call from the Gore campaign asking him if he would open up an office here in Florida and be the campaign person in Jacksonville. And the kid talked to them for a few minutes and finally said, 'Look, I'm only 14 years old.'" The students' parents were not Gore supporters, so the inquiry came to an abrupt end.

In focusing on the campaign and attempting to educate his sometimes trying pupils, Mr. Yerkes is keeping an eye on the future. "One kid made a comment the other day: 'You know, in the other history classes all we do is look at the past, and in Mr. Yerkes' class we look a lot toward the future.' That comment made me feel really good." He tries to stress to his students that they are the future. "Come the 1990s, they'll be running the country. I'm hoping that they will get involved."

Some of the students are looking at the future as well. In a class on the Constitution, they protested, "You mean we have to wait until we're 35 to be president?" The laid-back teacher has made a few of his students impatient to lead.   —M.C.

Joe Yerkes and his students watch C-SPAN on Continental Cablevision.

"The Big-City Mayor"

Andrew Young_____
Atlanta, Georgia

Against one wall of his office in Atlanta's 100-year-old city hall, Mayor Andrew Young keeps a television set. Whenever there are issues up before the Congress in which he is interested, the television set is simply left on "so that you catch it from time to time." Sometimes, like during the House debate on South African sanctions, one can find Mayor Young's office "filled with staffers, sitting there watching the debate."

Andrew Young is a big-city mayor, successfully winning two elections on a platform that promoted Atlanta as a major center of international finance and trade. Hence, to keep in touch with issues beyond the parochial, Mayor Young uses C-SPAN to help follow the decisions of the U.S. Congress.

About 12 years ago, however, he was a member of Congress himself. And an interview he agreed to grant to a little-known cable television project helped give C-SPAN its start.

Andrew Young, 56, first drew national attention in the 1960s when he served as executive director of the Southern Christian Leadership Conference and as senior aide to Dr. Martin Luther King Jr. A native of New Orleans, Mr. Young had received degrees from Howard University in Washington, D.C., and the Hartford Theological Seminary in Connecticut. In 1972, the people of the 5th District of Georgia elected Andrew Young as their representative to Congress. His official biography states that "he has rewritten history by becoming the first black congressman elected from Georgia in the 20th century."

During much of Andrew Young's tenure in Congress, the House was embroiled in debate over a seemingly internal issue—whether the U.S. House of Representatives should allow television cameras into its chamber. As a member of the House Rules Committee, Rep. Andrew Young was frequently involved in that debate. He brought to the discussion an affinity for the role television could play in illuminating public policy issues; as a civil rights activist, he had observed that "television had an impact on the audience and the constituency that was created for the civil rights movement."

"He was one of the early advocates of direct broadcasting of congressional debates," remembers longtime aide Stoney Cooks. Andrew Young felt strongly that "televising Congress would have the positive feature of getting people interested in politics."

About the same time Congress was debating House television, the cable industry was undergoing some internal debates of its own. Cable television was in transition. Domestic satellites became a reality in the mid-'70s, making cable-exclusive programming a possibility. In 1976, Home Box Office was already on satellite and was being beamed into the homes of cable subscribers across the nation. Industry executives cast about for original programming ideas that could help cable television differentiate itself from its broadcast competition.

One early suggestion was for cable to offer public affairs programming. Robert Titsch, then-publisher of a communications trade magazine called *CableVision,* saw promise in a project called Cable Video. Half-hour interviews with members of Congress would be taped to run, uncut and without editorial comment, on cable systems across the United States. Mr. Titsch donated $1,000 to the project and convinced 14 others in the cable industry to ante up a similar amount. In all, 10 members of Congress were interviewed for the Cable Video project—each about communications issues. Among them was Rules Committee member Andrew Young, who was asked to discuss the question of House television.

By January 1977, Andrew Young was gone from Congress; President Jimmy Carter asked him to serve as U.S.

ambassador to the United Nations. Just 10 months after he left the House, however—and after six years of discussion—members gave the okay to televised coverage of debates. Cable Video grew into a full-fledged concept called C-SPAN. And, as the House prepared for its television debut, members of the cable industry made plans to put C-SPAN's gavel-to-gavel coverage of the House on satellite. Cable Video interviews of Rep. Andrew Young, Sen. Howard Baker (R-Tennessee), and others had been one significant factor in selling the C-SPAN idea to the cable industry.

Andrew Young left the United Nations in 1979, but he has remained deeply interested in Third World development issues. To advance the concept, he organized a nonprofit group called Young Ideas Inc. Even after his 1982 election to mayor of Atlanta, Andrew Young continued to serve as president of the Washington-based group. Through it, he attempts to promote "greater U.S. involvement—particularly private sector—in developing Third World countries." Young Ideas has a small staff in Washington that "monitors legislation and produces a kind of legislative update on bills that we think are having a negative impact on world trade."

This interest in international issues frequently brings Andrew Young to Washington where C-SPAN viewers have seen him testifying before Congress. The network has also televised him addressing Washington's National Press Club, participating in the U.S. Conference of Mayor's meetings, and attending other public policy events.

And the summer of 1988, once again, gave Mr. Young a prominent place in C-SPAN telecasts—as the host mayor of the Democratic nominating convention.   —B.L.

Andrew Young keeps his eye on Congress at City Hall and at home through Prime Cable.

"The Political Rocker"

Frank Zappa
Los Angeles, California

"I have a fondness for American politics because of the anthropological implications. It can be pretty amusing," says the creator of songs and albums such as "Weasels Ripped My Flesh," "Don't Eat the Yellow Snow," and "Uncle Meat."

What, you might wonder, is a '60s counterculture hero like Frank Zappa, 47, doing studying inside-the-Beltway politics? The one-time Mothers of Invention band leader watches to keep an eye on what's happening in Washington so that he can understand "how and why people do certain things in government." While there's no particular programming that Mr. Zappa watches regularly on C-SPAN or any other station, he does have general criteria for what he considers watchable. He stays away from "rhetorical bilge" and "choreographed propaganda," saying that "you have to look through the data and figure out the spin—sometimes you can smell the spin." Even C-SPAN, which Mr. Zappa considers to be "the best television available," is "not without spin."

Mr. Zappa recognizes that his penchant for the absurd makes the "really, really deadly serious" content of C-SPAN's programming somewhat hard to handle at times. He believes "that since human beings have a mechanism built into them that allows for laughter, that mechanism should be used as frequently as possible." One of his favorite C-SPAN programs, for example, was a 1987 panel discussion with political strategists during which the host, CBS News correspondent Lesley Stahl, posed a hypothetical question to the presidential campaign managers: What would they advise their candidates to do if they were challenged to ride pigs to prove their manliness? "I was slapping my leg over that one," laughs Mr. Zappa. "Here are these adults talking seriously about being forced to ride a pig in order to get a vote. I think that describes a larger social condition in this country." Mr. Zappa was so impressed with the program he sent Lesley Stahl a bouquet of flowers.

Putting aside the entertainment value of politics, however, Frank Zappa makes it clear that he cares deeply about American government and has taken advantage of his celebrity to bring up what he believes are serious issues. The night he was scheduled to host the Fox network's late night talk show he lined up National Public Radio commentator Daniel Schorr and Gerard Straub, former "700 Club" producer and author of a book about TV evangelist Pat Robertson. "This was right after the contra hearings," he says. "I was going to bring these guys on in the context of an entertainment show and talk about the link between the fundamentalist right and Nicaragua. Just before he was scheduled to appear, however, Fox "pulled the plug" on the show.

In the summer of 1985, necessity brought the former Mother of Invention to Washington, D.C., to testify at a Senate hearing on the labeling of rock music lyrics, something he saw as censorship. Testifying at his side were musicians John Denver and Dee Snider of Twisted Sister. Tipper Gore, wife of Sen. Albert Gore (D-Tennessee) had formed a group of concerned parents called the Parents Music Resource Center, which wanted to monitor the contents of the lyrics. "The astonishing thing about having to testify was that such an idiotic event actually took place on public time," says Mr. Zappa. He describes his experience before Congress as an "absolute kangaroo court." Five of the senators sitting on the committee had wives who were involved with the PMRC, according to Mr. Zappa.

Besides giving him a chance to participate directly in the congressional process, the experience was worthwhile to Mr. Zappa because his children were able to see the "government in action right there in front of them. They woke up to the fact that everything is not going to parties and rock 'n' roll."

He says that his teen rock star son Dweezil actually does watch C-SPAN. "I can discuss this stuff with him and it's not like talking to your average teen-age party guy." His daughter Moon Unit, however, "is more into spiritual stuff."

His interest in politics does not stop with late night looks into Washington politics. Frank Zappa actually considered becoming the Libertarian candidate for president, even though he is a registered Democrat. "I said I would consider talking to them if I understood their platform and I agreed with it," Mr. Zappa says. But after some study, he declined. "While there are some things the Libertarians say that I'm enthusiastic about, it is far too dogmatic and doctrinaire. And certain things are absolutely contradictory. It seems to me that if you really dig into these people they're closet anarchists—they would be happy with zero government. I happen to think that, from a practical standpoint, you can't exist with zero government."

The exercise got him thinking about how he'd change things if he were president. "I'd look at the political landscape and try to say not whether the Democrats or Republicans are right, but what is practical and affordable. I would try to do serious business with the Congress, because times have changed."

Mr. Zappa says his respect for Congress comes from watching individual congressmen so often on C-SPAN. "It's easy to see how a common citizen, which I would say I am, would say that politicians are all crooks or jerks. But now I see they are not all that way. Some are real statesmen, and I'm glad they are there."

What advice does the professional musician have for C-SPAN? "You have to spend a little more time on sound," Mr. Zappa says. "You have to understand what music people have known for a long time—that with bad sound people lose interest. A mediocre picture and terrific sound work, but a terrific picture and bad sound will lose your audience. If your philosophy is to bring government to the people, let's bring it to them hi-fi."   —P.K.

Frank Zappa and his son Dweezil watch C-SPAN on Century Communications.

Appendix One
The C-SPAN Audience

In fall 1987, the University of Maryland Survey Research Center was commissioned by C-SPAN to conduct a national survey to update information about the size, practices, and composition of our audience.* The results confirmed what C-SPAN had learned from earlier surveys and provided some new insights as well.

At present, 10.9 million households (potentially over 27 million people) report watching C-SPAN. In a similar survey conducted in 1984, the Washington, D.C.-based Media Analysis Project found 7.6 million households watching C-SPAN. There was a 43 percent growth in the number of households watching C-SPAN over the last three years.

The C-SPAN audience continues to be better educated and more interested in news and politics than the general public. What follows is a summary report of major survey findings.

Viewership
C-SPAN viewers spend, on average, 9.5 hours per month watching C-SPAN and 6.5 hours per month watching C-SPAN II—the Senate television service. Sixty-four percent of all viewers tune into both C-SPAN networks. In addition, C-SPAN has a loyal following of approximately 1.3 million households (potentially over 3 million viewers) that tune in for 20 hours or more per month.

About how many hours of congressional floor proceedings do you watch per month on C-SPAN?
Average hours watched equals 4.5 per month; 17% watch 8 hours or more per month

---

* This study is based on a nationwide (excluding Alaska and Hawaii) random digit dial telephone survey of 3,944 U.S. households conducted during the last quarter of 1987. The sampling error for questions answered by C-SPAN viewers is plus or minus five percentage points. Maryland researchers simultaneously conducted a national survey of non-C-SPAN viewers for comparative purposes. With the exceptions of voting turnout questions and a measure of respondent's sex, all national comparisons are derived from Maryland data. The percentage of C-SPAN viewers who voted in 1984 and 1986 is compared to actual voter turnout; the sex of C-SPAN viewers is compared to 1986 Census Bureau estimates.

Did you watch either Judge Bork's Supreme Court nomination hearings or the Iran-contra hearings, or both, on C-SPAN? About how many hours . . .?

	Percent	Avg. Hours
Both hearings	72%	
Iran-contra hearings	16%	12.0
Bork hearings	5%	6.9
None/don't know	6%	

Which of the following C-SPAN programs do you watch on a regular basis?

"America & the Courts"	15%
Call-in shows	32%
Congressional hearings	69%
National Press Club speeches	36%
Public affairs seminars and conferences	33%

[Asked of those who choose not to watch C-SPAN] What are some of the reasons why you don't watch C-SPAN?

No interest in politics	26%
No time to watch	16%
Have other channels to choose from	13%
Boring	12%

How do you usually find out what programs will air on C-SPAN?

Flipping channels	63%
Cable TV guide	17%
Newspaper listings	11%

Have you ever called or attempted to call a call-in show?

No	96%
Yes	3%

[Of those who attempted to call/called a call-in show] What prompted you to call a C-SPAN call-in show?

To voice an opinion	63%
The issue discussed	25%
The call-in guest	12%

Have you ever changed your opinion on an issue or public official because of information you received from C-SPAN programming?

No	58%
Yes	40%

Do you think C-SPAN programming has a liberal bias, a conservative bias, or no bias at all?

Liberal bias	14%
Conservative bias	13%
No bias at all	73%

Do you consider cable television to be a good value for your money? (See Figure One.)

	C-SPAN	Cable Non-C-SPAN Viewers
Yes	92%	81%
No	8%	19%

Interest in Politics

C-SPAN viewers continue to express a greater interest in politics and news than the public at large—whether one examines electoral behavior, likelihood to engage in political discussion, or news consumption.

Are you registered to vote?

	C-SPAN	Nation
Yes	86%	76%
No	14%	24%

Did you vote in the 1984 presidential election?
Did you vote in the 1986 congressional elections?
(See Figure Two.)

	1984		1986	
	C-SPAN	Nation	C-SPAN	Nation
Yes	93%	53%	69%	37%
No	7%	47%	31%	63%

Within the last year, have you written to either a congressman or senator?

	C-SPAN	Nation
Yes	28%	21%
No	72%	79%

How often do you discuss politics with your family or friends? (Eighty-two percent of C-SPAN viewers discuss politics; 61% of the nation discusses politics.)

	C-SPAN	Nation
Every day	22%	11%
Three times a week	22%	10%
Once or twice a week	35%	36%
Less often	20%	43%

In politics today, do you consider yourself a Democrat, a Republican, an Independent, or something else?

	C-SPAN	Nation
Democrat	38%	31%
Republican	32%	30%
Independent	24%	31%
Other	5%	5%
Don't know	1%	3%

How many days in the past week did you read a daily paper? Watch news programs on television?

	Daily Paper		Television News	
	C-SPAN	Nation	C-SPAN	Nation
Every day	76%	44%	80%	55%
None	2%	18%	1%	10%

Audience Composition

C-SPAN viewers are also distinguished from the general population by their demography, rating above average in terms of education and income. (See Figure Three.)

In what year were you born?

Age	C-SPAN	Nation
18-24	8%	17%
25-44	50%	45%
45-64	31%	22%
65 and over	10%	15%

What is the highest grade in school you have completed?

	C-SPAN	Nation
Graduate school	12%	11%
College graduate	25%	13%
Some college	30%	24%
High school graduate	28%	39%
Less than high school graduate	5%	13%

Was the total income of all family members who live with you last year:

	C-SPAN	Nation
Under $10,000	4%	10%
Between $10,000 & $20,000	12%	20%
Between $20,000 & $30,000	19%	25%
Between $30,000 & $50,000	35%	28%
Between $50,000 & $75,000	15%	7%
Over $75,000	9%	6%

Last week, were you working full-time, part-time, going to school, keeping house, or some other activity?

	C-SPAN	Nation
Working full-time	61%	55%
Working part-time	9%	8%
Going to school	6%	6%
Keeping house	10%	14%
Retired	11%	13%

Sex:	C-SPAN	Nation
Male	54%	48%
Female	46%	52%

"Do You Consider Cable Television To Be A Good Value For Your Money?"

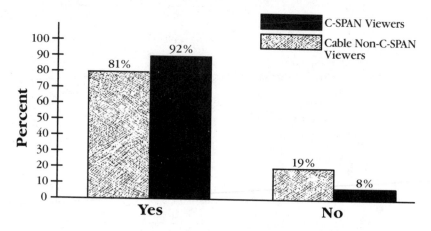

Percent of Electorate Voting in The 1984 Presidential & 1986 Congressional Elections

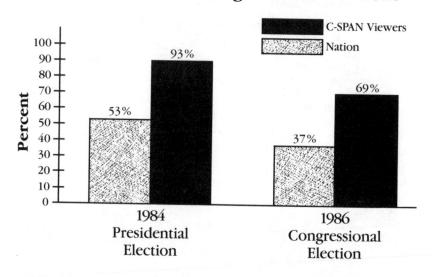

C-SPAN Audience Demographics

Education

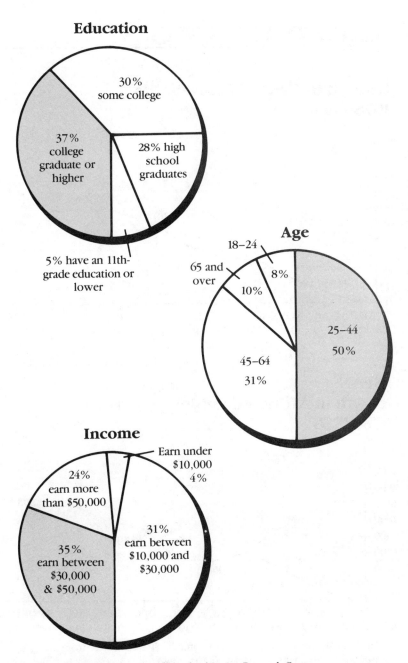

30% some college

37% college graduate or higher

28% high school graduates

5% have an 11th-grade education or lower

Age

18–24 8%

65 and over 10%

45–64 31%

25–44 50%

Income

Earn under $10,000 4%

24% earn more than $50,000

31% earn between $10,000 and $30,000

35% earn between $30,000 & $50,000

Source: December 1987 University of Maryland Survey Research Center

Appendix Two

Growth in C-SPAN Households
1978–1988

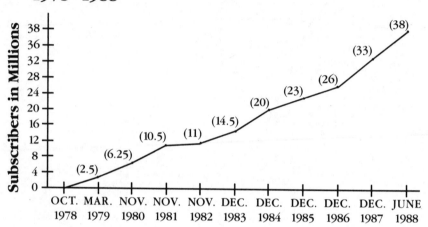

C-SPAN
Growth in Affiliated Cable Systems
1978–1988

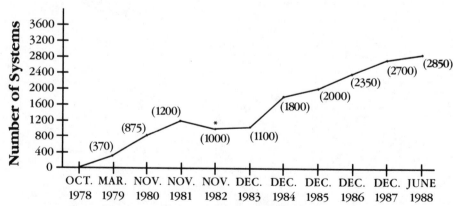

*Short term affiliate drop attributed to shift of C-SPAN's service from a
transponder shared with USA network to its own full time use of a transponder.

C-SPAN Penetration Into U.S. Households:
June 1988 State-by-State Breakdown

State	Total TV Households*	C-SPAN Cable Households	Satellite Households	C-SPAN Penetration
Alabama	1,486,770	473,800	54,030	35.5%
Alaska	142,990	64,700	3,820	47.9%
Arizona	1,270,150	493,370	31,690	41.3%
Arkansas	868,450	245,760	40,220	32.9%
California	9,886,080	4,130,410	123,380	43.0%
Colorado	1,283,390	584,740	33,190	48.1%
Connecticut	1,164,940	856,320	5,900	74.0%
Delaware	224,740	130,940	3,820	60.0%
District of Columbia	246,160	18,730	850	8.0%
Florida	4,737,280	2,596,250	78,970	56.5%
Georgia	2,182,460	679,830	54,270	33.6%
Hawaii	333,380	231,330	1,470	69.8%
Idaho	348,290	115,500	13,920	37.2%
Illinois	4,232,600	1,531,450	63,890	37.7%
Indiana	1,990,670	790,250	56,860	42.6%
Iowa	1,100,090	460,180	29,850	44.5%
Kansas	931,300	398,580	41,820	47.3%
Kentucky	1,334,710	532,450	62,290	44.6%
Louisiana	1,586,390	584,400	55,400	40.3%
Maine	435,300	93,500	8,490	23.4%
Maryland	1,618,950	500,220	15,420	31.9%
Massachusetts	2,173,930	1,280,890	8,630	59.3%
Michigan	3,316,510	1,392,110	85,620	44.6%
Minnesota	1,577,800	537,910	29,610	36.0%
Mississippi	915,880	159,840	47,620	22.7%
Missouri	1,867,350	684,130	56,860	39.7%
Montana	315,540	141,060	17,500	50.3%
Nebraska	607,910	291,110	20,570	51.3%
Nevada	394,820	125,860	12,690	35.1%
New Hampshire	380,870	226,130	20,470	64.7%
New Jersey	2,800,190	1,485,130	15,520	53.6%
New Mexico	526,280	158,760	18,860	33.7%
New York	6,632,170	2,360,180	93,120	37.0%
North Carolina	2,339,080	600,470	71,670	28.7%
North Dakota	248,290	52,970	9,620	25.2%
Ohio	4,013,020	1,757,430	94,250	46.1%
Oklahoma	1,266,010	463,310	43,800	40.1%

State	Total TV Households*	C-SPAN Cable Households	Satellite Households	C-SPAN Penetration
Oregon	1,019,180	444,690	25,410	46.1%
Pennsylvania	4,452,480	1,561,980	57,480	36.4%
Rhode Island	358,140	228,670	1,600	64.3%
South Carolina	1,226,290	396,910	35,130	35.2%
South Dakota	262,460	105,840	8,870	43.7%
Tennessee	1,786,050	533,830	75,010	34.1%
Texas	5,957,530	2,376,050	175,910	42.8%
Utah	526,770	206,950	15,420	42.2%
Vermont	198,390	68,490	8,250	38.7%
Virginia	2,056,890	969,050	48,100	49.5%
Washington	1,714,860	913,850	27,500	54.9%
West Virginia	719,010	194,620	41,680	32.9%
Wisconsin	1,786,020	705,040	41,310	41.8%
Wyoming	186,170	64,040	12,690	41.2%
Total	88,848,990	36,000,010	2,000,320	42.8%

*Nielsen television household estimates

1987 C-SPAN Call-In Program Participation

Top 25 States		Top 25 Cities	
State	# of Calls	City	# of Calls
California	3,101	Los Angeles	438
Texas	922	San Diego	327
Florida	845	New York City	268
New York	809	Seattle	257
Washington	614	Houston	174
Virginia	545	Portland	160
New Jersey	541	Tucson	141
Arizona	468	Denver	125
Ohio	379	San Francisco	109
Pennsylvania	350	Phoenix	105
Michigan	319	Las Vegas	97
Colorado	317	Pittsburgh	92
Oregon	312	Long Island, N.Y.	87
Illinois	310	Santa Barbara	86
Massachusetts	300	Indianapolis	83
North Carolina	268	Dallas	80
Georgia	259	New Orleans	79
Alabama	230	Austin	78
Connecticut	227	Albuquerque	68
Louisiana	223	Arlington, Va.	67
Indiana	196	Honolulu	67
New Mexico	193	Atlanta	66
Oklahoma	190	Miami	66
Missouri	165	San Antonio	65
Maryland	163	Boston	64

In 1987, 14,115 callers' questions were taken on C-SPAN programs.

1987 C-SPAN Programming "First Run" Hours

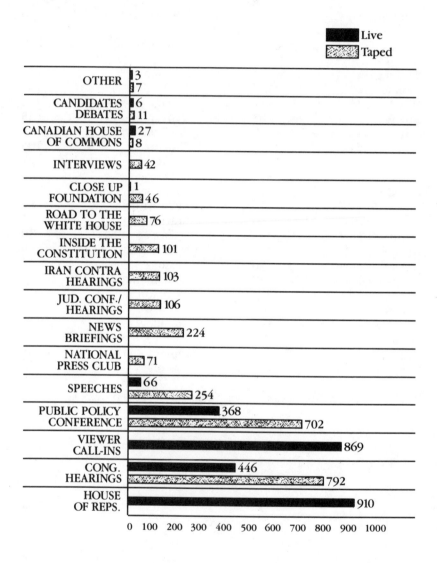

Legend: ■ Live　▨ Taped

Category	Live	Taped
OTHER	3	7
CANDIDATES DEBATES	6	11
CANADIAN HOUSE OF COMMONS	27	8
INTERVIEWS		42
CLOSE UP FOUNDATION	1	46
ROAD TO THE WHITE HOUSE		76
INSIDE THE CONSTITUTION		101
IRAN CONTRA HEARINGS		103
JUD. CONF./ HEARINGS		106
NEWS BRIEFINGS		224
NATIONAL PRESS CLUB		71
SPEECHES	66	254
PUBLIC POLICY CONFERENCE	368	702
VIEWER CALL-INS	869	
CONG. HEARINGS	446	792
HOUSE OF REPS.	910	

0 100 200 300 400 500 600 700 800 900 1000

U.S. Senate
Hours in Session 1975–1987

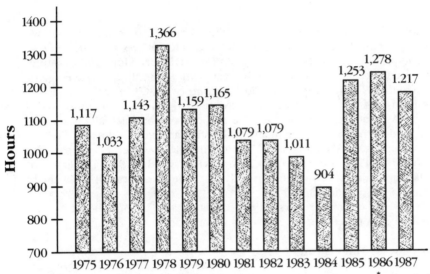

*Senate telecasts begin June 2, 1986.

U.S. House of Representatives
Hours in Session 1975–1987

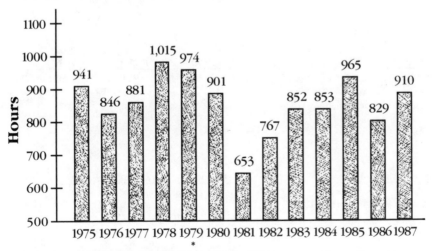

*Congressional telecasts begin March 19, 1979

Relative Sizes of Public Affairs Television Audiences

Public affairs programming—on either broadcast or cable television—draws relatively small viewing audiences. One of the nation's top rated public affairs programs, ABC's "This Week With David Brinkley," for example, finished the 1986-1987 television year with a 3.8 rating—an average of 3.3 million TV viewing households. By contrast, NBC's "The Cosby Show," earned a 34.9 rating, attracting an average 30.5 million TV households.

As a nonprofit public service without commercial advertisers, C-SPAN does not participate in any of the standard measurements of television audiences. We felt it would be instructive, however, to compare the overall C-SPAN audience estimates provided by the 1987 University of Maryland survey with certain readily available measures of public affairs television audiences.

Maryland researchers estimated that in 1987, 1.3 million cable TV households tuned in to C-SPAN for 20 or more hours per month.

Broadcast Television:

Network	Program	Measurement Period	Rating*	Size (TV HH)
ABC	"This Week with David Brinkley"	10/86–9/87	3.8	3.3 million
CBS	"Face the Nation"	10/86–9/87	2.8	2.4 million
NBC	"Meet the Press"	10/86–9/87	2.7	2.4 million

Source: A. C. Nielsen

Public Television:

Network	Program	Measurement Period	Rating*	Size (TV HH)
PBS	"McNeil-Lehrer Newshour"	10/86–9/87	1.9	1.7 million

Source: PBS, Washington, D.C.

Cable Television:

Network	Program	Measurement Period	Rating*	Size (TV HH)
CNN	"Crossfire" (prime-time)	1/87–12/87	1.4	585,000

Source: Cable Advertising Bureau

*Ratings are based on each network's universe.

The C-SPAN Board of Directors

Edward M. Allen
Walnut Creek, California

Kenneth L. Bagwell
President
STORER CABLE

Robert D. Bilodeau
Chairman
THREE SIXTY CORPORATION

David A. Bohmer
President
CENTEL CABLE TELEVISION

Harvey T. Boyd
Vice President
POST-NEWSWEEK CABLE

Gary S. Bryson
Executive Vice President
AMERICAN TELEVISION AND
    COMMUNICATIONS

Michael Callaghan
Vice President of Cable
SCRIPPS HOWARD

Douglas H. Dittrick
President
DOUGLAS COMMUNICATIONS
    CORP. II

Frank M. Drendel
President
GENERAL INSTRUMENT CABLE
    HOME GROUP

Barry R. Elson
Senior Vice President
    of Operations
COX CABLE COMMUNICATIONS

John D. Evans
President
HAUSER COMMUNICATIONS,
    INC.

Paul A. FitzPatrick
Wilton, Connecticut

John P. Frazee, Jr.
Chairman and Chief
    Executive Officer
CENTEL CORPORATION

Michael J. Fuchs
Chairman and Chief
    Executive Officer
HOME BOX OFFICE

Richard Gessner
Chairman
COMMUNITY ANTENNA
    TELEVISION ASSOCIATION

John W. Goddard
President
VIACOM CABLE

James L. Gray
President and Chief
    Operating Officer
WARNER CABLE
    COMMUNICATIONS, INC.

Robert Hosfeldt
President
GILL CABLE TV

Amos B. Hostetter, Jr.
Chairman and Chief
    Executive Officer
CONTINENTAL CABLEVISION,
    INC.

Glenn R. Jones
Chairman and Chief
    Executive Officer
JONES INTERCABLE

Marvin L. Jones
President and Chief
    Executive Officer
UNITED ARTISTS CABLE-
    SYSTEMS CORPORATION

Brian P. Lamb
Chairman and Chief
   Executive Officer
C-SPAN

Jerry D. Lindauer
Senior Vice President
PRIME CABLE

Sheila Mahony
Vice President, Government
   Relations and Public Affairs
CABLEVISION SYSTEMS
   CORPORATION

Robert Miron
Executive Vice President
NEWCHANNELS CORPORATION

David A. Oman
Vice President Development
HERITAGE COMMUNICATIONS

Philip R. Patterson
Vice President
MACLEAN HUNTER CABLE TV

Norval D. Reece
Senior Vice President
FRAZIER, GROSS & KADLEC

Brian L. Roberts
Executive Vice President
COMCAST CORPORATION

Robert M. Rosencrans
President
COLUMBIA INTERNATIONAL,
   INC.

John V. Saeman
Chief Executive Officer
DANIELS & ASSOCIATES, INC.

Robert L. Schmidt
McLean, Virginia

Gene W. Schneider
Chairman and Chief
   Executive Officer
UNITED CABLE TV
   CORPORATION

John J. Sie
Senior Vice President
TELE-COMMUNICATIONS INC.

Robert Titsch
VIRGO PUBLISHING, INC.

Donald E. Tykeson
Managing Partner
TYKESON ASSOCIATES
   ENTERPRISES

Larry W. Wangberg
President and Chief
   Executive Officer
TIMES MIRROR CABLE
   TELEVISION

Thomas E. Wheeler
Chairman and Chief
   Executive Officer
NUCABLE RESOURCES CORP.

James N. Whitson
President
SAMMONS COMMUNICATIONS,
   INC.

Researchers for America's Town Hall

GB	Greg Barker	BL	Brian Lamb
KB	Kathleen Brown	RL	Rob Lee
SB	Susan Bundock	CM	Chris Maloney
MC	Maura Clancey	LM	Lori McFarling
RC	Rosemarie Colao	MM	Mike Michaelson
JD	Jana Dabrowski	KM	Kathy Murphy
CD	Connie Doebele	PP	Penny Pagano
CE	Caroline Ely	EQ	Eileen Quinn
JE	Jenna Eudaley	PS	Paul Sinclair
MG	Martha Gallahue	TS	Terri Sorensen
NG	Nan Gibson	SS	Suzanne Stahl
MH	Mary Holley	SMS	Susan Swain
RK	Ruth Kane	PW	Pat Watson
PK	Peter Kiley		

1979

THE WALL STREET JOURNAL

Monday, March 26, 1979

Dull or Not, the Televising of 'Action' From House Floor Is Making History

By JAMES M. PERRY
Staff Reporter of THE WALL STREET JOURNAL

WASHINGTON – "They started it off with a good typical day," says Paul Duke, the veteran reporter for public television. "It was uninspiring and dull."

But it's making history. For the first time, "action" on the floor of the House of Representatives is being televised, by the House itself, and transmitted to the outside world. Public TV carried the inaugural show live – it lasted 2½ hours last Monday afternoon – and then bundled up its equipment and went home. But public TV may be back. So may NBC, CBS, ABC and anyone else who wants to take a "feed" from the House's telecast. Meanwhile, on cable TV the show goes on.

Six television cameras have been permanently positioned in the House chamber. They are focused, unwaveringly, on the Speaker's rostrum and the majority and minority tables. They are controlled by personnel working out of a basement in the Capitol. The whole system cost about $1.2 million to install. There is nothing like it in the Senate.

How many people watched the premiere show is anyone's guess. Rep. Charles Rose, the North Carolina Democrat who presided over the installation of the system, says his mother in Fayetteville, N.C, watched part of the show and spotted him. "She called me up and told me I needed a haircut." Mr. Rose was at the barber shop the next morning.

Public TV stations pre-empted their regular fare, such as "Sesame Street," to put the House on the air. Chuck Lichenstein, a vice president of the Public Broadcasting Service, says "no one here knows when we'll be back to do it again." The commercial networks have said all along they don't plan to use much more than video-tape snippets from time to time to be included in their regular news programs.

Gavel to Gavel

In some parts of the country, it's possible to watch the proceedings gavel to gavel every day. The "feed" is being provided live by the Cable Satellite Public Affairs Network (C-Span) to about 170 cable-TV systems around the country. C-Span officials say about 1,100 of the nation's 4,000 cable systems are capable of receiving the signal, which is bounced off a satellite.

(In Washington, where lobbyists, bureaucrats, and others might be interested in watching the routine proceedings on the House floor, the coverage can be seen only on Capitol Hill on closed-circuit TV.)

The maximum audience for the service, according to C-Span, is five million households.

"But I can't imagine how many people would sit down in front of their TV sets and tune in cable to watch it," says PBS's Mr. Lichenstein "It really is excruciatingly dull."

House Speaker Thomas O'Neill (D., Mass.) worries that the media will use the "feed" from the floor of the House to criticize the performance of Congress. But his insistence on having his own people control the cameras – others thought the networks should run the show – limits the damage. The way it is now, the fixed cameras aren't allowed to sweep the chamber and show how empty it normally is or how inattentive the handful of members lounging on the back benches usually are.

Thus, the cameras focus on the business at hand. "The idea," Rep. Rose says, "is to inform the American people about the way the Congress really works."

Looking at the "feed" provided by the new system doesn't do much to accomplish that.

Some Things Interesting

It isn't so much the routine business is dull. The surprising impression from the House's first week before the cameras is how interesting some of the routine business can be. The problem is, it is almost incomprehensible to someone who isn't seriously devoted to congressional procedure and the agenda.

On the first day, when public TV was on the job, the members debated the question of creating a special committee with a $500,000 budget to try to revise Congress's antiquated committee system. It may have been routine to some people, but it wasn't to Democratic Rep. Richard Bolling of Missouri, who defended the idea of a select committee. He said, accurately enough, that he has spent 25 years of his life trying to streamline Congress's machinery.

Recognizing that background, the vote the next day, when public TV had packed up, was moderately exciting. It lasted 15 minutes, during which not a sound came from the TV set. The screen was filled with a voting chart that was updated every 13 seconds. With two minutes and 59 seconds to go, the resolution to create the special committee was ahead, 192 to 190. With 2:33 left, it was dead even, 194 to 194. With 2:20 to go, it fell behind by a single vote.

In the end, the resolution passed, 208 to 200. It would have been interesting to see Mr. Bolling's reaction, but the cameras aren't allowed to take that kind of liberty.

Meanwhile, the House is providing another little service to members. They can purchase 30-minute video tapes of their performances. So can the media and members of the public. Though House members can't use the tapes for political purposes, they can send them to TV stations back home as a "public service." And there is an interesting loophole Rep. Rose is desperately trying to fill. There isn't any prohibition against a challenger purchasing House tapes and using them in a campaign against an incumbent Congressman.

His Unsteady Best

A striking example of that possibility occurred the other day when a veteran Congressman who is known to have a drinking problem did his unsteady best to manage a routine bill. The pitiless microphones and cameras recorded the quavering of his voice and the shaking of his hands. As the rules stand now, someone interested in challenging him next year could buy tapes of that performance and turn them into damaging political commercials.

Whether TV will be a negative or a positive force for Congress remains, almost literally, to be seen. So far, the reviews are mixed. Public TV's Mr. Duke is hopeful. "We were all encouraged," he says. "The feeling here is that we'll be back to cover the big events as they occur."

Others aren't so impressed. The chief counsel of an important House committee glanced at the TV set in his office the other day while the House show was on. "Look at them," he said, "all dressed up in their three-piece suits. It looks like a giant ad for Brooks Brothers. If it goes anywhere, it's the end of civilization as we have known it."

Reprinted by permission of The Wall Street Journal, @ Dow Jones & Company, Inc. 1979. All Rights Reserved

1988

The New York Times

C-SPAN: Electronic Sunshine

WHATEVER ELSE THIS PRESIDENTIAL campaign is, it is the first in which candidates, prominent supporters and even bit players are now fully wired for sound. C-SPAN seems ubiquitous and so, to a lesser degree, does the Cable News Network. Increasingly, we can comprehend government and politics live. About half of America's television households now receive cable television. C-SPAN, carried by 2,700 cable systems (the cable industry has more tributaries than the Amazon) reaches 33 million homes. Viewers seriously addicted to C-SPAN may keep it on all the time; the semi-addicted (this critic is one) watch at least once a day. The staple is Congress, although in recent months there were great chunks of Iowa and New Hampshire: debates to caucuses to Pete du Pont, say, hanging out at a Dunkin' Donuts. C-SPAN goes where no camera crews have gone before.

It's great stuff, of course. Everyone who talks about it praises C-SPAN. For years, citizens' groups and enlightened politicians have called for "sunshine laws" to open the governmental process to public scrutiny. That's what C-SPAN does. As it happens, this critic, along with only a few other tourists, was in the visitors' gallery of the House of Representatives one night last October; the press gallery was even more deserted than the visitors' gallery. On the floor, though,

---

Its ubiquitous cameras prompt politicians to measure their words and actions.

Jim Wright, the House Speaker, was conducting a vote on a $12 billion tax bill he favored. When the bill was rejected by a single vote, Mr. Wright simply refused to recognize the tally; he ruled that voting was still in progress.

Meanwhile, his lieutenants worked the House floor. They were looking for someone who would switch sides. Finally, they found him. Then the bill was passed 206 to 205. Republicans were so angry over Mr. Wright's tactics that they booed. Some Republicans literally climbed over chairs and shook their fists. Where were the other television networks when we needed them? Only C-SPAN was there. It showed the shenanigans live and also in rebroadcasts. When the House was voting on a contra-aid package recently, CBS was presenting "Kate & Allie," while NBC was offering "A Year in the Life" and ABC was giving us "Hooperman." Everyone to his or her own taste, but the contra vote was more exciting.

C-SPAN kept a running count of yeas and nays. It was clear that a number of House members did not want to commit themselves until they knew which side would win and whether their votes would be needed. Until the last minute or so in the 15 minutes of balloting, neither the pro- nor anti-contra forces were more than two or three votes apart.

Faint-of-heart Congressmen waited until the end before defeating the bill 219 to 211. Prior to that, however, it had been a gripping horse race. Some things in the governmental process just lend themselves to television.

Does the Presidential campaign lend itself to live television, too? Actually, it no longer seems to have much choice. George Bush and Jack Kemp declined C-SPAN's invitations to wear microphones at local events in Iowa and New Hampshire, but the other candidates accepted. That's how we were able to see and hear Mr. du Pont at the Dunkin' Donuts. He introduced himself to the customers. Most of them smiled politely. A waitress kept pouring coffee. It was just another day in the Presidential process. Nonetheless, every so often we saw the glare of television lights. Then we were reminded that Mr. du Pont wasn't campaigning just in a Dunkin' Donuts. Potentially, he could reach 33 million homes. Meanwhile, his every word and gesture was being recorded.

Did Mr. du Pont think about that? If he didn't, he has no business being in politics. Senator Joseph Biden forgot about the C-SPAN cameras and microphones one day in New Hampshire last April and exaggerated his academic honors. Months later, it caught up to him. The print press reported what he had said, and then the major networks replayed the C-SPAN tape. Mr. Biden eventually dropped out of the race.

■

Therefore, Mr. du Pont had to measure his words and actions, even in Dunkin' Donuts. One supposes that was good; maybe television keeps the candidates honest. But what about the supporting players in the camaign — aides, wives, voters and coffee drinkers in Dunkin' Donuts? Are they weighing everything, too? In the glare of TV lights, supporting players often seem to be actors in a sound-and-light show.

In Iowa, C-SPAN visited real caucuses. It showed good citizens expressing their preferences for President. This was inspiring. The democratic process was alive and well. Meanwhile, you began to like some of the caucus participants. Candor and good humor were upon them. Maybe, you thought, the U. S. Information Agency should transmit C-SPAN overseas to show everyone how the process works.

Well, that was a lovely thought. But how does the process now work? In the 67th precinct Democratic caucus in Des Moines, a man approached two caucus leaders. "He's got the lights — he's got the cameras," the man said with annoyance and pointed across the auditorium. He was distressed because someone else was getting too much television attention. A little later, C-SPAN visited the 18th precinct Republican caucus in Cedar Rapids. A dispute arose over when to start counting votes. "I think because of television we should go on," the caucus chairman said. What was happening here? Was television running the system or was the system running television, or didn't it matter? Maybe it didn't matter. Anyway, that's what you hoped. □

TV VIEW/John Corry

Copyright © 1988 by The New York Times Company. Reprinted by permission.